An Introduction to African Legal Philosophy

An Introduction to African Legal Philosophy

John Murungi

LEXINGTON BOOKS
Lanham • Boulder • New York • Toronto • Plymouth, UK

Published by Lexington Books
A wholly owned subsidiary of The Rowman & Littlefield Publishing Group, Inc.
4501 Forbes Boulevard, Suite 200, Lanham, Maryland 20706
www.rowman.com

10 Thornbury Road, Plymouth PL6 7PP, United Kingdom

British Library Cataloguing in Publication Information Available

Library of Congress Cataloging-in-Publication Data
Murungi, John, 1943-
An introduction to African legal philosophy / John Murungi.
pages cm
Includes bibliographical references.
ISBN 978-0-7391-7466-1 (cloth : alk. paper) -- ISBN 978-0-7391-7467-8 (electronic)
1. Law--Africa, Sub-Saharan--Philosophy. I. Title.
KQC90.M87 2013
340'.1--dc23
2013005256

The paper used in this publication meets the minimum requirements of American National Standard for Information Sciences—Permanence of Paper for Printed Library Materials, ANSI/NISO Z39.48-1992.

Printed in the United States of America

Table of Contents

Preface	vii
Introducing African Legal Philosophy	1
African Jurisprudence	29
Thinking Like an African Lawyer	71
African Legal Interpretation	137
Otieno Case and African Jurisprudence	173
Concluding an African Legal Philosophy	203
Notes	217
Bibliography	225
Index	229

Preface

A preface to a book on philosophy of law is an interface. Nothing flows out of it that does not flow into it. Nothing flows into it from the outside. The outside is inside, and the inside is the outside. Because this is a preface to this book, the book itself must appropriate it as its own, and echo it as its own. One must dwell in both, for it is such dwelling that renders both intelligible. Such dwelling makes it possible to bring into relief not only the sense of both but it also brings into relief he or she who seeks to understand what is said in both. By dwelling therein, one is in a position to understand oneself. Accordingly, there is what is autobiographical in the preface and in the book it prefaces. In other words, a preface to a book on philosophy of law is a preface to oneself, and similarly, a book on philosophy of law is a book on oneself. Thus, it should not come as a surprise that, at the center of a book on African philosophy of law, it is the African who is brought into focus. It is a book on philosophical anthropology with a focus on what it is to be an African.

Normally, in the West, conventional books on philosophy of law focus attention on law, and rarely on philosophy. Though not explicitly stated, the rarity of the focus on the latter appears to be based on the assumption that what philosophy is is either self-evident or will be self-evident in what is said about law. What philosophy is is projected as unproblematic. This book differs in that it explicitly focuses attention on both philosophy and law, and more specifically, on their interconnectedness. It problematizes both if only to call attention to the unfinished task of defining and constituting what they are, and on how they are connected to each other. What is said about law reflects what is said about philosophy and, conversely, what is said about philosophy reflects on what is said about law. This book demonstrates that this is the case in the context of African philosophy.

The qualification of philosophy of law by the word "African" is not to be taken as being nothing more than a geographical signifier, as appears to be the case in the manner in which books on philosophy of law are normally presented in the West. In books on Western philosophy of law, the word "Western" appears to be simply a geographical qualifier, or as is the case, generally, it is omitted. This is equally the case when the word "Western" is used to qualify philosophy in general. This is misleading in that the word "Western" is more than a geographical signifier. It refers to thinking as it is shaped by Western culture. This culture has much to say about what is said about philosophy in general and about what is said about the philosophy of law in particular. African philosophy of law is equally shaped by African culture, as is the case with African philosophy in general. Accordingly, what is said about African philosophy of law in what follows is presented and is to be taken in the context of a thinking that is deeply rooted in African culture. It must also be noted that what is said about African philosophy of law is a venue for understanding African culture. This contextualization of African philosophy of law is not unique. Each and every philosophy of law is to be understood in the context of the culture in which it exists. There are no exceptions. Moreover, to the extent that African culture does not exist in isolation from other cultures, what is said about it will reflect the relation it has with other cultures and hence, with other philosophies of law.

It is not to be assumed that what philosophy is is the same everywhere at all times, or that every concrete expression of philosophy is disconnected from every other concrete expression of philosophy, and this applies to philosophy of law. In philosophy, geography matters, but how it matters is not explicit. Geography of philosophy is a cultural geography. Geographical boundaries are cultural boundaries, and philosophy is prefigured in the network of these boundaries.

Another important point that needs to be made is that this book seeks to situate us where law and philosophy intersect. The intersection calls for multiple philosophico-cultural entrances. No one can enter this intersection by another's entrance. One enters it through one's own entrance. This leaves the intersection open to multiple perceptions and to multiple interpretations. The intersections of perception and interpretations are, likewise, subject to multiple perceptions and multiple interpretations. These aporias constitute the inner essence of both law and philosophy. Accordingly, it should not be a surprise that their intersections are aporetic.

Law and philosophy do not intersect at a point. They intersect at a lived-space or at a living space where each undergoes a metamorphosis prompted by the other. These promptings are not mechanical or a repetition of the same. New horizons come into being from the womb of the present and from the womb of the past. African philosophy of law is not exempt from this process and neither do those who concern themselves with it. There is a tomorrow and the day after tomorrow of the intersections. Time is the framework for these intersections.

To help in the entrance and in the following of what is said in this book, it may be important to state right at the outset that I write from a perspective of someone who has lived through a colonial phase of African history. For a good part of my early life, I was subjected to a colonial rule, and later, to neo-colonial rule. It is under these regimes that I was introduced to the study of philosophy and to the study of law. I have lived under a colonized and neo-colonized philosophical space, and in a colonized and neo-colonized legal space. The book is a contribution to the decolonization of these spaces. I have an intimate connection with the decolonization process. In this process, I am myself undergoing this same process. Hopefully, those who are not similarly situated will experience intimacy in what is said, for decolonization is an attempt to affirm the intimacy we have with each other as human beings.

Philosophers are not lawyers and lawyers are not philosophers. This double "not", which is not double, is the cowry shell out of which philosophy and law emerge and it is into which they return and in which they are preserved and conserved. It is in this context that one is to think about African philosophy of law. African philosophy, that out of which African philosophy of law comes into being, is not a body of knowledge produced by Africans for Africans and for non-Africans. It is a call to address and interrogate African life, to open it up in a way that calls for addressing and interrogating our own life. It opens us to ourselves and preserves and conserves us in openness.

I owe what I am to my ancestors. Out of the respect for them, and in accordance with my tradition, I dedicate this work to them. It is a token of my appreciation of what they have contributed to what I am. The living also have contributed and continue to contribute to what I am. They are inspirational. Accordingly, the work is also dedicated to them. In anticipation, it is also dedicated to those who are to come. They too are a part of my family. What is in the horizon has inspired me and continues to inspire me. African philosophy of law is, in this sense, to be understood horizonally.

Chapter 1
Introducing African Legal Philosophy

Introducing a work intended to be a contribution to the study of African legal philosophy is to be formulated in such a way that the manner of its formulation is in question. It is itself subject to study, for it is only in this way that it can make a significant contribution to what it seeks to introduce. It seeks to render explicit what is at work in the introduction as well as what is at work in what it seeks to introduce. In other words, in seeking to introduce what it seeks to introduce, it also seeks to introduce itself. It calls attention to what works itself out in the introduction, and also what is at work in what it introduces. Since what is being introduced here is African legal philosophy, it should be expected that what is African, what is legal, and what is philosophical will be introduced. Multiple introductions are unavoidable. What we have here are multiple pregnancies. That is, we have a pregnant introduction that necessarily will lead to multiple births if we have good pre-natal care. This calls for a good midwife, wise enough to carry out pre-natal care and, ultimately, provide assistance in the delivery. Whether I am good or wise enough to act as a midwife in this context remains to be seen. What I can confess right way is that I have doubts about my ability. If I did not have such doubts, I would not qualify as a philosopher, for a philosopher is a man or a woman who is constantly haunted by a living doubt. There is nothing that he or she says that is definitive. Certitude belongs to the gods if there are such beings, or to fools because they do not know any better. For a philosopher, certitude is and remains doubtful.

Is the meaning of law in Africa the same as it is everywhere? If it is, there should be demonstrable evidence that this is indeed the case. Such evidence would provide a basis for a rational study of the meaning of law. If the meaning of law in Africa is not the same as it is everywhere, equally, there is need for demonstrable evidence to allow for a rational study of the meaning of law. However, the assumption that the study of the meaning of law has to be rational requires scrutiny, for it is not self-evident what it means to refer to such a study as rational. Africans have suffered dearly as a result of European conception of what is rational. They have witnessed the trashing of their thinking and cultural practices which largely have been declared superstitious, irrational, or unscientific. Moreover, to the extent that Europeans have traditionally associated science and rationality exclusively with their civilization, this association has led them to declare Africans as uncivilized. The study of African legal philosophy cannot ignore what has happened to Africans or what is happening to them at the hands of Europeans in the name of law.

For those who are interested in the study of African legal philosophy, recourse to European and American legal philosophy cannot blindly be embraced. Doing so may render one a victim of the imperial aspect of this philosophy. The temptation here is to succumb to parasitism to this philosophy or to the paternalism in the domain of legal philosophy. It is to have undue aid in the form of legal philosophy. If Africa is an underdeveloped part of the world, or if it is a part of the developing world, it is tempting to offer aid in legal philosophy to help Africans catch up with the developed West where legal philosophy is apparently developed or is apparently more advanced. It makes sense to be paranoid about the words "scientific" and "rational" in the study of law in Africa if one is to avoid perpetuating dependence in thinking about legal philosophy, and if one is to avoid mistaking appearance for reality. This is a healthy paranoia rather than a mental illness that calls for a cure.

Under the delusion that Africans are law-less, Europeans have taken up the mission of sending missionaries of law in Africa. These missionaries have accompanied other European missionaries of civilization to Africa to uplift Africans from the state of savagery. They suffer from the illusion or the delusion that what law means has already been universally settled, and what remains is to have everyone else recognize and implement it. For most of them, what is ignored is what Africans have experienced and what they still experience in the regime and the empire of the Western conception of law. This conception has not only been consistent with the colonization of Africans but also with the enslavement of Africans. It has provided justification for the inhumane treatment of Africans. The truth of what Westerners in general understand by law is reflected in the way they treat Africans. Under the guise of law, anti-Africanism has found a fertile soil. Westerners have much to learn from Africans about themselves. As Sartre has noted about European self-knowledge, "Our victims know us by their scars and by their chains, and it is enough that they show us what we have made of them for us to realize what we have made of ourselves."[1] There is a missing aspect in the treatises on European legal philosophy that Africans and other victims of European colonial regime can supply to gain a deeper and broader understanding of the European sense of law. African legal philosophy can make a contribution to this end but, generally, expecting Europeans to accept such aid from Africa is truly farfetched. It is like carrying out a missionary activity among missionaries. Those who believe that they have ultimate truth in their hands do not see the need for a lesson on what truth is.

The questions we are raising regarding the nature of African legal philosophy are about what is at stake in the meaning of law in Africa. In so far as they deal with meaning of law, they bear on the nature of law, for what law means is what the nature of law is. If there is a multiplicity of the meaning of law, this multiplicity will be reflected in the nature of law. This possibility cannot be ruled out given the apparent current proclivity towards postmodernism which calls for suspicion on grand theorizing. Mono-theorizing in the West cannot be severed from Judeo-Christian theology where monotheism has fatally affected "secular" thinking. Post-modernism is incompatible with Judeo-Christian theology. For the most part, the kind of post-modernism that prevails in the West today is an internal pluralization of Judeo-Christian theology. It is yet to make a dent on the Christian monolithic discourse—a discourse that has played a prominent role in the shaping of Western thinking. Moreover, the "secular" in this part of the world is the "secular" within this theology—a secularism that is a secretion of this theology.

The questions that are raised above and their answers touch on geography. They deal with the cartography of law—how law is mapped out, or how it ought to be mapped out. When legal philosophy is qualified by the word "African" geographicity is brought to bear on it, or more specifically, geographicity appears to be integral to it. How geographicity is internally linked to African legal philosophy is not self-evident. What should be noted right at the outset is that one cannot leave the final determination of the sense of this linkage to African physical geographers, or to any other physical geographers. The final determination is to be made by students of African legal philosophy. The geogaphicity of African legal philosophy is a matter of African legal philosophy. It is legal philosophy that is to determine the nature and the province of African legal philosophy. The African parameters of legal philosophy are to be determined by African philosophy. That is, to the extent that it is conceded that there is a space in Africa for legal philosophy, the boundaries of such space is to be determined by geographers of the African philosophy of law. Physical geographers do not have a monopoly of demarcating geography or expressing the sense of geography. Those who concern themselves with philosophy, the poets, and the artists, and others have a role to play in this project.

Linking of law and geography may strike one as abnormal. What appears normal is the de-linking of law and geography. Africa is a geographical territory among other geographical territories. The community of Africans, as is the case with any other human community is earth-bound. It inhabits a specific territory. Moreover, like any and every other human being, an African is named after the geographical territory of his or her origin. How this affects the meaning of law is not self-evident. An inquiry into the nature of law may shed some light on this matter. However, it should be recognized at the outset that such an inquiry is highly problematic. One faces a challenging starting point. The starting point is challenging in part because how one starts fatefully determines what is to follow. It may be beneficial to look into the starting points of other human endeavors. We may be able to benefit from a brief reflection on musical and poetic starting points. Let us turn to music and poetry to help us in this reflection. There is what is poetic in music and there is what is musical in poetry. Both are a matter of language, and language has everything to do with everything that pertains to speech, to language.

How does a musician begin to compose music? How does a poet begin to compose a poem? There are some problematic answers that may readily come to mind. For example, it can be said, and correctly so, that a musician begins to compose music musically, and a poet begins to compose a poem poetically. If these answers are problematic, they are so in that if one does not know what it means to compose music musically or what it means to compose a poem poetically, the answers will not be satisfactory. If one does not have a pre-understanding of what it means to compose music or to compose a poem, one would have to ask what it means to compose music musically, or what it means to compose a poem poetically. Without such pre-understanding, meaningful communication with others would be difficult, if not impossible. There are times when one hopes that one will not be asked certain questions. Such hope haunts anyone who puts himself or herself in a position of being asked to respond to a fundamental question. As for those who seek answers to a fundamental question, it may be appropriate to bear in mind that one needs to have some pre-understanding of what one seeks to understand; otherwise, one would not understand what one seeks to understand. Even if this is borne in mind, when a fundamental question is raised, the question has to be raised in such a way that one who raises the question enters into a questioning that brings into relief an environment where one finds oneself in company with others. The question is directed not only to others but also to oneself. That is, raising such a question opens an environment in which the questioner is not alone in questioning, and in which he or she finds himself or herself in community with all others who are being addressed by that which is the subject to questioning. Moreover, to raise this question is to find oneself in a position where one's own being is in question. It is in such a situation in which I find myself as I attempt to compose a philosophical introduction to African legal philosophy. How is such composition to be undertaken?

I cannot be completely ignorant about this introduction, but at the same time, I am perplexed as to how I am to undertake it. Likewise, my audience must somewhat know and not know not only what is to be composed, but also how to go about composing it. We are to answer the question I am posing together. We must co-compose the introduction that I want to compose. My attempt cannot succeed if you are total strangers to what is said about African legal philosophy. I am reminded of a similar predicament in which Calvin Schrag found himself when trying to figure out how to introduce one of his books. He says

> In delineating portraits, composing narratives, or providing accounts of human action, one always finds it difficult to decide how to begin. Perplexity becomes intensified when one realizes that there are no necessary starting points. All starting points are contingent. One could always choose another beginning. And the quandary of this predicament is further compounded by the realization that in a consequential sense one is always already begun, situated in medias res, as it were searching for an entry into a conversation and a positioning in a state of affairs that is already on its way.[2]

The awareness that there are no necessary starting points, and that one can always choose another beginning, does not always guarantee unproblematic freedom for beginners. Beginners must still make a determination on how, where, and when to begin. Even if one is to enter into a conversation that is already on its way, one has to negotiate one's entrance. One must still figure out the right moment to make the entry, and how to make the entry. This figuring out is not solely a matter of reflection. What is being entered into also must facilitate the entry. One must, so to speak, be called upon by that into which one seeks entry. He or she who is to enter must be possessed or inspired by what is to be entered. One may prepare and must prepare oneself for such inspiration. One cannot force oneself into it. The preparation must be guided by that which one is after.

It has been said that where true poetizing is flourishing, the poet does not simply commit to paper finished thoughts that are stored up in his or her mind. This is not only because there may be no mind where anything can be stored, but also because a poem comes into being as the poet poetizes. Similarly, it can be said that in all truly philosophical compositions, a philosopher does not embark on philosophical writing or on philosophical speaking with thoughts that are already finished and stored somewhere. Writing or speaking philosophically is an event through which and in which philosophy comes into being. Thus, to the extent that an introduction to African legal philosophy is truly philosophical, such an introduction is constitutive of African legal philosophy. Understanding how such constituting of an introduction is to take place is an essential aspect of the task that lies ahead.

It may appear strange or anomalous that music and poetry are brought to bear on our thinking about African legal philosophy. The strangeness or the anomaly may have to do with what remains unthought in or about music, poetry, and philosophy, and also with what remains unthought about the relationship that these three works have in common with one another. What may appear as breeding of confusion in our understanding of these works and their interrelatedness may turn out to be precisely what is needed to clear such confusion. As long as it is assumed that what each of these works addresses is foreign to what the others address, such a possibility remains beyond the horizon of our understanding. We may be no better off by assuming the opposite, but, at least, we will be put on notice that the tendency to separate these works is not to be blindly embraced. What is essential about each of them remains to be thought. There is what is poetic about African legal philosophy just as there is what is musical about it.

When one thinks about legal philosophy, poetry and music do not readily come to mind, even though both are at the heart of legal philosophy. Neither can be foreign to the other for all speak about the kind of being that each one of us is. Language is the site where each is what it is and where each is constituted and expressed. And because each is the site for the constitution and expression of what it is to be a human being, to say that either is foreign to the others is to say that a human being is foreign to himself or to herself. This would not make sense, even if it must be conceded that, for a human being, making sense of what it is to be a human being is an issue.

Provided that the perplexity that I have referred to above is adequately grasped, a philosophical introduction to African legal philosophy is bound to be a formidable task. What is true of a philosophical introduction is true of what such an introduction introduces. What grows out of a seed bears what is essential in the seed. It is precisely for this reason that presenting a proper introduction to philosophy is such a formidable task. The composition of the introduction is to be undertaken in such a way that, in some manner, what is introduced is thereby composed. How what is introduced is already in the composition of the introduction is and remains an important question. Hopefully, with your assistance, the task will be less formidable. Where genuine philosophizing takes place sharing is indispensable. I seek your collaboration to protect myself from being exiled from the human community. As an African saying goes, he or she who is without a village is either mad, or is a witch. A philosopher is a fellow villager; that is to say, he or she is a social being. He or she philosophizes as a social being. The subject that he or she takes up for philosophical consideration is a social subject. A philosopher must write for and speak not only with and to fellow philosophers; he or she must write and speak in a way that brings into focus the entire village community. He or she must speak in a way that engages all villagers—both philosophical and non-philosophical. To write or to speak otherwise is to alienate oneself from fellow villagers, and consequently, from oneself.

Regardless of how specialized philosophical language is, if it is divorced from ordinary language, it loses what is vital about itself. In so far as it is philosophical, the language of African legal philosophy must be accessible not only to philosophers; it must also be accessible to non-philosophers. What is African about legal philosophy should be accessible to both philosophers and non-philosophers. The composition of African legal philosophy by an African philosopher is a joint project. It is co-composed by all Africans whether they are or are not philosophers. It must resonate in all Africans. Differently stated, fundamentally understood, African legal philosophy, understood as a sense of law or as a sense of legality in Africa, is not private domain open only to legal philosophers or to legal scholars. It is a domain where every African has a say, if only because it is matter of being African. It stands for the sense of being African—the consciousness of being African. But it is also more than this. African legal philosophy is a site where the Africanness of every African is constituted and exhibited. That is, there is what is African in every African, and it is what is African about every African that African legal philosophy seeks to articulate and bring into the open. Thus, if it is asked how one can speak of African legal philosophy in a situation that seems to call for multiple conceptions of legal philosophy, it may be worth remembering that, in the midst of their diversity, Africans remain African. To speak of African legal philosophy is to address that which paves the way for thinking about such remainder. Moreover, as members of the human community, thinking about such remainder opens the way for thinking about African legal philosophy in the context of the human community—in the context of human legal philosophy. To think of African legal philosophy in this context is to think of it in a manner in which the being of every human being is at stake. It is this manner of thinking that is at stake in legal philosophies. It is that by which every legal philosophy is to be judged.

African legal philosophy is a branch of African philosophy. I construe it as such to set it apart from other studies on African law that explicitly may have nothing to do with philosophy. As a branch of African philosophy, it cannot be fully understood unless one has a general understanding of African philosophy. Moreover, one cannot truly have a general understanding of African philosophy if one does not have a general understanding of philosophy. Success in exhibiting what is at stake in African legal philosophy will serve as an introduction to legal philosophy in general, to African philosophy in general, and to philosophy in general. In the course of this introduction, philosophy, in turn, will pave the way not only for the understanding of African legal philosophy, but also for understanding legal philosophy in general.

The idea that an introduction to legal philosophy is an introduction to philosophy is rarely if ever explicitly stated in most books on legal philosophy. Most legal philosophers jump right away into the illumination of the nature of law and its related aspects and ignore illuminating the nature of philosophy and its related aspects. This may have the virtue of calling attention to a better focus on the nature of law, but the virtue is compromised if one does not take into account the lens of philosophy that is at work in this focusing. Whether explicit or implicit, every text on legal philosophy bears and bares a conception of philosophy. Thus, most texts on legal philosophy in the Western world bear a Western conception of philosophy. Likewise, it should be expected that African texts on legal philosophy should bear an African conception of philosophy. To be sure, one can admit that every text book on legal philosophy bears a conception of philosophy without admitting that there is a plurality of conceptions of philosophy. There is a great temptation to adopt a universalist conception of philosophy and hence, a universalist conception of legal philosophy at the expense of regional conceptions of philosophy. One does not have to succumb to such a temptation. Reciprocal implication may be in order here. The universal is in the particular, and the particular is in the universal. One's concern should be the avoidance of dogmatism, for where dogmatism prevails philosophy is excluded. Philosophical thinking flourishes in the absence of dogmatism, or in the attack on dogmatism. In thinking about African legal philosophy or about any other legal philosophy, dogmatism has to be avoided and has to be constantly challenged. This is not an easy task for those who are called upon to philosophize. Philosophy is constantly in the process of being constituted.

As one looks at the history of philosophy, one finds a continuous dialogue, and at times, a continuous controversy on what the task of philosophy is, or on what that task ought to be. It can be expected that this state of affairs is reflected not only in legal philosophy, but also in other branches of philosophy. My own constituting reflection on African legal philosophy is not immune to this state of affairs. Indeed, the success of what I am trying to do here can be attained only if I am able to reinforce the continuation of the dialogue on the nature of philosophy in general, and on the nature of African legal philosophy in particular. Any closure of the dialogue on the nature of philosophy can only mean that philosophizing has come to an end. And were philosophizing to come to an end, it would not only mean that a discipline called philosophy has come to an end. The being that philosophizes would come to an end as a philosophizing being. Moreover, given the ongoing controversy that has characterized the nature or the function of philosophy, what would have come to an end in the end of philosophy would equally be controversial. To the extent that it has been claimed that philosophy exemplifies what it is for us to be what we are, we too, somehow, would have to come to an end with the end of philosophy. Whether there would be another form of practice that would henceforth claim what is essential about us, would all depend on what is entailed by the end of philosophy. In other words, what is entailed by the end of philosophy would depend on how philosophy is understood. We ask of African legal philosophy, as we do with any other legal philosophy: to put us on the right path to this understanding, or at least, to shed light on what constitutes the right path.

As a branch of legal philosophy, African legal philosophy is essentially linked to all other non-African branches of legal philosophy. Where all branches of legal philosophy intersect, is a place where African legal philosophy should take us, if what is true about it is made manifest. Moreover, where legal branches of philosophy intersect is also a place where legal branches of philosophy and non-legal branches of philosophy intersect, and thus, by taking us there, African legal philosophy makes it possible for us to have some access to philosophy in general. It is the internal unity of philosophy that preserves its integrity. It is the essential task of every branch of philosophy to claim and allow itself to be claimed by this unity if it is to have philosophical integrity. It is by bearing the entire weight of philosophy that African legal philosophy can be truly what it is. What is at stake in the bearing of the entire weight of philosophy depends on what is philosophically understood about the nature of philosophy. The question on the nature of philosophy remains unasked in an elemental way partly due to an endless proliferation of the branches of philosophy, whereby each branch of philosophy appears to be lost in self-obsession. Moreover, the question remains unasked since asking remains incapacitated due to the imprisonment of philosophy in the academy. Such imprisonment remains an important achievement of modern Euro-western culture. Without interrogating and challenging the presiding over philosophy by Euro-western philosophers, the true import of philosophy will remain elusive, and so will the success in opening a horizon where African philosophy in general, and where African legal philosophy in particular can come into relief. The academy is only one of the possible theaters of philosophy, and consequently, one of the possible theaters of legal philosophy. Philosophical life reaches beyond the boundaries of the academy and so does legal philosophical life. Hence, the study of African legal philosophy must reach beyond the confines of the academy.

At issue in the notion of African legal philosophy is not only what philosophy concerns itself with in general, or what legal philosophy concerns itself with in particular. At issue is also what is African about legal philosophy. We concern ourselves with the Africanness of philosophy with the hope that this concern will shed light on what constitutes the Africanness of legal philosophy. This way of putting matters may strike one as somewhat awkward. Texts on American legal philosophy do not explicitly concern themselves with the Americanness of American legal philosophy. Texts on German legal philosophy do not explicitly concern themselves with the Germanness of German legal philosophy, and texts on British legal philosophy do not explicitly concern themselves with the Britishness of British legal philosophy. Why then, one may ask, should African legal philosophy be burdened with the issue of what constitutes the Africanness of legal philosophy? Isn't this a diversion from the investigation of what is to constitute African legal philosophy? And isn't this likely to lead one to the error of essentialism? In response to these questions, it can simply be stated that a philosophical investigation of the Africanness of legal philosophy is a part of the investigation of African legal philosophy, and as such, it is not a diversion. This investigation permeates the work at hand. Hopefully, this will be done in collaboration with those who take what will be said thoughtfully. To take what is said thoughtfully is to reflect on it creatively. Moreover, it is only in a philosophical dialogue with what is said that what is said can be heard philosophically. When one dialogues with what is said, one thereby dialogues with others. It is worth repeating that one does not philosophize alone. Even at those moments when a thinker isolates himself or herself to ponder those matters that are of utmost importance in philosophy, one is not entirely cut off from other human beings. It is true that thinking is the site in which human individuality is constituted and made manifest; but it is also true that such constitution and manifestation is inevitably social. One cannot be human alone. It is only in the context of others that one is human.

As previously stated, as African legal philosophy, African legal philosophy is to be understood, as a branch of African philosophy. In thinking about it, one inevitably finds oneself thinking about African philosophy. How is one to think about African philosophy? There appears to be extensive literature on philosophy in some non-African philosophical traditions, thereby, making philosophy in this context better known to the readers, whereas in the African philosophical tradition there appears to be only meager literature on philosophy, thereby, making it less known to the readers. Also, in regard to legal philosophy, it could be said that there is little written literature on African legal philosophy, whereas there is ample written literature on some other non-African legal philosophy. However, it should be noted that the amount of literature available in a tradition is not necessarily a measure of the existence or non-existence of philosophy in it. Whether there is an African philosophical tradition in which one can locate African legal tradition has been an issue. The very existence of African philosophical tradition appears to have been controversial.[3] What a distinguished professor of history at Oxford said in response to the pressure to offer a course on African history may reinforce the contention of those who have had doubts about the existence of African philosophy. The professor said,

> Undergraduates, seduced, as always, by the changing breadth of journalistic fashion, demand that they should be taught the history of black Africa. Perhaps, in the future, there will be some African history to teach. But at present there is none, or very little; there is only the history of the Europeans in Africa. The rest is largely darkness, like the history of the pre-European, pre-Colombian America. And darkness is not a subject for history.[4]

Those of us who teach African philosophy often encounter questions such as what are the canonical texts in African philosophy. Who are the major African philosophers? In regard to African legal philosophy, the questions that one is likely to encounter are what are the canonical texts in African legal philosophy? Who are the major African legal philosophers? These questions appear disarming and are not easy to answer especially when asked in a philosophical spirit. To ask them in a philosophical spirit necessitates a philosophical pre-understanding of what philosophy is. It is not always evident that everyone who asks these questions already possesses this pre-understanding. Some of those who ask these questions would have a hard time articulating philosophically what they understand as philosophy. There are those who labor under the assumption that African thinking is yet to attain a philosophical status either due to the alleged racial constitution of Africans, or due to an alleged claim that African culture is yet to develop to a stage where African thinking would attain a philosophical status. It is indeed the case that, today it is no longer fashionable to openly adopt a racist attitude towards Africans. But it should not be forgotten that the projection of African thinking by non-Africans is not yet fully immunized from racist characterizations or from cultural chauvinism. To be sure, it is not always fair to suspect nasty motives in everyone who asks the above questions. In the case of those who honestly seek to know, there may be assumptions that must first be explored. These questions are for the most part posed in a comparative context. Those who ask them, already, may have in mind some legal philosophical canonical texts, or some major legal philosophers from other philosophical traditions. The comparison, however, may be philosophically suspect, for the standards that are used may contain an implicit prejudice. Despite conventional wisdom, what text is canonical or which is not, or what makes a philosopher major or minor may be in the eyes of the beholder. It may depend on standards that are specific to one's cultural tradition, and hence, without necessarily having universal validity. Moreover, academic historians of philosophy or academic philosophers may have appropriated undue authority in determining what is canonical and what is not, or who is a major legal philosopher and who is not. Contrary to what appears to be conventionally the case, the academy is not the only locus of such authority. Conventional determination of what is or is not a canonical text in philosophy or the conventional determination of who is and who is not a major philosopher may be different from a philosophical determination. A philosophical determination itself may be problematic in that what makes a determination philosophical may be subject to an endless philosophical controversy. The fact that there may be a community of philosophers who make the determination does not immunize the constitution of such a community from a critical appraisal, and it should not readily be assumed that there must be only one such community. Membership in a philosophical community depends on what is understood as a philosophical community and, in part, such understanding is subject to philosophical inquiry.

An African criterion for what constitutes a philosophical determination takes shape in the context of African philosophy. Today, it is evident that the discussion on African philosophy among Africans is affected by discussions on the nature of philosophy in non-African cultural traditions, and more specifically, it is affected by the Western European discussions on the nature of philosophy. This is largely due to European colonialism, or European cultural imperialism in Africa. Exploring the influence that Western European philosophers have on African discussions of the nature of philosophy is important if one is to have a better understanding of what Africans are saying about philosophy.

For the most part, African academic philosophers have been trained by Western academic professors of philosophy. Even those who have been trained by African professors of philosophy, the trainers of these trainers are for the most part Western academic professors. In this training, written texts on Western philosophy appear to be more widely read than philosophy texts from other traditions. In making a case for African philosophy in general, and for African legal philosophy in particular, one cannot ignore the domination of Western philosophers in the conception and setting up the criterion of what constitutes philosophical cannon. This domination has not only constrained African philosophical life. It has also effectively marginalized Asian philosophy as well as other traditions of philosophy. This state of affairs has institutionalized ignorance of other branches of philosophy among Africans, for they have been led to believe that the only branch of philosophy that matters is the Euro-Western branch. Today, where legal philosophy is taught in African institutions such legal philosophy is likely to be Western legal philosophy, or to be a footnoting of what Western legal philosophers have said. An exception may be found in those regions of Africa that have come under Islamic influence where Islamic legal philosophy is likely to be taught. One hardly hears of Taoist legal philosophy, Buddhist legal philosophy, or Hindu legal philosophy. In the same vein, speaking about African legal philosophy is likely to have no audience among European students of legal philosophy. African students of law are likely to be deaf to what is said about African legal philosophy primarily because they have been integrated into European audience, and have been equipped with Europhonic hearing aids.

Philosophical dialogue between the Africans who have received Western philosophical education and the Africans who have received Islamic philosophical education is rare. The former know little about Islamic jurisprudence, and the latter know little about Western jurisprudence, unless they happen to have been subjected to European colonial experience. Similarly, an elemental philosophical dialogue between Africans and Asians or between Africans and other non-Euro-western people has been aborted, suppressed, or inhibited. In the area of African legal philosophy, there appears to be a widespread impression that Africans have nothing, or have little to learn from Asian or from other non-Euro-Western people. On the other hand, the imperial nature of Euro-Western philosophical thinking has given the impression to Asian and other non-Euro-western people that Africans have nothing or have little to offer in philosophical thinking, and hence, in philosophical legal thinking. The difficulty of articulating indigenous African legal philosophy is thus compounded by the pressure that has been generated by Euro-western imperial thinking.

Imperialism, one must bear in mind, is not exclusively a matter of economics or politics. It has an intellectual/spiritual component. It has what appears to be a philosophical component. When in the name of philosophy some people, on account of their cultural tradition, race, or gender, are pre-judged to be non-philosophical, anti-philosophical, or pre-philosophical, we have a spurious and anti-philosophical conception of philosophy. Imperialism is incompatible with what it means to philosophize. Incompatibility can be minimized if it is recognized or admitted that no people are immunized from philosophical thinking. African philosophy has an impact on, and ought to have an impact not only on Western philosophy, but also to non-Euro-western philosophy. Such recognition and admission would undermine the prevailing domination of Western philosophy and prepare for and reinforce a genuine philosophical dialogue between African and non-African philosophers. The current environment in which African and Western philosophers engage in discussion on philosophy does not allow for a meaningful dialogue. Generally, Western philosophers appear to be dictatorial and paternalistic, and perhaps, at the root of this dictatorship and paternalism lies a crucial element that is anti-philosophical. Towards Africans, they act as missionaries of philosophy and recognize Africans as philosophers only to the extent that Africans learn philosophy from them. What is dictatorial is anti-philosophical. It is by challenging this dictatorship that Africans can position themselves where they can engage each other in a genuine dialogue on African philosophy, and where they can enter into a meaningful dialogue with non-Africans. The invasion of African thinking by Euro-western thinking has been so successful that what generally passes as African philosophical thinking is for the most part parasitic to Euro-western philosophical thinking. One of the tasks of African thinkers is to find or institute an African thinking that divorces African thinking from this parasitism. In demarcating the province of African philosophical legal thinking, one must be on guard lest one fall victim to this parasitism. An African, or anyone else for that matter, who seeks to think philosophically about African legal philosophy can successfully do so if he or she makes what is to think in an African way subject to an ongoing philosophical scrutiny. This would be consistent with being African, for being African is an ongoing process.

The dictatorial element in Western philosophy is partly a result of the shaping of the Western philosophical mind by the Christian religion. Whitehead has noted that "The safest general characteristic of European philosophical tradition is that it consists of a series of footnotes to Plato". He would have been more accurate had he said that "The safest general characteristic of European philosophical tradition is that it consists of a series of footnotes to Christianity"[5], which, essentially, makes it a Christian tradition rather than a philosophical tradition. Today, in the West, it may not be so outrageous to construe what is canonical in philosophical determination in an ecclesiastical context. The medievalization of Greek philosophy and of philosophy in general, may have robbed the word canon of its Hellenic (pagan) meaning.

In classical Greek philosophy reason was the canon. Philosophical life was construed as the life of reason. Reason was the standard rod of measuring human affairs. The canon was the lived reason. It was reason as exemplified in the way that human beings live or in the way they ought to live as human beings. For the Greeks, such a life was pre-eminently political. The life of reason was a political life. A philosophical determination of law was grounded in reason, and consequently, on the political. For medieval thinkers however, philosophy as the life of reason became subservient to Christian faith. Reason was subjected to Christian baptism. Philosophy became the handmaiden of theology. Legal philosophy was reduced to being nothing more than a branch of Christian theology. Divine law was the law of laws. It became the source of human laws and the basis of their validity. It was the proper province for jurisprudence. The canon was theological. Legal science was ultimately a species of divine science. Taking the cue from the New Testament, Christian thinkers appropriated logos, and shrouded it in unfathomable and unquestionable religious mystery. Logos, as the written sacred word, was rendered absolutely authoritative. The written sacred word became an object of veneration. It is true that medieval Christian thinkers did not originate the veneration of the written word. Before them, the Hebrews, their religious ancestors, had Yahweh's Commandments handed to Moses in writing. These Commandments had the force of law, as did the Old Testament in general. As evidenced in the New Testament, Christians took over the authoritarianism of the Old Testament and liberalized it to bring those who were not Christians under the umbrella of this authoritarianism. The spread of Christianity brought with it the imperial reign of the sacred written word. Medieval Christian thinkers embarked on a historic mission of transforming philosophy to the handmaiden of this religious imperialism. Neither European Renaissance, nor the Age of Reason, nor the rise of Scientific Spirit succeeded in divorcing Christian religion from philosophy, and consequently, in divorcing Western legal philosophy from Christian theology. It is the absence of this divorce that leads modern Western scholars of natural law to look up to St. Thomas Aquinas' legal philosophy and jurisprudence for inspiration. Legal positivism has not succeeded in bringing about this divorce. By blindly embracing modern Western legal philosophy and Western jurisprudence, African legal philosophers are likely to end up embracing a Christo-centric legal philosophy or a Christo-centric jurisprudence—a legal philosophy and its attendant jurisprudence that is essentially religious but that poses as non-religious or as anti-religious.

It should not be forgotten that there is nothing European about the so-called European Renaissance. It was an attempt by Europeans to resurrect the Greco-Roman classical world. Neither the Romans nor the Greeks were Europeans. Neither was Western. The renaissance was not a renaissance of ancient classical European world. In the story of European people there was no classical thinking to be reborn. If there were such thinking Europeans are yet to tell the world what it was. Moreover, the Greco-Roman classical world they want to give birth again was mediated by Christian interpretation. They used the Greco-Roman classical world to constitute their identity and to cover up what could be interpreted as the poverty of their being. In matters that pertain to legal philosophy, they keep Africans and other non-European peoples in the dark about this state of affairs. It must be recalled that the humanism of the so-called European Renaissance was deeply rooted in Christianity, and when this humanism was used as a founding stone for the so-called secular European legal philosophy of jurisprudence, Christianity played a major role in the construction of this stone. Renaissance flowered from Christian Medievalism.

The consecration of the marriage between philosophy and Christianity gave birth to European culture. The missionary / evangelical element took root in this culture. European culture became the Chosen culture, the Culture of all cultures, and became the Culture to be propagated throughout the world. Absolutism in the reign of the written word in Christian religion was readily transferred to philosophy, and in this transference philosophy, as henceforth understood in the West, acquired absolutist tendency.[6] This tendency was captured with greater perfection by Hegel for whom all history is the realization of the Absolute, the absolute of Westernism. If anyone wanted to philosophize, he or she had to turn to the West for inspiration. It is in this context that an unemancipated African philosophy appears to be an offspring or parasitic to Western philosophy. In demarcating the province of African philosophy in general and hence, the province of African legal philosophy, it is essential to combat this paternity and parasitism. The combat calls for a firm grounding not only on African philosophy but also on the history of African philosophy. This is the grounding of African legal philosophy and of its history.

In combating colonial mentality in African philosophy, Africans find themselves in a situation that is similar to the one in which some Latin Americans find themselves. Leopoldo Zea, a Mexican philosopher has noted that,

> The man who had lived with so much confidence under a tree he had not planted now finds himself in the open when the planter cuts down the tree, and throws into the fire as useless. The man now has to plant his own cultural tree, create his own ideas. But a culture does not emerge miraculously; the seed of that culture must be taken somewhere, it must belong to someone.[7]

For the African, it must be asked, where is this somewhere? And who is this someone? The obvious and easy answer in this case, is somewhere is Africa, and the someone is the African. But the obvious and the easy answer may take for granted what ought not to be taken for granted. By Africa are we to understand simply a geographical location? By African are we simply to understand a biological designation? The somewhere we are after is a philosophical Africa and the someone we are looking for is a philosophical African. In this case, to look intelligently we are to look philosophically. And how is an African or anyone else to look at Africa and at the African philosophically? Without such a look African legal philosophy will not fully yield its truth. African legal philosophy constitutes not only a legal definition of Africa but also a legal definition of an African. An inquiry into what it is is at the same time, an inquiry into what Africa is, and into what an African is. Jurisprudence, African or non-African, has an ontological significance.

The colonialists projected pre-colonial Africa as devoid of philosophy. With the end of colonialism the African philosopher now finds himself or herself face to face with pre-colonial Africa, and what is at stake here is his or her own identity as an African. Is he or she to search for a written philosophy in pre-colonial Africa to vindicate himself or herself in the eyes of those who have deprived him or her of a philosophical past? To whom is he or she to vindicate himself or herself? A philosophical answer to the latter question must be that he or she is to vindicate himself or herself to himself or to herself. But this cannot be done intelligently without an authentic conception of an African self. Must such a self be inscribed in writing the way his or her European counterpart believes? To do so would be to succumb to the dogmatic attachment to what is written, which would be unphilosophical. But this does not mean the African is to establish his or her philosophical identity by being anti-writing. There is nothing anti-African or non-African about writing. There is nothing wrong with writing as such. What is wrong is a conception of writing that mystifies writing and transforms it into an ideological weapon in the struggle against the humanity of others. As African nations scramble to ground law on a written constitution, it should not be forgotten that what is written is but one source of testifying at what law is. This source may even be derivative, not elemental. To the extent that legal philosophy concerns itself with what is human, what is human is not confined to what is written. Being human pre-dates what is written, and consequently, in so far as it seeks to articulate the human, legal philosophy pre-dates the written. The oral legal philosophy has a more primordial place than written jurisprudence. Textuality signifies what is human in a non-exhaustive way. There are other signifiers of the human.

The appropriation of the canon by the holy written word appears to have had enormous influence in the formation of the Western European legal mind. It was Sir William Blackstone, the author of the Commentaries on the Laws of England, and a man who has had enormous influence in the formation of the ideas of law in the Anglo-American world, who stated that,

> This law of nature being coeval with mankind and dictated by God himself, is of course superior in obligation to any other. It is binding all over the globe, in all countries, and at all times, no human laws are of any validity if contrary to this; and such of them as are valid derive all their force, and all their authority, mediately or immediately, from this original.[8]

The nature that Blackstone has in mind is no longer nature as was understood by the pre-Christian Romans, or as was understood by the pre-Christian Greeks, and clearly, it was not nature as understood by Africans. He had in mind nature as understood by Judeo-Christians, nature that was created by God. Imprinted in this nature by God were laws that regulated it. Accordingly, natural law was ultimately grounded in and was intelligible in Christian theology. Moreover, the God Blackstone had in mind is God as construed by Judeo-Christians. It is that Old Testament God, the jealous God, who will not tolerate the worship of any other God, and who has singled out a specific group of people in the human community as his people. Africans are not among the select people, and their Gods are reduced to non-Gods and as anti-God. As non-Gods, they have no binding effect on the affairs of men—the true men of God. They are not legally authoritative. The laws that they author have no validity. When the God of the Old Testament is liberalized in the New Testament, he retains the same jealousy, continues to view himself as the only God, but now, he can embrace Africans, but only if they renounce their Gods and also renounce whatever commands may have issued from these Gods. With the emergence of the New Testament, the Israelites—the chosen people of the Old Testament, are effectively replaced by Romans when they become Christian converts, and later, by Europeans. That is, Europeans become the Chosen people—the people of God. In modern history, it has been the mission of Europeans to convince Africans and other non-Europeans that they (Europeans) are, indeed, the Chosen people. Africans and other non-Europeans have been forced and pressured to swallow this religious myth. It is a myth that, as a myth, has corrupted and distorted philosophical life to the point at which philosophical jurisprudence has become almost indistinguishable from Judeo-Christian theological jurisprudence. Whereas Islamic jurisprudence explicitly embraces theology as the foundation of jurisprudence, Euro-Westerners conceal the fact their jurisprudence equally rests on theology. Secularism, among Euro-westerners, conceals this concealment. It is a whitewashing of a theological outlook that makes it look as if it is non-theological or anti-theological. It is another element in the Euro-western toolbox of cosmetic paraphernalia. Euro-western modernity has attempted to end the matrimony of philosophy and Christian theology but with little success, perhaps, because the moderns did not fully grasp the extent to which philosophy was compromised in this matrimony. Despite the Austinian attempt to separate divine law from positive law, legal philosophy in the West has remained trapped in this marriage. The notion of the uncommanded commander (the sovereign) who is to issue commands that are genuinely legal is an earthly being patterned after the God of the Judeo-Christians. The Man of Europe has proclaimed himself as the heir of this God and has taken his jurisprudence to be His jurisprudence.

Although it is projected as a version of secularism, the legal philosophy that Europeans have imposed on Africans is a legal philosophy that is deeply rooted in a European version of Christianity. The unmasking of this rootedness is not only an essential for the understanding of this legal philosophy; it is also an essential step towards the demarcation of an authentic African legal philosophy. In an attempt to avoid or to solve problems that are raised by legal relativism, legal subjectivism, and by conflicting views about the nature of law, the quest for objectivity in the study of law has become an attractive proposition. The appeal of natural law appears to be irresistible. After all, what is natural is not bound to this or that society or culture. It is not subject to spatial temporal or historical contingencies. Moreover, it reinforces the so-called rule of law when it is set apart from the rule of man. Impartiality, neutrality and non-partisanship are projected as virtues of the rule of law. Obedience to the rule of law is then set up and viewed as a part of the bedrock of justice. What remains concealed in the modern seduction is the Judeo-Christian theological and the religious aspect of natural law. As understood in the West, Natural law is deeply medievalized. St. Thomas Aquinas is the major force in the formulation of this project. When African students of law forget this their embrace of natural law role amounts to the embrace of this medievalization. Thereby, they contribute to the continuing rape and destruction of African culture. It is a form of cultural suicide. Unwittingly, they continue to look for jurisprudential inspiration in legal philosophy in the Christianized West. They continue to be parasitic to Western legal philosophy. They continue to render support to Western imperial theo-naturology. Jurisprudential naturalism is a part of the Christian mythology—a mythology that has been fully integrated into Western jurisprudential imperialism. Western legal philosophy is yet to be immunized from this imperialism.

In authentic African legal philosophy, it is essential that writing be demythologized. The continued worship of the written word by philosophers reflects the extent to which legal philosophy continues to labor under the yoke of religion or quasi-religion (secularism). Although it can be granted that the codification of law has practical benefit, it is erroneous to claim that coded law and only coded law is law. Written law does not exhaust what law is, and what is essential about law pre-dates writing. The failure to see philosophy in Africa may be due to a failed sight or a failing sight in the looker, or it may be due to a misconstruction of philosophy, and hence, a misconstruction of where and how philosophy appears. An eye trained to look at philosophy only in the written word may fail to notice African philosophy since it is generally believed that Africans are not people of the book. This belief is held despite the fact that writing in Africa, as evidenced in Egypt, predates the existence of writing in Europe and in many other parts of the world. Construing the written word as the only testimony for the existence of philosophy is a dogmatic construction that ought to have no place in philosophy. The dogmatism is not simply a mental stagnation. To think of it this way is to overlook the fact that writing is more than arrangements of alphabets, marks, or characters on a surface. In writing, we announce who we are, and what we value. Descartes, the French philosopher and the alleged founder of modern Western philosophy, said I think therefore I am. For those who derive their identity from writing or those whose identity is constituted in and by writing, it could similarly be said that I write therefore I am. A human being is a being that writes. But, it must not be forgotten that writing is but one of the many ways in which human beings constitute and announce themselves as human beings. Being unable to write does not attest to one's lack in being human. To be sure, there are those who have sought to deny the humanity of others by denying them membership in the writing community, and there are those who do not recognize the humanity of those who cannot write.

When Africans were slaves in the United States they were forbidden from knowing how to read and how to write. This was a way of undermining their humanity. It is not that one has to be able to read or write to be a human being. The problem here is the deliberate racist suppression of the actualization of the Africans' ability to read and write out of the fear that they can claim human equality. At one time, women were kept out of schools where they could learn how to read and write for the same reason. An openness where women could express or constitute who or what they were was put off limits to them. This was a way of keeping them from being who they were as human beings. Writing is a way of exhibiting and deploying power. It is a power base that is in the hands of those who wield power in society. To understand writing one must look at its politics. Committing philosophy into writing, as is the case with the codification of law, is a way of deploying power. In an oppressive world such as the one we live in today, prioritizing what is written over what is not is a deployment of power in the human hierarchical manner. Such deployment privileges the group that is at the top of the hierarchy. The challenge of the view that writing is the only place for philosophy or the only place for legal philosophy is the challenge of the way in which power is deployed in society. Writing may be an instrumental good. It must be evaluated in the light of the good that it seeks to realize. The hunt for African legal philosophy exclusively in the terrain of writing may yield inconclusive or may yield distorted results. It may fail to take cognizance of the technology of power that writing is. The modern European inspired distrust of the word of mouth in the construction of law and the belief that what is put in writing deserves more serious legal attention than what is uttered by the word of mouth is, for the most part, a legal fiction in the service of fetishism. Must the non-western world be sucked into this fetishism too? The worship of the written word marginalizes millions of Africans since they cannot read or write or because they can barely do so. This leaves essential matter of law at the hands of the few who can read or write. It is they who write the law for all; it is they who interpret the law for all. It gives the few the power to determine and direct the destiny for all. Their written pronouncements become the law. African legal philosophy or African jurisprudence is reduced to the study of the interpretations of these pronouncements. Such legal philosophy is incompatible with the proper province of African legal philosophy which must be a philosophy for all and not just for a few. Authentic African legal philosophy is a philosophy that affirms and empowers the humanity of every African, a philosophy in which the material expression of the dignity of every African is recognized and affirmed. This is the landscape of African legal philosophy.

It is not enough to say that the existence of African philosophy in general, or the existence of African legal philosophy in particular, is problematic in that there is scarcity of written literature on African philosophy. Must one not ask whether the written word constitutes the only place for philosophy? Why shouldn't philosophy have a place in the oral word too? The claim that philosophy must have a place only in the written word may be a reflection of the imperialism of writing cultures. Such imperialism may obscure the multiplicity and heterogeneity of the theaters of philosophy, and may be a violation of what is essential about philosophy. The abundance of written philosophical works, and more particularly in our case, the abundance of written legal philosophical works in some cultural traditions does not necessarily prove that cultural traditions without writing do not have an abundance of philosophical literature in general or legal literature in particular. The idea of looking for philosophy only in books may be symptomatic of a cult of those who have made a fetish out of books. If Socrates is correct in seeing the primary task of philosophy as the examination of one's life for the sake of leading a virtuous life, then it is in our lives that what is philosophical announces itself. If we must make a fetish out of a book let that book be the book of life. It is also worth bearing in mind that literacy has multiple theaters. It does not show itself exclusively in writing. The oral is an essential theater, and so is social and cultural life in general. Law has its place in life. That is, the life of law is ultimately the law of life. Life is the proper subject matter of legal philosophy. The oral is closer to life than writing. Without a proper interpretation of writing, writing becomes where life ceases to be life, where life dies.

Raising the issues of the existence of legal canonical texts in African legal philosophy, or highlighting the lack of major African legal philosophers may betray an unreflective attitude towards what constitutes legal philosophy, and also towards the location of legal philosophy. It may reflect a lack of reflection on what philosophy is, and on how it is exhibited. How and where philosophy manifests itself depends on what is understood as philosophy. If properly understood, what is said herein in the name of African jurisprudence, or in the name of African legal philosophy, should lead us to a reflection on what is said in the name of philosophy. In other words, what is said should be understood as an invitation to philosophize. The response to this invitation is a response to participate in determining how philosophy is to be constituted and understood. I do not have in mind solely what academic philosophers say about philosophy for, as previously stated, it is not philosophically evident that the academy is the only place where philosophy is constituted, or the only place where it is exhibited. Heidegger must be given some credit for observing that,

> The misinterpretations with which philosophy is perpetually beset are promoted most of all by people of our kind, that is by professors of philosophy. It is our customary business—which may be said to be justified and even useful—to transmit a certain knowledge of the philosophy of the past, as a part of the general education. Many people suppose that this is philosophy, whereas at best it is the technique of philosophy.[9]

What Heidegger says about the contribution that professors of philosophy make in perpetuating misinterpretations of philosophy is applicable to misconception of legal philosophy. Professors of legal philosophy or professors of law are not necessarily legal philosophers. They may be simply producing information on law, or they may be disseminating information on what philosophers have said about law. They may have in their possession a body of knowledge about law that they pass on to their students, to their academic colleagues, or to members of society in general. It is not difficult to imagine how professors of law, in this sense, would naturally fit into the post-colonial (neo-colonial Africa). In colonial Africa, education, especially the education introduced by colonialism, was in the service of colonialism. It was an education whose mission was to keep Africans under colonial bondage. Initially, low level vocational training was sparingly offered to Africans. Men were taught carpentry and other handcrafts, and later, women were taught domestic science. Such an education had the full support of the United States, and indeed was patterned after Booker T. Washington's Tuskegee model of education.[10] This model of education discouraged African students from pursuing academic subjects. It trained students for vocational jobs—the kind of jobs that the slave economy needed. When elementary or primary education was introduced, it was run by Christian missionaries whose primary mission was to offer religious education—an education that sought to erase indigenous African religions, to sow the seeds of Christianity and inculcate obedience to colonial government. Education consisted of rote memorization. Bright African students were those students who excelled in this kind of education. A few of them entered the few secondary or high schools that were established. Post-secondary education was largely non-existent during the colonial period. When it was established in the post-colonial period, it was largely an inferior imitation of the education offered in Europe. Its primary mission was not to de-colonize African education. It was to fit Africans into a neo-colonial world.

During the colonial world of law Africans were subjects of colonial law. They were to obey colonial law. They were excluded from legislating and from adjudicating except in matters that did not impede the constitution and administration of the colonial world. They could participate in low-level enforcement of law. There were no African law schools. In the latter period of colonialism, the few Africans who had an access to legal education had to go abroad. The legal education they received was tailored to needs of non-Africans, and when they returned to Africa they perpetuated the olonialist and later, the neo-colonialist mission. The legal training consisted of rote-memorization of both substantive and procedural law—law that was largely alien to Africans.

When law schools were established in post-colonial Africa, they were staffed by foreign professors of law. These professors were purveyors and even today continue to be purveyors of knowledge about law. Professors of law, who for the most part, distinguished themselves in the knowledge of foreign law, became the captains of legal education. Even when they turned attention to African law, such law consisted of nothing more than a body of knowledge about African customary law. This is largely the case today. And as Mamdani has pointed out, African customary law was applicable only to "tribal" Africans and not to European residents in the colonies.[11] In the African world—a world that Europeans projected as a tribal world, and a world that was under the regime of customary law, there were no legal philosophers. In the eyes of Europeans there was no legal philosophy. Apparently, Africans were too stupid to understand any philosophy. But even in post-colonial legal education, generally, legal philosophers have no place. This is not radically different from the situation in the West where legal philosophers are generally ignored in law schools, or treated as if they were lepers. Following the reigning ideology in the legal academy in the West, African professors of law have come to view law schools as trade or vocational schools where young men and women are trained to practice law. A philosophical investigation of what it is that they practice in the name of law appears to be a diversion. Their mission is accomplished when they pass on vocational knowledge about law, and when students assimilate this knowledge. Unlike professors of law, legal philosophers are those women and men who go beyond the call of knowledge and open up an elemental dialogue and conversation on who and what we are. Law is one of the places where this dialogue and conversation ought to be carried out. By emphasizing the production of knowledge, the search for knowledge, the dissemination and acquisition of knowledge, prevailing education about law has led to the marginalization of such a dialogue and conversation. If this state of affairs is taken into consideration, one may readily notice the plight of legal education in Africa.

For the most part, today, in Africa, African philosophical education is taking place in the academic setting. The teaching and learning about African legal philosophy has moved from the rural setting to the urban setting. It is headquartered in this setting—a setting that has distinguished itself and that continues to distinguish itself as the center for the de-Africanization of the African, and as the center for the de-Africanization of African culture. Indigenous schools of law, and indigenous schools of philosophy, formerly located in rural areas, have increasingly been rendered anachronistic. The wisdom of elders that was found in these schools has now been replaced by the knowledge that is produced in the urban academic institutions that perhaps should be referred to more appropriately as industries of knowledge.

Young men and women who want to study philosophy or law are forced to abandon the rural area and head on to the city. Traditionally, young people were not entrusted with the practice of law. They were expected to observe law as it was construed and practiced by the elders. The practice of law was entrusted to the elders. It is the elders who, due to extensive experience, had a more mature understanding of human nature, and who had the understanding of the customs of their people. Today, the elders are regarded as disposables. They are perceived as obstacles to legal education and to legal practice. Their lack of academic legal education disqualifies them from the life of law. What the life of law seems to require today is clever young men and women—the ones who excel in gobbling and spitting out information on law—law as defined by the academy. As long as young men and women excel in high school and enter the university, the doors of legal education are opened to them. After a few years of academic legal training, those who begin practicing law start referring to one another as my "Learned Brother" (in formerly British colonized parts of Africa), and later, those who become judges, expect to be referred to as "Your Honor". Because they lack academic credentials, African elders are no longer the learned. Moreover, since honor has increasingly become a privilege of the academically trained, African elders lose respect in the eyes of the young since they lack academic education. Even law-making has become a matter for the academically learned. African elders are excluded from it because they lack academic training. They are treated as idiots who do not know what is good for themselves or what is good for the country. They cannot understand the new language of law—a language that is rooted in non-African cultures and that is corrosive of African culture. They have become systematically marginalized and infantilized. They have been rendered dependent on the youth, and are subject to youthocracy, to a dictatorship of the young. The majority of them languish in the rural areas—an area that largely preserves most of what remains of African culture. In many parts of Africa the language of law is not an indigenous language. It is a foreign language, a language that for the most part flourishes in the city. It is this language that is the medium of education in the law school, and in higher education generally.

In the rural area, there languishes not only indigenous African legal sensibility, but also the indigenous African philosophical sensibility. The rural area has been projected as a lawless jungle from which the African must arise and enter modernity, the modernity that is symbolized by the city. Law is projected as one of the vehicles to transport one from the jungle to the city. The city has become a big mouth that devours whatever remains of African culture. In devouring of African culture, African legal philosophy is thereby devoured too. The crisis of African identity as exemplified in the crisis of African legal philosophy is rarely if ever taken up by those who concern themselves with contemporary legal education in Africa. The Africanness of a philosophy that is in complicity with this education cannot but be suspect. Resistance to this kind of education is an important aspect of the Africanness of an authentic African legal philosophy. Genuine African legal philosophy, in part, is a part of the struggle to stem the tide of the destruction of the Africanness of the African. The objective of the struggle is not to return students of authentic African legal philosophy to the rural area. I am not advocating Cambodianization of African legal philosophy where professors of law and legal philosophers are to be forced to go to the African countryside for re-education. The African rural area was not and is not a paradise. What is called for is not a recovery of the African past lock, stock and barrel. As Aime Cesaire notes in his anti-colonial crusade,

> For us, the problem is not to make a utopian and sterile attempt to repeat the past, but to go beyond. It is not a dead society that we want to revive. We leave that to those who go for exoticism. Nor is the present society that we wish to prolong, the most putrid carrion that ever rotted under the sun. It is a new society that we must create, with the help of our brother slaves, a society rich with all the productive power of modern times, warm with all the fraternity of the old days.[12]

As we attempt to de-colonize ourselves, there are many pitfalls that we have to avoid. One of them is a pitfall that is common to all those who have been victims of European domination. Vine Deloria, Jr., a Native American, has observed,

> Experts paint us the way they would like us to be. Often we paint ourselves as we wish we were or as we might have been. The more we try to be ourselves the more we are forced to defend what we have never been.[13]

We cannot fool ourselves or anybody else into believing that pre-colonial Africa was a human paradise and it is dangerously ridiculous to blame the plight of Africans entirely on colonialism or on European imperialism. We must assume responsibility for what has been dehumanizing and what is dehumanizing in African society. We must not make the erroneous assumption that indigenous African legal sensibility is without fault, or that it is entirely without merit. To do either is to do an injustice to the indigenous African and also to do an injustice to the post-indigenous African. An emancipatory African philosophy and its attendant emancipatory African jurisprudence is the anti-dote to this injustice. A call for the Africanness of philosophy or for the Africanness of African legal philosophy is a call to awaken Africans to the condition under which they live, so that they can identify and remove whatever stands in their way to being members of a human community—a community in which no one human being lives at the expense of another human being, and in which no one human community lives at the expense of any other human community.

It is a part of the conventional wisdom in the West that Africa is not a geographical territory that is normally associated with philosophy. This conception and drawing of the map of philosophy depends on how philosophy is understood. The conception and drawing of the map of philosophy in the West is based on a unilateral understanding of philosophy. The West has monopolized the understanding of philosophy and has precluded any meaningful dialogue on how philosophy is to be geographically situated. As a result of this monopoly an empire of the Western view of philosophy has emerged. If Non-westerners dare philosophize, they are forced to philosophize in the context of this empire; they are expected to be in its service. It is in this context that the West has been projected as the normal home of philosophy. It is apparently from the West that the missionaries of philosophy span the globe planting the seeds of philosophy. But it is not self-evident that what is normal in the West ought to be necessarily normal in the West or in Africa. Possibly, what is normal in the West could be abnormal not only in the West but also in Africa. It may not be a misconstruction to construe philosophy along the lines of psychoanalysis or psychotherapy. Such a construction may contribute to a diagnosis and identification of the false notions that have settled in the landscape of philosophy. The construction of the landscape of philosophy is not itself immune to false notions, and it must itself be brought under philosophical scrutiny.

Thinking of philosophy as an imperial project tends to generate the possibility of a philosopher. The realization of this possibility has found a fertile place in Africa, where Western missionaries of philosophy have been active. But, it should not be forgotten that there is something absurd in having a "missionary" of philosophy. It may be quite normal to have religious missionaries, as is the case in some religions such as Christianity, but having a missionary of philosophy, perhaps, reflects a contradictory thought. A philosopher is not a missionary and a missionary is not a philosopher. There are no geographical territories that are philosophically virgin such as to invite missionaries of philosophy. Philosophical education proceeds by the way of dialogue whereas the missionary's education is a monologue that assumes that those who are to be educated are mere receptacles who have nothing to give except their attention. The depiction of Africa as philosophically barren may tempt those who profess to be in philosophy to see an opportunity to plant the seeds of philosophy, but those who succumb to this temptation disqualify themselves as philosophers. The depiction of Africa as philosophically barren is unphilosophical. It is only by engaging Africans and by being engaged by Africans in a philosophical dialogue that the correctness of such a depiction can be intelligently evaluated. Such an engagement however already concedes to the very opposite of this depiction. One cannot engage another in a philosophical dialogue without expecting reciprocal engagement by the other. To engage an African in a philosophical dialogue, or to be engaged by an African in a philosophical dialogue, the African must be presumed to be philosophical. An African legal philosopher must be recognized as such.

Those who are involved in legal philosophy in the West may be tempted to see Africa as lacking legal philosophy, and thus be tempted to adopt a missionary attitude towards Africans. Succumbing to this temptation may render one's philosophical status suspect. Western paternalism towards Africa appears to be boundless. Africa is poor. Africa is diseased. Africa is illiterate. Africa is lawless. Africa is godless. Africa is moral-less. Africa is powerless. An Africa so painted is irresistible to those who are prone to a missionary complex. Of all the peoples of the world, Africans appear to be the most vulnerable to missionary cannibalism, and the temptation to be cannibalistic appears to be more pronounced among Westerners. Westerners try to do their best to save Africans from being African. It is precisely because of this situation that a philosophical dialogue between Africans and Westerners is so difficult. This state of affairs has also complicated intra-African dialogue. African legal philosophy comes across as imitative legal philosophy. The Dependence theory that developed largely in Latin America in the Sixties has a place for dependence legal philosophy, and since this theory was inevitably relevant to Africa, dependence legal philosophy that was a part of it is relevant to Africa. Breaking away from this dependence is necessary if African legal philosophy is to see the light of day. The coming into the light of day of African legal philosophy calls for a broader resistance to the world-view that the West has attempted to impose on Africans.

As previously indicated, law schools, generally, tend to be inhospitable to philosophy. They tend to banish philosophy from law. If philosophy is to be true to itself, however, it cannot accept this banishment, or go into exile. It must struggle for its rightful place in the life of law. The dwelling that philosophy constitutes in law is a home or ought to be a home for all of us whether we are or are not professional philosophers. Here is where we constitute ourselves as human beings. Yes, in Africa, there is a home for philosophy, a home not only for Africans but also for the humanity of all human beings. When law is taken up in African philosophy we ask of it that it lead us and secure us in this home. This is what is at stake in African legal philosophy. It is where a truly thought provoking African legal philosophy takes us. It is this taking that is at stake in African legal philosophy. An introduction to African legal philosophy is to be understood as this taking. As a philosophical taking, it is a taking in which one is not pulled or dragged. It is a taking into which one is automatically driven. Strictly speaking, one is not taken to this taking by someone else. One finds oneself already on the way to this taking. It is this way of taking and being taken that constitutes what is essential about philosophical teaching and learning. Philosophy teachers are assistants of philosophy students. It is only students who recognize this who can truly benefit from philosophy teachers.

Philosophizing, it must always be borne in mind, is autobiographical. It mirrors he or she who philosophizes. It is more than an individual undertaking. It brings into relief what is human about the philosopher. It is an undertaking that tells the story of being human. It is this story that legal philosophy tells in the province that it marks out for itself. In the case of African legal philosophy, what we have is a human story being told in an African context. It is a part of the task of African philosophy to constitute and define this context. To make sense of it, it is not essential that one be African. Provided that each one of us understands who he or she is, each one of us has already a pre-understanding of this context. In being what each one of us is, each one of us participates or must participate in constituting what I am constituting. The work of philosophy is the work of all of us. It is our autobiography, a webiogaphy that does not consist of a collection of individuals that exists independent of one another but as members of an organic community.

Now, it remains to be seen whether you will see yourself in what follows. If you do not see yourself in what follows, make room for yourself, and in doing so, make sure that you make room for all of us; otherwise, you would not be making a room for yourself. A room that is inhabited by philosophy has a place for all of us whether we are or are not in academic philosophy. It is unfortunate that the rise of academic philosophy, or the disciplining of philosophy in the academy has resulted in alienating us from one another, and has rendered us homeless in that home that holds us together as human beings. When applied to law, such a philosophy gives rise to a view of law that alienates us from one another and that renders us homeless where we all ought to be at home. Whenever we exclusively associate law with lawyers, judges, jurists, lawmakers, law professors, and law enforcement officers, we miss out on what is essential to law. What is essential to law is what constitutes us as human beings, and what defines us as such. In such a view of law, none of us is a stranger to any one of us. Such a view of law is what is pursued under the umbrella of African legal philosophy. Welcome to yourself. The otherness of African legal philosophy should not be used by Africans to sever their kinship with non-Africans and should not be used by non-Africans to sever their kinship with Africans. Today, the recognition and rehabilitation of this kinship is a central task of African legal philosophy. This kinship is unlike the kinship that is celebrated in Western modernity. The kinship that is celebrated in Western modernity is a product of social contract. In the West, the province of law is carved out of the environment created by social contract. Western legal philosophy, as is the case with Western jurisprudence, is largely a product of this environment. The kinship to which we are led by African legal philosophy, and which generates and nourishes African jurisprudence, is a primordial kinship. Social contract presupposes it. It is a kinship that is not readily accessible to modern social science. It is not a kinship in an ethnic god—whether the god of Judeo-Christians or the god of Islam. Regardless of how widespread the belief in either of these gods is, these gods remain ethnic and will never form a foundation for human kinship. Moreover, reason cannot be the foundation of human kinship. As construed in the West, kinship in reason has distinguished itself by excluding Africans from the human community, or by projecting Africans as if they are junior members of this human community. Any attempt to liberalize the conception of the Judeo-Christian god or Allah, or to liberalize reason to accommodate Africans is doomed a priori. An assimilationist thinking or way of life cannot gain access to an authentic human kinship. In addition to violating the humanity of those who are assimilated, it conceals the violence of those who seek to assimilate others. Authentic human kinship is mytho-poietic. This kinship makes each of us a mytho-poietic being. Reducing this mode of being to an aggregate of commands, rules, or rules and principles is to miss out on what ought to be claimed in the name of law. Law names us and preserves what is mytho-poietic about us. What law names and preserves can be named and preserved heterogeneously. To be faithful to what it names and what it preserves, there must be unity in this heterogeneity. The integrity of law lies in naming and preserving this heterogeneous unity, or this united heterogeneity. African legal philosophy is a path to this naming. It is a path in which the becoming of an African comes into relief. It is this becoming that embodies African legal thinking. In such thinking, thinking is not simply a matter of making inferences from presupposed premises. It is a matter of opening that horizon in which an African can be an African, in which the African can become a human being. One is human only in the process of becoming human.

If an introduction is a part of what is introduced, it remains a part of what is introduced. This means that it never goes beyond itself, and it is also a part of the conclusion. Consequently, if one is to take what is introduced seriously one must equally take the introduction seriously. One must commence the African legal philosophical journey where the African is at home and end at the same place—the place where the African is at home. At this home, it should not be forgotten that there is a place for every human being. It is a human home.

Beneath African legal philosophy, beneath what is African, there is the soil that nourishes both African legal philosophy and what is African. The beneath is not apart from what it nourishes. It is what makes what it nourished be what it is. What is this beneath? An African child comes into the world the same way that any other child comes into the world. It comes into the world without the consciousness of being African, and does not even come into the world with the consciousness of being a child. This coming into the world is the beneath of the African legal philosophy, the beneath of being African. It is a stream of silence that remains at the core of African legal philosophy, at the core of being African. Anything that is said to dam this stream or to stop its flow erases what is said and as soon as it is said. Normally, a child begins to speak from not being able to speak, from silence. Speaking is inherent in the child. It is the maturing of the child. As maturing, however, speaking never overcomes silence. Even in our speaking, we remain the silent ones. At death, our speaking reverts to silence, to what has been accompanying it all along: to its mother, for silence is the mother of speech. Our ancestors are the custodians of speech.

Chapter 2
African Jurisprudence

The peculiarity of African character is difficult to comprehend, for the very reason that in reference to it, we must quite give up the principle which naturally accompanies all our ideas—the category of Universality. In Negro life the characteristic point is the fact that consciousness has not yet attained to the realization of any substantial objective of existence—as for example, God, or law in which the interests of man's volition is involved and in which he realizes his own being. This distinction between himself as an individual and the universality of his essential being, the African in the uniform, undeveloped oneness of his existence has not yet attained; so that the Knowledge of an absolute being, an Other and Higher than his individual self, is entirely wanting. The Negro, as already observed, exhibits the natural man in his completely wild and untamed state. We must lay aside all thought of reverence and morality—all that we call feeling—if we would rightly comprehend him; there is nothing harmonious with humanity to be found in this type of character.[14]

By dint of trying to defend our civilizations at all costs, we have petrified them. We have betrayed our original cultures by showing them off, offering them as topics of myths for external consumption. In doing so we have unwittingly played European game—the Europe against which we first claimed we were setting out to defend ourselves. And what do we find at the end of the road? The same subservience, the same wretchedness, the same tragic abandonment of thinking by ourselves and for ourselves: slavery.[15]

> For Europe has never expected anything from us in cultural terms, except that we should offer her our civilizations as showpieces and alienate ourselves in a fictitious dialogue with her, over the heads of our own people.[16]

In the light of the above passages, those who are familiar with modern Western thinking and with modern African thinking will not find it too difficult to see the connection between Hegel's thought and Hountondji's thought. As exemplified by Hegel, modern Western thought has had a historic significance in denying the humanity of Africans, and generally, in denying the humanity of non-Westerners. The Western conception of law has been used as a means of exemplifying and furthering this denial. In Hegel, it appears that the perceived absence of law among Africans disqualifies them from membership in the community of human beings. In his eyes, such a community is one in which human beings are fully conscious of being human. An understanding of what he understands as law can lead us to an understanding of what disqualifies Africans from being members of the human community.

Those who are familiar with modern African history will also readily recognize that Africans have contested and resisted this disqualification. Contestation and resistance to the disqualification have taken many forms. Unfortunately, some of these forms have only reinforced what is being contested or resisted. The observations that Hountondji makes target those Africans whose responses to Hegel serve to reinforce what Hegel says about Africans. The belief that Africans will be recognized as members of the human community if and only if Westerners can be persuaded that African cultures too are human has proved to be ridiculous and tragic. The attempt to persuade Westerners that Africans are just as human as Westerners has met with indifference on the part of Westerners, or has transformed Africans and African cultures into sub-human curios for Western consumption and voyeurism. In the name of promoting tourism, cash-starved African countries have embarked on projects of promoting this transformation without taking into consideration the de-humanization that may be entailed in this process. Moreover, the attempt by Africans to demonstrate to Westerners that they too are human beings continues to be dictated by Western criteria of what constitutes being human. What is forgotten is that the Hegelian types are immunized from any attempt by Africans to gain genuine recognition as human beings. Any effort by Africans to persuade Westerners that Africans too are members of the human community has failed and will continue to fail a priori because, for the Hegelians, being African and being human are mutually exclusive. It is important to keep in mind that Hegelianism is a religious faith, more specifically a Christian religious faith. Because it is a faith, a philosophical argument against its claims is a priori irrelevant. Philosophy and faith are like day and night. By Hegelian definition, human community consists exclusively of those who have attained consciousness of being human, and apparently, for him, it is only Westerners who qualify. That is, if one is not Western, one is not fully human. Although one can argue that Hegel's belief expresses a nineteenth century European view that is no longer held today, this view has been so entrenched in the Western European psyche that nothing short of a Copernican revolutionary transformation of the European psyche warrants such a conclusion. The degree to which the African psyche has been harmed by this view is such that the African psyche itself needs a radical transformation to reflect the degree to which it can be cured of this harm. African jurisprudence must incorporate the diagnostic and therapeutic dimensions in bringing about this transformation. It must be a medical science. To understand it one must go to medical school, to an African medical school.

Hegel has not been alone in expressing this point of view. It is a view that was a part of the mainstream thought in Europe during his time. The view that Africans are not members of the human community was used to rationalize the enslavement of Africans and to colonize them. In *The Spirit of the Laws*, Montesquieu tells us that if he were to vindicate Europeans' right to make slaves of Negroes (by which he meant Africans) his arguments would be,

> These creatures are all over black, and with such a flat nose that they can scarcely be pitied. It is hardly to be believed that God, who is a wise Being, should place a soul, especially a good soul, in such a black ugly body....It is impossible for us to suppose these creatures to be men, because, allowing them to be men, a suspicion would follow that we ourselves are not Christians.[17]

Clearly, he believes that to be human is to be Christian, and to be a Christian is to be human. In his eyes, Africans are neither. They are not human. It also appears clear that to be human is to be white, and to be Christian is to be white. Christianity is Whitianity. Africans are neither. Therefore Africans fail the test of being human. Apparently, skin complexion has played a major role in the European imagination in the construction of who is and who is not human. The lighter one's body is the more human one is, and the darker one is the less human one is. That is, the consciousness of being human is predicated on color consciousness. A racist ideology has played a major role in determining who is and who is not a human being. Western jurisprudence has played a major role in validating, promoting, and enforcing this ideology. Subjecting Africans to slavery, to colonialism, and to apartheid provides unassailable evidence that this was indeed the case. Law, as understood in the West, legitimized these heinous institutions.

According to Christian/philosophical Hegel, one of the qualifications for being human is the possession of consciousness of oneself. That is, legal consciousness is consciousness of being human. Those who do not possess such consciousness are not conscious of being human; they are not human, and have to be treated by those who possess this consciousness as such. This conception of law sets Hegel apart from those contemporary Western students of jurisprudence who fail to see the inadequacy of defining law either as the command of the sovereign, as a set of rules, or as a set of rules plus principles. If it is assumed that law pertains more appropriately to human beings, then it is not adequate to think of law simply as the command of the sovereign (Austin), or as a special system of rules (Hart), or as a special system of rules buttressed by some principles (Dworkin). Whether consciously or unconsciously these post-Hegelian students of Western jurisprudence define jurisprudence in a way that ignores or that leaves out the African contribution to jurisprudence. It is not unreasonable to assume that they intend their definitions to end up in a Western missionary basket that is sent to Africa as a part of Western foreign aid.

In spite of his distortion of what a human being is, Hegel appears to hold a correct opinion, namely, the knowledge of law leads to the knowledge of what it is to be a human being. Jurisprudence, as the study of law, is ultimately the study of what it is to be a human being. Legal science is the science of being human. It is anthropology. This is precisely what conventional jurisprudence in the West has either ignored, or has relegated to the background in its pursuit of the study of law. Although Hegel errs in conceiving human ontology, at least he deserves some credit in pointing out that jurisprudence seeks to articulate what is distinctive about being human. Conventional legal education, as it has been institutionalized in the West, has institutionally failed to incorporate this view, and it is this failure that conventional Western law professors have embarked on propagating throughout the world. For the most part, this is the idea of law that has been institutionalized in Africa, and it is the idea that is largely taught to African law students.

In conventional legal education in the West (and this has increasingly become the case in the Western dominated world), one enters law school to study what legal rules are, how to distinguish them from other types of rules, how to interpret them, how to apply them, how they are made, or who makes them, the scope of their authority, and why they are obligatory. Law professors are expected to provide this conventional education. They do not normally concern themselves with the knowledge or with the understanding of what a human being is, and do not expect their students to get out of law school having mastered such a knowledge or understanding to the extent that such a knowledge or understanding can be mastered. In short, it is not a part of the mission of the law schools to provide such knowledge or understanding. To be sure, this does not mean that law schools do not operate under the assumption of what a human being is. After all, it cannot be denied that the rules that are the subject of study are not rules made by animals for animals. They are rules made by human beings for human beings. Even when they are derived from the Gods by human beings, or from nature, they are derived by and are applicable to human beings. To the extent that conventional legal education relegates being human to the background or to the margins, the education that is offered in law schools deprives students of an opportunity to examine who they are, and also deprives them of an opportunity to critically examine the kind of education they are getting. They are deprived of an opportunity to examine the veracity of the Socratic claim that an unexamined life is not worth living. To be sure, law professors are not to be mistaken for philosophy professors, and law students are not to be mistaken for philosophy students. Nevertheless, the exclusion of philosophy from legal education may shield legal education from a critical examination of its underlying practice and mission. It may shield both law professors and law students from examining themselves.

To be sure, not everyone who professes to be a philosopher accepts the Socratic claim that self-examination is the central task of philosophy. However, those who adopt a Socratic view of philosophy will approach the study of jurisprudence as a means to self-knowledge and also as a means to a good life. Those who adopt this view teach law or study law with the aim of getting to know themselves and with the aim of becoming virtuous. Moreover, in line with Socratic thinking, the self-knowledge that is sought is intended to lead to human well-being, a part of which includes leading a just life. It makes those who concern themselves with law examine their ethical and moral identity with a view of determining how to live well not only as legal practitioners but as human beings. Legal practice ought to be a practice of virtuous living. It is precisely this objective in the study of law, whether theoretical or practical, that is widely neglected or marginalized in the prevailing Western dominated legal education. For example, in his essay on the authority of law, Joseph Raz has claimed that,

> It is also to be insisted that the rule of law is just one of the virtues which a legal system may possess and by which it is to be judged. It is not to be confused with democracy, justice, equality (before the law or otherwise), human rights or any kind of respect for persons or for the dignity of man. A non-democratic legal system, based on the denial of human rights, on extensive poverty, on racial segregation, sexual inequalities, and religious persecution may, in principle, conform to the requirements of the rule of law better than any of the legal systems of the more enlightened Western democracies.[18]

This is quite a mouthful. What is undeniable is that it is readily used as a rationale to excuse and justify social systems that perpetrate crimes against humanity. One can imagine the horror of a judicial system that enforces the rule of law that Raz has in mind. Africans and other oppressed people are all too familiar with the kind of rule of law he speaks about.

In the reduction of law schools to being nothing more than trade schools where students are trained to acquire technical skills for successful legal practice, and where law professors do nothing more than impart these skills, self-examination with a view of leading a virtuous life has largely been set aside. By its insistence on the separation of law from morality or the separation of law from ethics, or more generally, by its insistence on the separation of law from the humanities, the jurisprudence that is embodied in legal education today subverts a Socratic-centered jurisprudence. This is the type of jurisprudence embodied by legal positivism.[19] A jurisprudence that would call for a study of law that takes morality or ethics into account would annul the separation of the study of law from humanities. Since traditionally, the study of morality and the study of ethics are studies within humanities, such jurisprudence would make the study of law a humanistic study. It would rescue the study of law from the dream of scientism, a dream that has given us the illusion that the way to make progress in legal education, and the way to make legal education respectable as an academic subject is by scientizing it. Authentic African jurisprudence does not take shape apart from other concerns with the human and the human good. It is thoroughly humanistic. The kind of rule of law that the West promotes in Africa today, and indeed to the world at large, as is the case with the rule of law that Africans are attempting to institute in Africa today, must be judged in terms of this standard. The well-being of Africans must be the cornerstone of legal education in Africa.

It is undeniable that contemporary legal education in Africa is heavily influenced by non-humanistic considerations. For the most part, it is construed as professional education, the type that appears to dispense with humanistic consideration. It is a trade school education that appears overtly as amoral and apolitical. It is inseparable from modern capitalist needs. It is deeply influenced by Western capitalist culture, and is subversive of indigenous African culture. Social justice is not one of its virtues. For the most part, it caters to the individualistic or self-serving interests of those who are attracted to it. African magistrates and judges may be identified as civil servants, but the Africanness of the civil society they serve is yet to be subjected to dialectical scrutiny. The very notion of the rule of law, as construed in the West and extended to Africa and to other parts of the world, dispenses with dialectical social and cultural differences. Although projected as faceless, the rule of law is essentially the rule of the Western jurisprudence. That is, it has a Western face. It brings with it Western social and cultural influences that are shielded from critical inquiry.

Under the current legal education in Africa, the qualification of law as "African" is a mere veneer to cover up this state of affairs. Even if it is not the case at present, the objective of the development of legal consciousness is to render the notion of being African inconsequential in the conception and practice of law. This inconsequentiality is a part of the process of the so-called globalization of law or the globalization of the rule of law. Globalization of the rule of law is not necessarily globalization of social justice. It can be an obstacle to social justice. Accordingly, it is worth bearing in mind that a rule of law is not necessarily a rule of just law. This is readily demonstrated by the colonialist rule of law, and by the rule of law that prevailed when Africans were under the Apartheid regime.

If there is resistance to Western conventional legal education in Africa, it is partly because such education is subversive of African societies and African cultures. In indigenous African societies and cultures, the humanities form the core of legal education. The mission of legal education is to preserve and enhance the well-being of the community. Instruction of what constitutes the well-being of the community is the principal objective of legal education. The mastery of legal skills is geared towards using the skills not only for individual gains, but also for the good of the community in which one is a member. In African thought, the community is not merely an aggregate of individuals, and the community good is not solely an aggregate of the goods of individuals. The community is an organic whole in which the individual has his or her being. This organic whole is not a primitive whole and it is not inhospitable to authentic individual autonomy. Moreover, this sense of being human has to be reinforced by the community for, on occasion, individuals stray from it. It preserves and nurtures the humanness of the individuals and the personal autonomy that arises from it. Although it appears that in the West autonomy is incompatible with communitarianism, the incompatibility appears to be a product of Western cultural history. It may be imposed on other societies, and it may even independently develop in them, but it is not intrinsic in human existence. Westerners are not inherently individualistic and neither are Africans inherently communalistic. Human existence offers us the possibility of a variety of social modes of being. Opting for individualistic or communalistic modes of social existence are choices that human beings make in the course of their social existence.

In our effort to understand or to constitute African jurisprudence, our quarrel with Hegel is not primarily about rules. In this we differ from the Western official doctrine that law is primarily about rules emanating from the sovereign. Our quarrel is with the view of being human that is central to his jurisprudence. To the extent that he speaks in the name of his fellow Westerners, our quarrel is with the view of being human that is expressed in Western jurisprudence.[20] As should be expected, the quarrel from an African perspective is that, in Western jurisprudence, we have a view of being human that Westerners believe is paradigmatic of what being human universally is, a view that Westerners impose not only on Africans, but also on other non-Westerners. It is precisely a rejection of and resistance to this paradigm that ought to inform genuine African jurisprudence. But this is not all there is to African jurisprudence. African jurisprudence has the task of constituting and understanding who and what an African is. It is a task that must be carried out in such a way that it does not exclude other human beings from the community of human beings, the way that traditional Western jurisprudence has. It construes the humanity of Africans without privileging it over the humanity of other human beings. It recognizes the non-hierarchical and indivisible humanity that all human beings share. It is a joint task that is to be carried out in conjunction with other human beings, since they too are implicated in African jurisprudence. Non-Africans have an important role in interpreting and constituting African jurisprudence.

By excluding Africans from membership in the human community, Hegel indicts himself. To use his own words, he exhibits himself as "the natural man in his completely wild and untamed state. We must lay aside all thought of reverence and morality—all that we call feeling—if we would rightly comprehend him; there is nothing harmonious with humanity to be found in this type of character. Hegel is a man who fails to grasp the essence of what it is to be human. He is a wild Western European man who has not been adequately domesticated into the community of human beings. He misconceives what he is, and mistakes his idiosyncrasy for what is essential about being human. The tradition in which he has his being shares this exaggeration and mistake. One must view the modern European project in Africa as a project of barbarization of Europeans, and this is evidenced by the European barbarization of Africa and of Africans. How else is one to think about the European colonial regime in Africa or the enslavement of millions of Africans in the so-called New World? These two European adventures are among the most barbaric undertakings in human history. By no stretch of imagination can one truly think of these adventures as being other than adventures of barbarians. Yet Europeans have portrayed them as if they were the projects of humanization, as if they were civilizing projects aimed at bringing light to those who lived in utter darkness. The view that these projects are manifestations of lawlessness is obscured in conventional European legal literature. It is precisely this view that Africans must recover if they are to understand the European conception of the criterion for distinguishing legality from lawlessness. Such an understanding may pave the way for the emergence of a liberating African framework for distinguishing legality from lawlessness.

In modern history, the Dark Continent that Europeans had in mind referred not to Africa as they believed. What they had in mind was their own Continent: Europe. That is, the Dark Continent was Europe not Africa. Somehow, they had succeeded in concealing this fact to their consciousness, and it is not without concerted psychoanalytic work that the children of European modernity can be made to come to terms with this historic mystification of human consciousness. If properly understood, African jurisprudence can make a significant contribution to this work. This contribution can be made indirectly as Africans try to rescue Africa from the Darkness into which she was cast by Europeans. By rescuing Africa, they thereby not only rescue Europe for Europeans, but also rescue themselves and indirectly assist Europeans in rescuing themselves, if indeed Europeans can manage to recognize that in barbarizing Africans they have barbarized themselves. Joseph Conrad, the Nineteenth Century British writer, was clearly mistaken in placing the Heart of Darkness in Africa. It is in Europe where this Heart was to be found. Europe was a Dark Continent. The so-called Age of European Discovery and Exploration is an Age of Historic Mystification: a Self-mystification on the part of Europeans and a Mystification of non-European peoples by Europeans. If from a European perspective the modern age in Europe can be construed as the Age of enlightenment, from an African perspective, it can be construed more appropriately as the Age of Darkness. From an African perspective, it is an age of European terrorism. It is an age of unparalleled genocide, an age in which millions of Africans and other non-Westerners died at the hands of Westerners. If Westerners view it as an age in which the seeds of liberty are planted, to Africans it is an age in which the seeds of the bondage of Africans are planted. As Westerners institutionalize liberty and equality in their own societies, at the same time, they institutionalize bondage and inequality in African societies. As they celebrate the orations on the dignity of man, they celebrate the degradation of Africans. The proverbial man they had in mind was the Western man, and not man in extension. It was not man everywhere. It was the European male. They equate the European male with the universal male, the Western man with the universal man.

From the perspective of Africans, the law that Hegel believes is the hallmark of being human is nothing more than the hallmark of a parochial and distorted humanism. If it is a law at all, it is the law of the jungle. The proverbial jungle that Westerners talked about in the heyday of colonialism and slavery is not the home of Africans. It was the home of Europeans. Contrary to the claim of modern Western social scientists, the existence of law was not a part of the evidence that man has risen out of the state of nature. It was rather an affirmation of the Western man's inability to rise out of the state of nature. This was made evident by explicit or implicit declaration of war against Africans, and against Non-western people in general. If the distinction between the state of nature and the civil/political state is to be maintained, a conception of law that would provide evidence that man has gotten out of the state of nature would be one that is not based on one segment of the human community declaring war on another segment of the human community. It would be a conception of law that would lead to the domestication of the Western man that Western modernity has constructed. When Europeans invaded Africa, the lawlessness they professed to see among Africans was mostly nothing more than the lawlessness among themselves. Their own culture had made them blind to this state of affairs. From the African perspective, the historic effort by Hobbes to raise man from the state of nature accomplished the opposite: it returned man to the state of nature. It was a declaration of war on Africans by Europeans. In relation to Africans, European rulers were sovereigns by conquest and maintained their rule over Africans by force. Social compact and social contract did not apply to Africans in relation to Europeans, and the jurisprudence that arose from these social institutions gave validity to the brutalization of Africans. Africa could have provided John Austin a good example of his view that law is a command of the uncommanded commander directed to the inferior by the superior. The colonial power was the political superior that directed commands to Africans (political inferiors), and by force, Africans had to be compelled to develop a habit of obeying.

The critique of Hegel's barbarization of Africa and of Africans creates one of the tasks that African jurisprudence must take up. African jurisprudence must not only expose this barbarism; it must pave the way for eradicating it. In the course of carrying out this project, it must be recognized that Hegel does not condemn this or that part of Africa to lawlessness. It is the entire continent that is condemned. Hence, the negation of Hegel's condemnation must be continent-wide. It is the entire continent that is to be indivisibly the locus of African jurisprudence. This is not a trivial observation, especially given the emphasis on a balkanized Africa, a balkanization that has been promoted at the expense of Africa. The need for Africans to get together on a Continental basis was already noted by Kwame Nkrumah during the early struggles for African independence. He recognized that the securing of the African liberty and the preservation of African liberty demanded that Africans raise the consciousness of their identity to a Continental level and translate such consciousness to social practice. It is in this context that he said,

> Our essential bulwark against such sinister threats and the other multifarious designs of the neo-colonialists is in our political union. If we are to remain free, if we are to enjoy the full benefits of Africa's rich resources, we must unite to plan for our total defense and the full exploitation of material and human means, in the full interests of all our peoples. To go it alone will limit our horizons, curtail our expectations, and threaten our liberty.[21]

It is precisely such a point of view that Fanon expressed in his classic anti-colonialist text. He observed,

> The native intellectual who decides to give battle to colonial lies fights on the field of the whole continent. The past is given back its value. Culture extracted from the past to be displayed in its entire splendor, is not necessarily that of his own country. Colonialism which has not bothered to put too fine a point on its efforts, has never ceased to maintain that the Negro is a savage; and for the colonist, the Negro was neither an Angolan nor a Nigerian, for he simply spoke of the Negro. For colonialism, this vast continent was the haunt of the savages, a country riddled with superstitions and fanaticism, destined for contempt, weighed down by the curse of God, a country of cannibals—in short, the Negro country. Colonialism's condemnation was continental in scope. The contention by colonialism that the darkest night of humanity lay over pre-colonial history concerns the whole of the African continent. The efforts of the native to rehabilitate himself and to escape from the claws of colonialism are logically inscribed from the same point of view as that of colonialism. The native intellectual who has gone far beyond the domains of Western culture and who has got into his head to proclaim the existence of another culture never does so in the name of Angola or of Dahomey. The culture which is affirmed is African culture.[22]

The union that Nkrumah called for, and the continental wide vision that Fanon had in mind necessitate a unified African jurisprudence. This cannot come about if the balkanization of African jurisprudence prevails. Just as the Western media dismissed Nkrumah as an ideologue and as a megalomaniac, those who call for a unified African jurisprudence are likely to be similarly dismissed simply as wallowing in illusion and in delusion. In post-colonial Africa, nation-state-centered jurisprudence is what is assumed to be a more realist jurisprudence, the proper African jurisprudential realism. Anyone who dares to think of continental jurisprudence is dismissed as a demagogue or as a silly dreamer. Apparently, being African in the truest sense of being African is too unrealistic for an African. If an African cannot be an African in the context of other Africans, how is he or she expected to be a human being in the context of other human beings? Should it be said that being human is too much for an African? It is in the interest of those who do not have the welfare of Africans in mind to encourage a balkanized jurisprudence in Africa. Although it cannot be denied that divisiveness is a present feature of African people, it should not be assumed that this divisiveness is natural, or that African jurisprudence is genuine only and if only it embraces such divisiveness as its essential nature. African jurisprudence is a part of the African's self-creation, and non-divisiveness remains a possible creation for Africans.

Normally, political balkanization of Africa is associated with the Berlin Conference of 1884/1885. Having depicted Africa and Africans as European property, European powers met to divide up this property and assign property rights to themselves. This division was made legal by European powers and provided jurisdiction to the parties involved in the conference, and the parties expected that the world, at large, would recognize this jurisdiction. But it is not only the entire Continent that was construed as a property to be partitioned among European powers. Africans themselves were deemed to be property of the European powers that took ownership of the territory of Africa they inhabited. Thus, the transformation of non-colonial Africa into colonial Africa that was accomplished in the course of colonization entailed the transformation of Africans into property. The same transformation took place in the course of slavery. As slaves of European settlers in the so-called New World, Africans were subjected to the same transformation. It is in the context of this transformation, for example, that for slave owners, it did not make sense for Africans to be accorded human rights by freeing them from slavery, since, strictly speaking, a piece of property cannot be said to be free or to have human rights. It was in the name of protecting property that those who enslaved Africans resisted anti-slavery forces. When runaway enslaved Africans were captured, by law, they had to be returned to their owners, the same way that a runaway horse or a bull had to be returned to its rightful owner.

The study of African jurisprudence should include the study of this propertization of Africans as a part of the history of African legal history. Currently, the law of property in African law schools does not cover this significant dimension of African legal history. It is to be found neither in the property text books nor in the lectures that are given by law professors. Legal training to which African students are subjected does not expose students to this dimension of legal education. To this extent, one can legitimately wonder about what is African in the legal education that is fed to Africans. This is the case not only in Africa; it is also the case in the African diaspora. When they go through legal education, African Americans, for example, do not learn about this dimension of the law of property. Property law texts and property law courses are silent on propertizaton of Africans in America. Law students are not taught how the law of property touched the core of the being of Africans or how in some ways, it continues to touch the core of their being. Property is important not only as one of the substantive areas to be covered in legal education, but even more so, because it is at the core of what law is, and as the core of what law is, it is at the core of what being human is. However, how property is to be construed remains a contested matter.

If we recall correctly, it is John Locke, one of the architects of the prevailing Western jurisprudence, who asserted that "The great and chief end, therefore, of men's uniting into commonwealths and putting themselves under government is the preservation of their property".[23] Western modernity, an institution that, in part, owes its genesis to Locke's thought, places the idea of law within what today we call the nation-state—the nation-state being the highest embodiment of government. For moderns, law cannot be understood apart from the governmental institution. It is the soul or the heart of this institution. Locke asserts that,

> The great end of men entering into society being the enjoyment of their property in peace and safety, and the great instrument and means of that being laws established in that society, the first and fundamental positive law of all commonwealth is the establishment of the legislative power, as the first and the fundamental natural law which is to govern even the legislature itself is the preservation of society, and as far as will consist with every public good, of every person in it.[24]

The other two branches that make up the government (the judiciary and the executive) are intended to facilitate the overall objective of government; that is to protect property and make it possible for citizens to enjoy it in peace and safety. The judiciary is not to make laws but to interpret laws in ways that preserve peace and ensure safety so that citizens can enjoy their property in peace. The executive branch of government is to enforce the laws made by the legislative branch with the overall governmental objective in view, and as interpreted by the judiciary. The so-called separation of powers whose objective is to check tyranny on the part of any of the branches of government has the underlying objective of preserving property and ensuring that it is enjoyed by property owners in peace and safety. The separation of powers is intended to prevent tyranny that is likely to arise from any of the branches of government: tyranny arising from the legislative branch, from the executive branch and from the judicial branch. Montesquieu tells us that,

> When the legislative and executive powers are united in the same person, or in the same body of magistrates, there can be no liberty; because apprehension may arise. Lest the same monarch or senate enact tyrannical laws, or execute laws in a tyrannical manner.

> Again, there is no liberty, if judicial power be not separated from the legislative and executive. Were it joined with the legislative, the life and liberty of the subject would be exposed to arbitrary control; for the judge would be then the legislator. Were it joined to the executive power, the judge might behave with violence and oppression.[25]

The separation of powers benefits those who are free and those who intend to remain free. It is meaningless, if not an insult, to those whose humanity the government has decided to violate. One whose humanity has been intentionally violated by all the branches of government cannot turn to any of them, or to all of them collectively to secure his or her humanity from violation. Since according to Locke, the chief aim of government is the protection of property, the three branches of government collaborate in the protection of property. When Africans are reduced to property, the three branches of government collaborate in protecting owners of Africans so that they can be secure in their property, and thereby enjoy it in peace. Separation of powers itself becomes a property of the property owners, a property they use to ensure to secure other properties so that they can be enjoyed in peace. The judiciary, as is the case with each of the other branches of government, is not truly independent. All branches of government collaborate in defining and protecting property.

Instead of protecting Africans from tyranny, during the time Africans were held in captivity in the United States, the doctrine of the separation of powers was an instrument of containing Africans in a state of servitude and tyranny. The three branches of government collaborated to secure the slavery of Africans for the benefit of European slave owners. In this situation, it would have been meaningless and tragically misleading to assert the independence of the judiciary. If judicial review was established to enable the judiciary to contain or inhibit tyranny on the part of the other branches of government, it was primarily for the benefit of the European settler community. It did not prevent the other branches of government from subjecting Africans to tyranny.

Similarly, in Africa, during the colonial period, European colonizers mobilized the powers of the three branches of government to keep Africans under colonial subjection. It did not take much effort to undertake this mobilization since colonial regimes did not pay any attention to the separation of powers except when intra-European interests in Africa were involved. In British colonies, the judiciary, as was the case with the other branches of government, was under Her or His Majesty's Colonial Service. In Belgian, French and Portuguese colonial territories, the judicial branch, likewise, collaborated with the other branches of government in servicing colonialism. More recently, in Apartheid South Africa, the oppression of Africans was orchestrated by the three branches of government.[26] The concept of law that prevailed was in many ways similar to the concept of law under the Nazi regime. The independence of the judiciary was severely compromised since whatever the Nationalist Party dominated South

African Parliament enacted as law is what the South African judiciary was bound to enforce. In other words, under the apartheid regime, the South African judiciary was under the direction of Apartheid jurisprudence. The South African judiciary assisted in the administration of the inhumane laws passed by the apartheid regime. As John Dugard has suggested, under apartheid, law was construed in the Austinian sense; that is, law was the command of the Sovereign—the sovereign, in this case, being the Apartheid Parliament.[27] Under the Apartheid regime, the judiciary was an instrument of the Parliament. Its task was to enforce the laws that the apartheid Parliament enacted. Although Afrikaners formed the majority in the Apartheid Parliament they were a minority in the total population of South Africa.

The supremacy of the Parliament in Afrikaner South Africa was not an exception in the so-called democratic European world. In England, A.V. Dicey, Professor of English law at Oxford University, had already promoted the idea that in Government, Parliament is supreme. In his book, *The Law of Constitution*, he claimed that Parliament has the right to make and unmake any law whatever; and, further, that "no person or body is recognized by the law of England as having a right to override or set aside the legislation of Parliament".[28] He further adds,

> There is no person or body of persons who can, under English Constitution, make rules which override or derogate from an Act of Parliament, or which (to express the same thing in other words) will be enforced by the courts in contravention of an Act of Parliament.[29]

In post-colonial Africa, the so-called separation of powers is yet to be fully institutionalized. In many instances, the judiciary has largely become an instrument of the executive branch of Government. Leaders of the countries where this has become the case take themselves seriously as the Commanders in Chief. They command not only the executive branch of government, but also the legislative and the judicial branches of government. In democratic states, where the Parliament or the legislative branch is supreme, at least, it can be argued that the will of the majority is taken into consideration. Where the executive is supreme, as it appears to be the case in many African States, the governing will is the will of whoever is in the executive seat. The will of the executive is the law, and the judiciary is compelled to cater to this will. The judicial will is the will of the Commander. Where this is the case, the province of jurisprudence is precisely what Austin says it is; namely, the study of the Command of the Uncommanded Commander. For the most part, in post-colonial Africa, African regimes have amply exemplified Austinism. Law has been the command of African dictators. Law has been the private property of these dictators. Various forms of kleptocracy have been institutionalized. Pervasive corruption has been one of the faces of this regime. Between many African leaders and the masses they lead, there prevails a state of nature; there is a state of war. The law that prevails has been the law of the jungle. What Europeans said about Africans in the Nineteenth Century may be more applicable today than then, but it is a characteristic that fits them as well, since the way they treated Africans was no better than the way Africans are treated today. In fact they were worse.

From the above observation, it should be clear that the judicial branch of government could be viewed as property. The owners of this property in any society are determined by those in power. Thus, whether it is viewed as an independent branch of government, or as subordinate to either of the other branches of government, it is a property of those who wield power in any society. It is used to secure and promote the interests of those in power. In England, for example, those who represented Royal interests, the interests of the House of Lords and the House of Commons, were the beneficiaries of the judiciary. In the British colonies in Africa, the judiciary was the property of the British Government. It secured and promoted the interest of the British Crown, usually at the expense of Africans. The same situation prevailed in other European colonies. The judiciary in these colonies was at the service of the colonizing European powers. In colonial America, the judiciary was at the service of European colonial interests. It was the property of the European settler community. When the colonies freed themselves, the judiciary was at the service of those who seized power—the European males. Since it was in the interest of these settlers to hold Africans into slavery, and to rob Native Americans of their land and marginalize them in their own native land, the United States judiciary was used to accomplish these objectives.

With the ascendancy of Afrikaners in South Africa, the judiciary was the property of Afrikaners. It was an instrument of securing and promoting their supremacy both accomplished by ensuring that Africans were kept homeless in their native land, and was also an instrument of preserving them in a state of bondage and of forcefully depriving them of their property. As a settler community in Africa, they monopolized the judiciary in the same way that the European settler community monopolized the judiciary in colonial Africa, in colonial America, in colonial South East Asia, and in colonial Latin America. The judiciary became instrumental in the construction of the Bantustans which were largely concentration camps into which Africans were herded and which, on occasion, provided labor to serve the European settler community. When Africans took up arms to fight against the Apartheid tyranny their fight was criminalized and they were defined as terrorists. Their fight was declared illegal. Clearly, here we get some evidence illustrating the idea of legality under the Apartheid regime. Let us also recall that when Jomo Kenyatta, the Kenyan nationalist, became a major force in anti-colonial struggle, the British colonial legality depicted him as a terrorist who was out to lead the country into darkness.

The judiciary is inevitably caught up in the conflicts that beset society. In colonial Africa, as it was the case in the period in which Africans were enslaved in the Americas, a judiciary that was positively responsive to the needs of Africans had to be anti-thetical to the judiciary that served the needs of those who deprived Africans of their life, liberty and property. An African-based judiciary had to be an instrument of African liberation. Africans had to seize it and make it a property to serve their interests. In this case, it had both a political and economic dimension. This called for a recovery of political and economic dimensions of jurisprudence. A jurisprudence that truly addressed the interests of Africans has to be emancipatory. This should also be an aspect of post-colonial and post-slavery African jurisprudence, if only because the work of emancipating Africans is not yet over. It is not possible to have a truly independent the judiciary in an oppressive society unless such a judiciary stands in opposition to oppression. Even in such a case, the judiciary is inseparably bound to a political regime—a non-oppressive political regime. Judiciary cannot exist in a political vacuum. All jurisprudence, not only African jurisprudence, is political. Beneath and permeating every jurisprudential theory is a political theory. The architecture of African jurisprudence is a political architecture.

As is the case with the judiciary, jurisprudence itself is a form of property. The ruling group in any society has the possession of this property, and it uses it to secure itself and promote its interests. An authentic African jurisprudence must be a jurisprudence of liberation. There is scarcely a mention of this function of jurisprudence among the leading scholars of jurisprudence in the West. Jurisprudence is not viewed as the jurisprudence of liberation. One does not hear about it in the works of H.L.A Hart, Ronald Dworkin, or in the other leading jurisprudential scholars in the West. Perhaps, the assumption that guides their views on jurisprudence is that human beings are free, and it is the primary function of law to safeguard freedom and its exercise. However, those who are not free, have nothing to safeguard other than their right to struggle to be free. In a few cases where jurisprudence of liberation is mentioned in the West, for example, in Feminist Jurisprudence, in Critical Legal Studies, or in Critical Race Theory, what is said is said from the margins of the mainstream jurisprudence—the jurisprudence that is insensitive to the call of liberation. The critique of mainstream jurisprudence by Westerners, moreover, remains largely within the ambit of the oppressive West. It reinforces the hegemony of Western jurisprudence by white washing its oppressive feature. It is a form of Phariseeism.

Unmasked, modern European jurisprudence, is incomprehensible if it is not seen as having a foundation on property, a foundation which, when adequately understood, presupposes a specific delineation of what constitutes a human being as well as what the human good is. Differently stated, as a theory of law, jurisprudence is based on a theory of property, and the theory of property is itself based on a theory of what it is to be a human being. The conflict between socialist/communist jurisprudence and Western jurisprudence rests on the conflict between two opposing views on property which ultimately is based on a conflict between two views on being human. Since the Second World War jurisprudence in Africa has been shaped by this conflict. The assertion or the creation of an autonomous African jurisprudence was blocked by the pressure applied by the West and by the Socialist/Communist camp as each side sought to impose its version of jurisprudence on Africans. A meaningful easing of this pressure after the end of the Cold War provided Africans with an opportunity of re-asserting or of constituting an autonomous African jurisprudence. However, the opportunity has emerged under multiple dangers. The Western presence antedates the rise of the Socialist/Communist presence and so does the conflict between the West and the Socialist/Communist camp. Western jurisprudence, as illustrated in the Western view on property, and hence, on the Western view of what it is to be a human being continues to be dominant in Africa. This domination appears to have a clear sailing after the collapse of the Soviet Union. The Soviet Union arose from the womb of the West, and its collapse has only helped the West to eliminate an internal parasite, thereby re-energizing the West. The Socialist/Communist jurisprudence was for the most part a secretion of Western capitalist jurisprudence. The former was an internal critique within the latter. It was not a radical alternative to the latter.

The difference and the conflicts between African and Western views on jurisprudence is a difference and conflict on how property is to be understood, which, ultimately, is a conflict on how being human is to be understood. Since understanding reveals itself in practice, the conflict lies in the practices of being human. The European enterprise of balkanizing Africa and balkanizing Africans blocks the emergence of the type of consciousness and practice that Africans need in order to find ways to resolve these conflicts. The conflict cannot be resolved if it is solely seen as a conflict of the rules of law. Ultimately, the conflict is a conflict in how to constitute the practice of being human.

As a work of the European colonial regime in Africa, the balkanization of Africa and the balkanization of Africans have been strengthened by European social anthropologists who construed Africa as consisting of autonomous social and cultural units—the so-called tribes. This construction concealed the underlying unified view that Europeans had of African social and cultural existence. The concealment continues to have sway over European/Western social science. In this social science, when African legal studies are taken up, the emphasis is on African customary laws. With the emergence of modern nation-states in Africa, one of the main issues is how these customary laws are to be integrated into the understanding of modern law. Such integration is perceived as essential for African development. What is understood as modern law is nothing more than Euro-American understanding of law that is disguised as a universal understanding of law. What African customary laws are being integrated into is Euro-American law. Accordingly, Euro-American development is the paradigm of African development. Seen from this perspective, African jurisprudence is an infantile or an adolescent jurisprudence that lacks the maturity that is exemplified by Euro-American jurisprudence. Or, strictly speaking, there is no African jurisprudence. If there is one, it consists of an aggregate of jurisprudences each of which is located in this or that African ethnic group. In other words, African jurisprudence consists of ethno-jurisprudence. Where several ethnic groups have been amalgamated into a nation-state, one may speak of this or that national jurisprudence, but even in this case, national jurisprudence is either an amalgamation of the jurisprudences of various ethnic groups, or it is a jurisprudence that the political elite with the advice of non-African political elites have imposed on Africans in the name of legal modernization. In other words, in post-colonial Africa, the colonial logic still pervades, although it is not as blatant as it was during the colonial period. The African is still languishing at the infancy of humanity and stands in need to the Euro-American jurisprudential tutelage.

To counter the destructive balkanization that has plagued Africa since colonial days, an anti-balkanizing jurisprudence is needed. Such jurisprudence should not be mistaken for a jurisprudence that would deny the heterogeneity of African customary law. It would be a jurisprudence that would be constructed in the context of the entire continent taking into consideration the heterogeneity of African customary law. To speak jurisprudentially about Africa, one must speak about the entire continent. Such a speech should not be readily dismissed for being devoid of substance, or for being sheer fantasy. If an African cannot think about or see his or her being African as implicated in or as implicating the being of other Africans, he or she will not think about or see his or her being as being implicated or as implicating the being of other human beings. He or she will think that, in being human, he or she is a total stranger to other human beings, which is a manifest contradiction. There is nothing fantastic in thinking that one's being is what it is by being linked with the being of every other human being. What is fantastic is thinking against such thinking. An African who thinks that his or her being is not linked with the being of other Africans engages in fantastic thinking, and such fantastic thinking is not only a liability to him or her, it is also a liability to all Africans, and indeed to the humanity of all other human beings.

Even if one were to grant some truth to the claim that, at present, Africa lacks jurisprudential unity, it does not follow that working towards such a unity is absurd. For an African, it is a way of working towards what he or she is, or a way of working towards what he or she ought to be as a way of being himself or herself. It should also be pointed out that one must avoid being dogmatic in speaking about the human being that is at stake in African jurisprudence. An open African jurisprudence attests to the openness of being African. Out of self-assertion and self-respect, Africans have an obligation to preserve or reconstruct the jurisprudential integrity of their continent. The Continent bears their identity and when they work for her integrity they work for the integrity of their own being. Working, in this context, points to an on-going construction of African identity—a construction that is an essential feature in African jurisprudential thinking.

It is noteworthy that Hegel does not condemn this or that African to lawlessness. He does not condemn this or that segment of the African community to lawlessness. He condemns all Africans and all segments of African community. An African who isolates himself or herself in his or her challenge of Hegel or the Hegelian tradition misunderstands what he or she challenges. The challenge is likely to prove futile. Equally, a segment of the African community that isolates itself from the entire African community and from that standpoint challenges Hegel's condemnation of Africans misunderstands the scope of his condemnation. Mounting a challenge from such a standpoint is likely to prove futile. If one understands the scope of Hegel's condemnation, there is no alternative to adopting a pan-African standpoint and to mounting a pan-African challenge. That is, to adequately address the problem of African jurisprudence, one must adopt a pan-African perspective. Adopting such a perspective is not a denial of multiple perspectives on African jurisprudence. It is, in part, to safeguard the multiple levels of jurisprudential thinking. The African must be cognizant of the material conditions in which he or she finds himself or herself. He or she has a jurisprudential identity not only in his or her distinct African community, but also a jurisprudential identity in the community of African communities. He or she needs to be aware of the latter identity if he or she is to successfully take up the challenge that is posed by other communities such as Hegel's. It must be borne in mind that Hegel's condemnation of Africa and of Africans is a condemnation that is deeply rooted in the European community. Approaching his challenge as it is an individual challenge, or as it is a German challenge, misunderstands the European dimension of his challenge.

Hegelian jurisprudence is not only the theater of man's expression of his true being. It is also where the Divine is realized in the truth of man's being. It is where the truth of man is realized in the truth of God, and where the truth of God is realized in the truth of man. Thus, by portraying the African as lawless, Hegel portrays the African not only as removed from the truth of being human, but also as removed from the truth of the Divine. Since according to Hegel, the African lacks a sense of the Divine, he or she lacks the sense of the truth of what he or she is. Hegel has a theological conception of jurisprudence. Just as he thinks of Africa as jurisprudential wilderness or a jungle without jurisprudence, he thinks of Africa as a wilderness or jungle without theology. He is not alone in thinking this way. It has been and continues to be a part of the modern European mission to project Africa as a Godless Continent, that is, as a continent that is inhabited by a Godless people—a people whose peoplehood is problematic. It is in the light of this projection that, for centuries, European Christian missionaries have invaded and flooded Africa. It has been the contention of these missionaries that they have come to Africa to bring the Christian light—a light by which the truth of being human is to shine so that man can truly see himself the way he is. Man, the Christians believe, is created in the image of God and it is only when he sees himself as such that he can truly know himself. As anthropology, jurisprudence is then to be understood not simply as a Christian theological perspective, but as the theological perspective since for the Christians there is only one God, and that is their God. From this belief, it follows that there is only one jurisprudence, and that is their jurisprudence. Among Christians, God is not only the Chief Law maker; He is also the Chief Judge and the Chief Executor of the laws that He makes. When Constantine, who initially persecuted Christians, became the first Roman Emperor to convert to Christianity, a door was opened for the transformation of Roman law into Christian law. He became not only a protector of Christians but became the propagator and propagandist of the Christian Divine law in the Roman Empire.

The study of Roman jurisprudence especially its Christianized version is indispensable for anyone who wants to truly understand the evolution of European jurisprudence. Such an understanding is also indispensable for understanding the claim that is made by Europeans that Africans have no jurisprudence. There is a religious aspect to this claim that one can easily miss if one does not take into account the context in which it is made. Overcoming Christian religious oppression in Africa may contribute to the paving of the way for the renaissance or the rise of African jurisprudence. It is especially important to take the claim advanced by European Christians seriously. It is their claim that man was created in the image of God. Since according to Hegel and his fellow European missionaries, Africans are Godless, they are not to be perceived as reflecting the image of God. The image of God is reflected exclusively in Europeans. Differently stated, Europeans and only Europeans are created in the image of God.

Anyone who believes that he or she is created in the image of God is likely to end up worshiping himself or herself. After all when he looks at himself or when she looks at herself he or she sees the image of God. As Christians, Westerners appear to have succumbed to the temptation of self-worship. If this is a central feature of sacrilege, then they are to be construed as sacrilegious. Theocentric jurisprudence, in this case, is a jurisprudence of self-worship. Herein lies the danger of blindly embracing Western jurisprudence. When Africans blindly embrace Western jurisprudence they are likely to end up worshiping Westerners. They are likely to implicate themselves in sacrilege. The conceptions of human beings in indigenous Africa do not project being human as a being in the image of God. If a human being is in the image of any being, it is in the image of being human. In this context, it is important to note the historic distortion of how Africans understood themselves prior to the imposition of the Judeo-Christian conception of being human on Africans.

If this is borne in mind, again, one can see the relevance of Hountondji's caution. There are those Africans who attempt to overcome European religious oppression of Africans by imitating European religiosity. In the course of being Christians, some Africans have not only abandoned their names (which they have come to believe are pagan) in favor of European names—which they understand as Christian names, but have given up African culture in favor of European culture that they understand to be Christian culture. In so doing, they have found themselves embracing Eurocentric Christian jurisprudence either explicitly or implicitly. Alternatively, there are those Africans who may have been tempted to prove to Europeans that Afro-centric theology is just as important as Euro-centric Christian theology. They may also be tempted to prove to Europeans that such a theology and theologies are just as good as the Eurocentric Christian theology. They may be tempted to encourage Europeans to go on a safari to the African world of theologies from which they can have splendid opportunities to witness the exciting world of African jurisprudence. The proofs however have no persuasive force. They can only serve as ridiculous entertainment for Europeans, or reinforce European theological and religious paternalism in Africa.

The role that Europeans have created for God in European jurisprudence has served to secure and promote European identity. In this jurisprudence, divine law is construed and is to be construed as European law. The jurisprudence that articulates this law is European jurisprudence. Failure to construe it as such may lead to a mistaken identity. In due course, an attempt will be made to show how this failure has been deceptively institutionalized in the European jurisprudential tradition. For the moment, let us turn to the role that the conception of philosophy in the West has played in this deception.

We need to constantly remind ourselves that contrary to conventional wisdom, Greece is not the cradle of Western philosophy. The construction of Western philosophy begins to take a definite shape within the course of the history of Christianity. An important milestone in this construction is erected in medieval Europe. At this period, philosophy succumbs to Christian theology. There is a systematic denouncing of philosophy as a pagan enterprise that is radically removed from Truth. In the eyes of Christians, the Christian way of understanding truth becomes the only path to truth, and Christian truth becomes the Truth. All other paths to truth are ruled out a priori. This message is to be propagated throughout the entire world by any means necessary including the use or misuse of philosophical skills. Hellenic philosophy is henceforth to be read selectively deriving from it those aspects that serve to promote Christianity. St. Augustine, an African who forgot his African roots, and St. Thomas Aquinas played a pivotal role in plundering philosophy to nurture Christian thinking and Christian life. In Augustinian jurisprudence, a law that contradicts divine law or that is inconsistent with divine law or that is without divine sanction is no law at all. Evidently, by divine law, St. Augustine does not have in mind any of the many African Gods since these Gods, like the Greek Gods or the Roman Gods, are not true Gods. For Augustine there is only one and one true god, and that god is his god—the Judeo-Christian God. A similar view is held by St. Thomas Aquinas, a man who has been very important as an authority on Divine law and natural law. The latter, that is, natural law, is itself nothing but the Divine law that human reason (understood exclusively as Christian reason since the philosophical or the pagan conception of reason obscures the truth of reason) discovered within itself.

What the so-called Christian philosophers such as Augustine and Aquinas have understood as the divine is the Judeo-Christian divine. It is not any one of the many Gods and Goddesses to be found in Africa, and clearly, it is not any one of the Greek Gods or Goddesses, or Roman Gods and goddesses. It is not Onyame, Ngai, Murungu, Shango, Siva, Krsna, Ra, Great Spirit, or any of the Gods of the non-European peoples. Accordingly, when Christian jurisprudence embraces natural law or manmade law, the nature that is at stake is construed from a Judeo-Christian perspective, and the man at stake is man construed from a Judeo-Christian perspective. If one bears in mind that the Christian perspective introduced to Africa by Europeans is European, the construction of nature, as is the case with the construction of man that Europeans imposed on Africans, is European. Africans should not make the kind of mistake that some Asian legal scholars have made. For example, Hyung I. Kim appears to claim that the Chinese concepts of The Way, Heaven, and Tao are analogous to the concept of nature as understood in Western natural law jurisprudence.[30] As understood in the Christian West the notion of nature is no longer the notion that the Greeks had in mind. The notion has been Christianized, and consequently, as understood in Western jurisprudence, nature has a meaning entirely different from the meaning it had in Greek jurisprudence. To this extent, Kim's understanding of nature in Chinese thought is suspect. Anyone who has read the Tao text cannot but be shocked by the cavalier attitude that Kim adopts when he equates Tao with the Western understanding of nature. Unwisely, Kim dispels the enigma and the paradox that Tao is. In The Daodejing of Laozi it is said,

> The Way is like empty vessel
> No use could ever fill it up,
> Vast and Deep!
> It seems to be the ancestor of myriad creatures.
> It blunts their sharpness;
> Untangles their tangles;
> Softens their glare;
> Merges with their dust.
> Deep and Clear!
> It seems to be there.
> I do not know whose child it is;
> It is the image of what was before the Supreme Spirit itself![31]

There is nothing in Thomistic thought, or in any aspect of the Judeo-Christian conception of nature that comes close to this Taoist thought, not even Aristotle's' nature as understood by St. Thomas Aquinas. Any attempt to equate the two misunderstands both the Western concept of nature and the Tao. Any comparative thinking presupposes a thinking that is yet to take place. Without the emergence of such thinking comparative thinking is likely to be unilluminating. It is also such a thinking that is needed to get a sense of African jurisprudence.

In examining the ground of African jurisprudence one must ward off the cannibalistic aspect of Western jurisprudence, especially because it has been largely shaped by Christian theology. Christian theology, as is the case with Christian religion, is dictatorial. It tolerates no other theology, and seeks the annihilation of every other theology. It propagates its own construction of nature as the only true construction of nature. It seeks to annihilate all other constructions of nature. It propagates its construction of what a human being is as the only true construction of what a human being is, and seeks to annihilate every other construction of a human being. It presents its version of jurisprudence (whether divine, natural, or man-based) as the only true jurisprudence, and seeks to annihilate all other versions of jurisprudence. It suppresses or rules out any philosophical dialogue on the nature of jurisprudence since it is in possession of true jurisprudence. It has been the unfortunate fate of philosophy in the Western world to fall under the regime of Christian thinking, for once it comes under the jurisdiction of Christian thinking, it loses its critical edge and is transformed into the handmaiden of Christian thinking. Such a philosophy becomes incapable of generating and sustaining an open dialogue on the nature of jurisprudence. It becomes dogmatic, and thereby, disqualifies itself as philosophy.

If an African philosophical presentation of African jurisprudence falls into deaf Western ears, or if it does not have a receptive ear among European engineered African ears, this should not come as a surprise. For centuries, Europeans have domesticated themselves into deafness when it comes to things African, and they have been domesticating Africans into deafness when it comes to things African. To the extent that the divine has a role to play in the constitution or in the understanding of African jurisprudence, the African divine has to be rescued from the Euro-Christian divine. To the extent that nature has a role to play in the constitution and understanding of African jurisprudence, the African conception of nature has to be rescued from the Euro-Christian conception of nature. To the extent that being human is the focus of African jurisprudence, the African conception of being human has to be rescued from the Euro-Christian conception of being human.

When Westerners teach jurisprudence to Africans, the jurisprudence that is taught is not without a missionary element. Western teachers are preachers who teach the true conception of law, and hence, the true conception of what a human being is. The teaching, which is indistinguishable from preaching, does not invite a dialogue on what law is, and thus, on what a human being is. It inhibits the emergence of a dialogue and paralyzes the critical spirit that should inform such a dialogue. Christianity and Christianized philosophy have contributed significantly to this state of affairs. The rush by African nations to embrace Western legal expertise in drafting constitutional law poses a threat to African jurisprudence. This expertise is likely to remain rooted in a Western construction of jurisprudence, and in all that is entailed in this construction in regard to human ontology. Constitutional drafting is a construction of social existence. The assumption that those who have been recognized as experts in their own societies have the qualifications to offer jurisprudential expertise in African societies is to assume an unwarranted similarity in the two types of societies. African societies are not replicas of Euro-American societies.

The European Christian Protestant Reformation did not truly free the individual from Christian theology or from Christian religion. It only freed the individual to decide his or her stake in Christian theology and Christian religion. The liberalism it unleashed was a Christian liberalism. The emergence of a secular individual in modern Europe was a Christian emergence. If this strikes one as contradictory, one should bear in mind that what appears to be the case may not be the case. Western secularism or atheism should be highly suspect. Christianity has contributed significantly to the integration of the European peoples and in giving them an identity as Europeans. Similarly, European jurisprudence has played the same role. It has served to integrate and provide Europeans with a European identity. These two forces did not operate in isolation from each other. The Roman Empire played a historic role in uniting them. After their conversion to Christianity, the Romans were instrumental in spreading Christianity throughout the Roman Empire. Roman law became Christianized, and Christianity became Romanized. The study of law at Bologna, the first modern European University, included the study of both the Roman law and Canon law. Students from all over Europe came to study and returned home to teach both laws. The study of law became a means of being Christianized, if one was not already a Christian. The medievalization of jurisprudence, which for the most part meant Christianization of jurisprudence, is still evidenced by the juridical vestments in the Western world. Many judges in the Western world still wear clerical garments, and where Western legal practice has been imposed on Westerners, one will also see officers of the court wearing similar garments. Walking into a Western courtroom one has the feeling of walking into a church. Even the place where the jury or the judge sits is elevated and looks down on everyone else in the courtroom. The elevated place looks more or less like a place reserved for a choir, or for the pastor or the church minister. With such organization of space, and taking into consideration the regalia of the court officials, one cannot help but sense an aura of the sacred—the Christian sacred.[32] The collaboration of Christian jurisprudence and what appeared to be secular jurisprudence was and is still evident in Africa. In colonial Africa the missionary with Christian Bible in hand and the colonial government agent with the law (gun) in hand collaborated in the same objective: terrorizing and subduing the African. Both the Bible and gun were made legal. They were the voice of European legality in Africa. The same collaboration took place in the Americas. The life of Africans in the Americas was the life of terror and the life of death. In the eyes of Africans during slavery, the agents of law and Christian missionaries were terrorists. One does not readily think of Christian missionaries as terrorists, but this is due to narrow construction of what terrorism is. There is religious terrorism whose objective is to terrorize its victim into obedience to God and to the so-called God's missionaries. The message of the pit of fire with unquenchable flames that consumes sinners will drive most men into submission. This aspect of Christianity was drilled into Africans giving them no acceptable alternative but to surrender to the Christian God. Undoubtedly, the God of the Old Testament was a terrifying God; that is, he was a terrorist to those he had not chosen to be his people, and to those who were obstacles to the realization of the interests and dreams of his chosen people. It was the way he was perceived by those who were not his people. In this case, for example, one should think of what this god meant to the Canaanites, to the Hittites, to the Amalekites and to Egyptians (Africans). Although the God of the New Testament is depicted as a god of love, and not as mean or vicious as the God of the Old Testament, the fundamentalist reading of the New Testament reminds us that after the Second Coming of Christ, those who will not have accepted Christ as Savior will burn in Hell for ever and ever. Thus, the God of the New Testament is also a terrifying god; he is a terrorist. It is unconscionable to spread this terrorism in the name of religion. African psychologists have yet to fully study the implication of the terror inflicted on African children by this Christian message. Prevailing law either in Africa or in the African diaspora is yet to address this offense. The freedom of religion is not an absolute freedom, especially if it is exercised at the expense of the mental well-being of children.

Why, it may be asked, should a study of African jurisprudence concern itself with Western jurisprudence or with Western legal history? Isn't this a digression? Several answers can be given. In the first place, anyone who is concerned with the study of African jurisprudence needs to understand Western jurisprudence and Western legal history, for both are in some significant ways implicated in African jurisprudence and constitute significant obstacles in the study of this jurisprudence. Western jurisprudential imperialism and the role that Western law has played in the subjugation of Africans must be understood if Africans are to make for an independent African jurisprudence. One cannot intelligently struggle against what one does not understand. African jurisprudence must be fought for by Africans, and the fight cannot be successful without the knowledge of what is being fought. Just as Africans had to fight for political independence, they must fight for the independence of African jurisprudence. Genuine African jurisprudence is not yet free. Those who want it on the cheap are digging their own jurisprudential grave.

In constructing a place where African jurisprudence is to take shape, it is not enough to remove the obstacles that have been created by Western jurisprudence. One must also remove the obstacles created by Islamic jurisprudence. The influence of Islamic jurisprudence on Africans is a lot older than the influence of modern Western jurisprudence. For centuries, millions of Africans have been Muslims, and have lived under Islamic jurisprudence. They have embraced the Koran as the basic foundation of jurisprudence. They have accepted Allah not only as the Supreme Law Maker, but also as the Supreme Judge. Islamic theology is the cornerstone of Islamic jurisprudence. If jurisprudence concerns itself with the nature of law, for Muslims the concern with the nature of law is ultimately the concern with Divine law. Differently stated, the study of Islamic jurisprudence leads to the study of Allah. Since Allah has revealed Himself in the Koran, the study of the Koran and the Sunna are indispensable for those who are interested in the true understanding of Islamic jurisprudence. The Koran is the basic text of Islamic jurisprudence. To the extent that jurisprudence concerns itself with human beings an understanding of human beings in Islam leads to the understanding of Allah. Islam asks of man that he totally submit himself to Allah. It is only where there is this submission that one can understand oneself. Now, Arabia is the birthplace of Islam. Allah's revelation to Mohammed that is the Koran did not take place in Africa. To this extent, regardless of how long it has been in existence in Africa, Islam is not a religion that is indigenous to Africa. Islam was imposed on Africans just as Christianity was imposed on them. Moreover, to the extent that the Koran is the basic text of Islamic jurisprudence Islamic jurisprudence was imposed on Africans just as Western jurisprudence was imposed on Africans. Islamic jurisprudence is not indigenous to Africa. The view of man that is found in Islamic jurisprudence was imposed on Africans just as the view of man in Western jurisprudence was imposed on Africans. The extreme monotheism of Islam was imposed on Africans. The Islamic view that there is no God but God, meaning the Islamic God, led to the categorical rejection and denigration of African Gods and African religions. Followers of Islam construed African Gods as heathen Gods, and sought their destruction. They denounced African beliefs about Gods as well as African religious beliefs as heathen beliefs, and systematically sought to convert Africans into Islam by any means necessary. Since in Islam, jurisprudence is inevitably theo-centric, and since the view of man expressed in this jurisprudence is accordingly theo-centric, the conversion of Africans into Islam called for an imposition of Islamic jurisprudence on Africans. The conversion of Africans called for the imposition of the Islamic view of man on Africans, and thereby, sought the eradication of the African view of man. Moreover, since the Prophet codified Allah's revelation in Arabic, Arabic became the language that one has to study and master if one were to truly get the message in the Koran. The language of the Koranic jurisprudence is Arabic, and it is this language that has to be adequately understood if true jurisprudence is to be adequately understood. African languages were not the languages of the truly sacred, and had to give way to Arabic. The sacred aspect of being human which was the true essence of being human could not adequately be captured by African languages. One has to turn to Arabic. For the African being religious, and hence being truly human, he or she had to succumb to being Arabized. Where Islam has been firmly established in Africa, it is difficult to distinguish a Muslim from an Arab. An African Muslim can readily pass for an Arab, and occasionally even deny that he or she is African. This is especially the case in the northern part of Africa where it is assumed that this part of Africa is the territory occupied by Arabs whereas the southern part of the continent is assumed to be a territory of the so-called Black Africans. It is an incontrovertible fact that some Arabs are Africans, and some Africans are Arabs. Some Africans who are Arabs are Muslims, and some Arabs who are Africans are Muslims, and some are not. To the extent that some Africans are Muslims whether they are or are not Arabs, Islamic jurisprudence must be taken into account in demarcating the province of African jurisprudence. Sharia'h or Islamic jurisprudence must be taken as what it is. It is not synonymous with African jurisprudence and may even be an obstacle in the affirmation of African jurisprudence despite the extent to which it has become indigenized in Africa. Where it is claimed that Allah is the only God and that the Prophet is the true and the last Messenger of God, there is no room to make a case for autonomous African jurisprudence. The threat that Islamic jurisprudence poses in Africa is yet to be fully explored.

Even in the case of Africans who are not Muslims, there are aspects of Islamic jurisprudence that have analogs in African jurisprudence. For example, the inseparability of religion from jurisprudence that one finds in the Islamic community is also found in African jurisprudence. Also the inseparability of ethics and morality from law that one finds in the Islamic community is also found in African communities. In modern Western jurisprudence, there is clear effort to establish the separation from everything else that is not law with the intention of establishing a clear conception of law and also with the intention of obviating political, social, moral and other problems that are likely to arise if the separation is not made. In the Constitution of the United States (the highest expression and locus of law in the United States), for example, there is a clear statement that religion is to be separated from the State. It is important to note that the separation of State from the Church or the exclusion of religion from jurisprudence in the Western world came about as a result of internal conflicts in the Western societies. It should not be assumed that these conflicts exist or must exist in every other society. The endless religious controversies that one finds in Western societies, the extension of these controversies to non-religious social spheres, and the intolerances that are to be found in some of the religious practices necessitate separation of religion from what is viewed as the secular world. Christian missionaries have introduced these controversies in Africa and everywhere else they have established a foothold. Western missionaries of Western jurisprudence have also introduced the separation of jurisprudence from religion in Africa and elsewhere where their missionary activities have taken them. They seek to extend the institutionalization of the secularization of jurisprudence in Africa. Ultimately, this is an effort to destroy African societies and constitute them in the manner of Western societies. If the implicit objective is not the destruction of

African societies, it is, at least, to render African societies parasitic to Western societies. In either case, it is not only African jurisprudence that is undermined. Religious practices in Africa are thereby undermined.

Since in indigenous Africa religion is inseparable from jurisprudence, one can understand why Islamic jurisprudence would tend to attract Africans. It is also noteworthy that the unity of religion and the rest of the socio-cultural life was a part of the pre-Islamic Arab world. Nearly all ancient societies and cultures did not make the distinction that Western Christian societies and cultures make. The Islamic community resists the thesis of separation not just to preserve the religion of Islam, or to preserve Islamic jurisprudence, but to preserve the autonomy of the Islamic society and culture. This resistance has resonance in Africa. The resistance is an effort to arrest the tide of Western cultural imperialism. The so-called virtues in the Western conception of the rule of law—neutrality, impartiality, and equality sugarcoat this imperialism so that it can be readily accepted by the members of non-Western communities. If Africans tend to be sympathetic to Islamic resistance to the separation thesis, it is because they too see the danger to the autonomy of African societies and culture. In the course of the history of Western societies, there has emerged a specific conception of religion just as there has emerged a specific conception of jurisprudence. Given the fact that the history of Islamic societies has taken on a different course, as has been the case with African societies, the construction of society, as has been the case with the construction of religion, has taken on a different course.

The fact that both in the Islamic world and in the African world there are some similarities does not in every respect entail similar constructions of jurisprudence. Thus, although in Islamic communities religion is integrated in the whole of social life and in the African world indigenous African religions are similarly integrated in the whole of African social life, it does not follow that there is a common understanding of religion, or that there is a common understanding of jurisprudence. Moreover, the absence of separation between religion and jurisprudence in Islamic communities and the absence of separation of religion from jurisprudence in African communities does not imply that there is a common conception of jurisprudence in Islamic communities and in African communities.

Na'im has attempted to make a case for a sharp distinction between Islamic law as a religious law and state law as a secular law but I believe the case is weak. Although one should be aware of the harm that may be caused by the declaration of religious law as state law or the declaration of state law as the religious law, the distinction may be illusory. As a secular law, state law may be a camouflage of religious law. What appears to intrigue Na'im is European modernity that he associates with liberty and self-determination. In Africa, and I am sure elsewhere, European modernity has been a curse. It is modernity that has given us slavery, colonialism, apartheid, and imperialism. For many Africans,

European liberty has meant the liberty to oppress Africans. European modernity should not be immunized from multiple and dialectical interpretation. The split between the religious and the secular is not like the split of a yam. It is significant. Students of jurisprudence should inquire into what is signified, and in doing so what jurisprudence itself signifies should be a subject of inquiry. Much has been said justifiably about the evils of radical Islamicists or Jihadists. Equally, much should be said about the evils of radical Christians who often pass as liberals. For Africans, the choice is not choose either of the two. There is much to be said justifiably about the evils the two have unleashed on Africans. The distinction between what is religious and what is not is itself religious. The Religious is total.

Traditionally, followers of Islam have condemned African religions and Africans gods, and in doing so, they condemned the view that Africans had of themselves. Basic to their belief is that there is one and only one God, and that God is their God. From this God, there emanates the fundamental source of true jurisprudence. Whatever it is that human beings construe as jurisprudence, if it is true jurisprudence, it must be consistent with and must not be in opposition to a jurisprudence that is theo-centric. This view is not radically different from the prevailing conception of jurisprudence in the Judeo-Christian West. As previously indicated, Judeo-Christian West jurisprudence is theo-centric. With the secularization of the West, Western jurisprudence is deprived of a theological foundation and a secular foundation is erected. Austin is one of the architects of this foundation. Hence, his exclusion of Divine law in strictly mapping out the province of jurisprudence.[33]

Given the fact that the followers of Islam and the followers of Judeo-Christianity discredit and denounce African theology and African religions, an authentic African theo-centric jurisprudence can be affirmed only in opposition to the theo-centric jurisprudence of both Muslims and Judeo-Christians. Africans do not have the same conception of God as Muslims or as Judeo-Christians. African theology and African religions are deeply rooted in African cultures, and to the extent that African jurisprudence is shaped by African theologies and African religions, it is deeply rooted in African cultures. Whether the followers of Judeo-Christianity or the followers of Islam believe it or not, their own theologies and religions are deeply rooted in their respective cultures, and so is the jurisprudence that is shaped by these theologies and religions. In the case of Judeo-Christianity, European culture is the dominant factor. Jurisprudence in this culture is characteristically European. In Islam, especially in African Islam, jurisprudence is characteristically Arabic. Those who seek to establish the province of Islamic jurisprudence in Africa have the unenviable task of distinguishing what is African from what is Arabic in it. To a degree, this holds true of those who want to establish African jurisprudence. They must take into account what is African in African Islamic jurisprudence. As pointed out earlier, the matter is complicated in that there are Africans who are Arabic, and there are Arabs who are African. Given the intolerance of Judeo-Christians and also the intolerance of Islam, it is exceedingly difficult to be authentically African, and at the same time, to be a Muslim, to be a Christian, or to be a follower of Judaism. Hybridity here tends to work at the disadvantage of Africans given the lingering effects of traditional subjugation by these non-African forces.

Today, it is not possible to examine or to constitute African jurisprudence in isolation from other traditions of jurisprudence. The barriers that separate one tradition of jurisprudence from other traditions of jurisprudence are collapsing as the barriers that separate one human community from other human communities collapse. In the light of the ongoing process of globalization, it is increasingly becoming senseless to think that one can study African jurisprudence or write about it without the influence of those studying and writing about other traditions of jurisprudence. In this influence, an African who studies or writes about African jurisprudence has more than a passive role to play. He or she can influence the course of jurisprudential thinking not only in Africa but also in the world. It is also important for him or for her to bear in mind that at stake in African jurisprudence is his or her own self—a self that is not fully what it is outside other Africans or outside other human beings. Essential to his or her task in jurisprudence is to map out the province of African jurisprudence making sure that it includes all that needs to be included. It is also important to bear in mind that the collapsing of the barriers that set African jurisprudence apart from other types of jurisprudence is problematic in that it may conceal an imperial jurisprudence. It may conceal an attempt to impose a conception of jurisprudence in one cultural tradition on all other cultural traditions. As the barriers that separate one tradition of jurisprudence from other traditions of jurisprudence collapse, there arises a danger that is likely to be obscured. This is the danger of a disguised imperialistic tradition of jurisprudence whereby such tradition cannibalizes, marginalizes, or renders other traditions of jurisprudence anachronistic. Students and guardians of African jurisprudence should be particularly sensitive to this possibility given the economic, political, and cultural vulnerabilities of African societies. Most African societies are economically exposed to these vulnerabilities. To pursue economic growth they are compelled to depend on economically powerful countries for aid, and such aid comes with strings attached. Some of these strings include allowing the donors to have cheap access to raw material in Africa, and meeting strategic needs of the donor countries. Also given their weak political status in international relations, they are compelled to align themselves with the politically stronger nations to pursue their international interests. Under these circumstances African jurisprudence is under enormous pressure to toe the line. Africans are put in a position where their jurisprudence is shaped by those from whom they get or seek aid. They are pressured to seek jurisprudential aid from those who give them other types of aid. There is a jurisprudential aspect of globalism that is designed and controlled by powerful non-African actors to establish and police the contours of global jurisprudence. In this context, the pursuit of authentic African jurisprudence is easily cast away as fantasy or as anachronistic, and as an impediment to the institutionalization of global jurisprudence. Essentially, this global jurisprudence caters to provincial interests that are disguised as the interests of the entire human community. It is projected as universal legal philosophy that serves the interest of all regardless of race, nation, creed, or culture. It is projected as a cosmopolitan jurisprudence that is apparently freed from the terrestrial social and cultural forces. This is the tide against which the advocates of the African jurisprudence must ride. African jurisprudence is an essential resource not only in the reconstruction of African societies and culture, but also in the reconstruction of the African self. Construing it solely as an intellectual or a theoretical endeavor makes it vulnerable to what stands in the way of the reconstruction project. It takes oxygen out of the spirit of African renaissance.

Part II

What then is the province of African jurisprudence? Some features of this province have already been highlighted in previous remarks. The question is raised at this juncture to allow for further determination of this province. Central to this question is what constitutes the Africanness of jurisprudence. The exploration of the answer to this question cannot dispense with the exploration of what jurisprudence is. The two questions are mutually implicated, and are implicated in a manner in which each sheds the light on the other. In trying to determine what is African about jurisprudence, it is important to stay away from geography and from biology—the two indicia that are in vogue in determining Africanness. Africans are not blacks who live in Africa, and African jurisprudence is not black jurisprudence that is practiced by blacks who live in Africa. Africans are Africans and the jurisprudence they practice is African jurisprudence. It may be claimed that these are tautological statements that do not tell us anything substantive about Africans or about African jurisprudence. One does not move away from what one seeks to understand. To understand oneself one cannot move away from oneself. One must reside in oneself. To be African is to be African; it is not to be in one's skin as is ordained by racism, and it is not simply a matter of being located in a geographical territory known as Africa. The former mystifies one's skin making it appear as if it is an outer statement of what one is. Being human is not to be found in human "skins". Except in objectivist biology, strictly speaking, human beings do not have skins. The latter objectifies the African and puts him or her on a territory as if he or she were one thing among other things in an objective space. The misconstruction of what being African is was institutionalized by European racists who sought to place the Africanness of the African on the African's skin, and to place the African so-determined on a geographical territory called Africa. Being African is not reducible to biology or to geography, and it is not a generalization of empirical phenomena. If one were to ask an African what an African is, it would be absurd to ask him or her to enumerate all the characteristics that make him or her African, just as it would be absurd to ask a Chinese to enumerate what makes him or her Chinese. An African who would proffer such enumeration would be testifying to the fact that he or she has no clue about what makes him or her African. Being African is a pre-synthetic mode of being. It is an indeterminate mode of being that is in constant process of becoming. It is only as such that it can be grasped. It is grasped in not being grasped. This is why it is so difficult to define. One cannot define oneself for others, if only because one cannot define oneself for oneself. This is not a matter of cognitive incapacity that lies in the subject. The incapacity is triggered by what is to be defined. Moreover, one cannot look for a definition of oneself in the dictionary. One derives one's meaning by how one lives, and one is understood by others by how one lives. Being African, which is a mode of being with others, is to be understood in and by how an African lives. If, as was said earlier, in the expression "African jurisprudence" what is African sheds light on what is jurisprudence and vice versa, what we are saying about being African applies to what we are to understand as jurisprudence if it is qualified by "African". In this context, jurisprudence is a pre-synthetic whole. It cannot be reduced to the study of a collection of rules, a collection of principles or to a collection of rules and principles. It is indefinable. This does not mean that it is devoid of life-force. It animates the African world in the same way that the indefinability of being African animates jurisprudence. There is a pre-cognitive awareness of what constitutes being African, and there is a pre-cognitive awareness of African jurisprudence. The attempt to cognitively trespass the pre-cognitive realm results in absurdity. The pre-cognitive life that claims the being of the African is not the same as or identical with the life of emotion. The distinction between what is cognitive and what is emotional does not address radically what is at stake in being African. It is a conceptual/cultural construction that is derived from what is essential about being African. Constructions seek to delimit, and in delimiting they undermine what they seek to delimit. What they seek to delimit overflows the delimitation. This mode of being of the African lies at the core of African jurisprudence. It may be argued that thinking of the being of the African in this manner obscures what is African, and once jurisprudence is predicated on this mode of being, it too becomes obscured. This argument, however, obscures more than it enlightens. There are different types of enlightenments. Conceptual delimitation is one type of enlightenment. It is an error to believe that it is the only type of enlightenment. A non-conceptual enlightenment is also a possibility for us if we can emancipate ourselves from the tyranny of conceptualization. How, one may ask, can such enlightenment be thought and expressed in language. It appears that thinking and language are the means by which human beings can express whatever it is that needs to be expressed. Conventional wisdom tells us to think and to express ourselves in language is inescapably to do so conceptually. How then are we to think and express what is at stake in being African and in African jurisprudence without contradicting ourselves. Obviously, to express myself the way I am expressing myself goes against conventional wisdom. I am expressing myself in a way that deliberately challenges the limits of our conventional understanding of thinking and our conventional understanding of language. Conceptualization does not exhaust the life of thinking, and it does not exhaust the life of language. In short, it does not exhaust what it is to be a human being. It is in this realm of inexhaustibility that I want to situate the being of the African and consequently, African jurisprudence. And where the African is, is also where other human beings are. Where African jurisprudence is, is where other branches of jurisprudence are. The resistance to reducing the study of jurisprudence to the study of rules or to the study of rules and principles is intended to bring into relief this state of affairs. The resistance may appear to be problematic in that, for many, jurisprudence makes sense only when there are rules or principles to reckon with. Moreover, without rules or principles it may be claimed that the distinction between legal validity and legal invalidity would equally be senseless. However, the distinction between legal validity and legal invalidity need not necessarily presuppose rules or principles. What makes the distinction meaningful is what is intended by law, and what is intended by law is a particular form of human life. In Africa such a form comes into relief in the African's lived world—a world that expresses the African's notion of good life.

When it is asked, what is the province of African jurisprudence? The word "African" qualifies jurisprudence. The qualification implies that there are other provinces of jurisprudence. The further implication of this implication is that the province of African jurisprudence is what it is, in part, by intersecting with other provinces of jurisprudence. It is tempting to think of this intersection as what the provinces of jurisprudence have in common, or to think of it as expressing a matter of family resemblances. Succumbing to this temptation may provoke another temptation. The temptation is to inquire what is it that these provinces have in common, or what is to constitute their familial ties. However seductive these temptations are, we will set them aside, not because the quest for the answers is not philosophically challenging, but because it may be more challenging to take up what is at stake in philosophical interrogation. If properly grasped, the character of philosophical interrogation may throw light to the challenge that these questions pose. That is, to ask what is the province of African jurisprudence in a philosophical sense is to place this question in the province of philosophical interrogation. Understanding the nature of this interrogation is essential if the question is to be adequately understood and if it is to be adequately answered.

What the province of philosophical interrogation is is not self-evident, and perhaps, what it is will never become self-evident unless philosophy comes to an end. What this claim states will readily become evident if one pays attention to any philosophical tradition. In any one philosophical tradition, one notices an on-going effort to establish the nature of philosophy, a nature that must be established if an adequate conception of the province of philosophical interrogation is to be attained. In addition to the existence of this ongoing effort, within each and every tradition, there is an ongoing inter-tradition effort to accomplish the same task. To be sure, this latter effort is not as evident as the former, and this may be primarily due to the fact the effort that is undertaken in each tradition has for the most part remained an internal affair, cut off from the efforts that are being undertaken in other traditions. For the most part, each philosophical tradition has concerned itself with its internal effort in clarifying what is to be understood as philosophy. With the gradual crumbling of the walls that have kept traditions of philosophy apart, a horizon is opening up where the intersection of the efforts at clarifying the province of philosophical interrogation has become increasingly inevitable. It is in the context of these efforts that one is to place the clarification and the constitution of the province of African jurisprudence. However it is designated, the province of African jurisprudence will take shape at this intersection. Moreover, the lack of closure to a true philosophical discourse is integral to African jurisprudence to the extent that it is constituted or understood in philosophical context.

The intersection of the provinces of jurisprudence exemplifies a location for a revelation of one of the basic aspects of philosophizing. It opens a horizon where both African and non-African students of jurisprudence can legitimately engage one another in a meaningful dialogue about jurisprudence. In this location, it is made explicit that, in every sense, non-Africans are not *personas non grata* in the province of African jurisprudence, just as Africans are not *personas non grata*, in every sense, in any other province of jurisprudence. That is, in a sense, non-Africans can justifiably critique what is said about African jurisprudence just as Africans, in a sense, can justifiably critique what is said in other provinces of jurisprudence. It is precisely this situation that makes inter-provincial dialogue on jurisprudence possible. This inter-provinciality makes it possible to make an inquiry on the nature of jurisprudence in a manner that is intelligible to all inquirers about the nature of jurisprudence regardless of the province that they inhabit. Thus, as a branch of African philosophy, African jurisprudence does not isolate the African tradition of philosophy from other traditions of philosophy. The openness that African jurisprudence has in relation to other traditions of jurisprudence is mirrored in the openness that African philosophy has in relation to other traditions of philosophy. When African jurisprudence is investigated by philosophers, it should be expected to reveal the investigator's understanding of philosophy, and when investigated from the standpoint of African philosophy, the investigation should reveal the investigator's understanding of African philosophy.

African jurisprudence, as is the case with every other jurisprudence, is largely intelligible if it is put into a historical context. Today, it is undeniable that African jurisprudence is significantly influenced by Western or European jurisprudence. As previously indicated, in colonial Africa, European jurisprudential views were imposed on Africans as a part of the overall European colonial enterprise in Africa. In post-colonial Africa, this influence has remained as a component of African jurisprudence. Today, any discourse on African jurisprudence must take this state of affairs into account. In taking this state of affairs into account, it is noteworthy that one of the casualties of the imposition of Western jurisprudence on Africans was the indigenous African jurisprudential views. In colonial Africa, there was systematic destruction or erasure of pre-colonial African jurisprudential views. The destruction and erasure was for the most part indirect, in the sense that Europeans denied that there was an African jurisprudence. Historians remind us that modern Europeans thought of Africa as a Dark Continent, and it can reasonably be assumed that in the context of this historic Darkness there was no jurisprudence to be seen or to be spoken of. Since according to Europeans, the inhabitants of the Dark Continent were savages and heathens, there was no civilization which would create and sustain jurisprudence. If it is borne in mind that, in the West, conventional jurisprudence is associated with the existence of a nation-state, and moreover, if it is borne in mind that Westerners have claimed that the nation-state is largely their creation, it should not come as a surprise that Africa proper has been projected by Westerners as devoid of nation-state, and consequently, projected as devoid of jurisprudence. Westerners projected Africans as living in a state of nature—a state that was devoid of the rule of law. Since Westerners generally associate jurisprudence with the rule of law, it would seem to follow that it is meaningless to speak of African jurisprudence unless one has in mind a jurisprudence that Westerners have imposed on Africans. That is, if it is granted that in pre-colonial Africa there was no jurisprudence, what may be regarded as African jurisprudence in colonial, and perhaps in post-colonial Africa, is nothing more than an exportation of European jurisprudence to Africa. Wherever and whenever possible, the exported jurisprudence was adapted to local African conditions. African native tribunals, African chiefs, kings and other African leaders were used to facilitate this adaptation. Where adaptation of exported jurisprudence was resisted, or where this jurisprudence was rejected, force was used. It is in this context that the rise of the police force in modern Africa is to be understood. Colonial jurisprudence in Africa, as was the case in other colonized parts of the world, was largely the jurisprudence of subjugation. Violence was an essential feature of jurisprudence. It is precisely this kind of jurisprudence that is well captured in Frantz Fanon's work. As he points out in his important study of colonial Africa, the language that the colonialist understands is the language of violence.[34] Colonial jurisprudence had a terrorizing effect in the eyes of Africans. It was a form of Jurisprudential terrorism—a form of terrorism that was sanctioned by the colonial judiciary.

In colonial Africa, force, or more specifically violence, was a key element in the jurisprudence the European colonizers sought to institute. Violence is force without justice. It is precisely such violence that Westerners had to get rid of in their own societies as a prerequisite for the emergence of a modernity in which the rule of law had a place. It is ironic that what these societies sought to get rid of is precisely what they sought to impose on African societies. The colonization of Africa institutionalized violence in African societies and inhibited the rise of the rule of law as understood by Europeans. The resistance of this violence was taken to be inimical to the rule of law. In the context of colonialism the rule of law meant colonial order. Post-colonial Africa is yet to do away with this sort of violence. In many African countries, one continues to see the sort of brutish force that was the major aspect of colonial African society. Rulers in these countries have not invented this force. They are merely continuing an instrument of social control that was instituted by European colonial powers. It is important to bear in mind colonialism did not introduce violence in Africa. In Africa violence predates European colonialism. What was new is the form that violence took in colonial Africa. Violence became a feature of the nation-state—a social formation that had its genesis in modern Europe.

An authentic African jurisprudence contests the Eurocentric perception and conception of jurisprudence in Africa. It challenges the Eurocentric conception of the history of jurisprudence in Africa. It rejects the view that Europeans initiated jurisprudence in Africa. The rejection and the resistance of this view is a part of African jurisprudence today. Authentic African jurisprudence must take to task those who deny the existence of African jurisprudence in pre-colonial Africa and those who believe that modern African jurisprudence is nothing more than the jurisprudence that Europeans have exported to or instituted in Africa. It calls for a reading of African history from an African perspective. It challenges the historic ignorance that led Europeans to characterize Africa as a Dark Continent. It challenges the arrogance exemplified by Europeans in their claim that modern African history is nothing more than a civilizing effort by which Africans are brought by Europeans into the mainstream of human civilization. It challenges the depiction of pre-colonial Africans as savages, heathens, and barbarians who distinguish themselves in lawlessness. It challenges the colonial and post-colonial civilizing mission of Europeans in Africa. In short, authentic African jurisprudence must be an anti-colonial process. Although formal colonialism has come to an end, it is not to be assumed that the anti-colonial process is anachronistic. Genuine anti-colonial process must take into account the difficult process of de-colonizing of the African mind. The mind to be de-colonized is not that proverbial mind that Descartes constructed and instituted. Rather, it is the African self-consciousness as it is exhibited in African life and culture. This de-colonizing process is an essential element of African jurisprudence.

The de-colonizing dimension of African jurisprudence is not the only dimension of African jurisprudence. That is, African jurisprudence is not solely a reaction to European colonialism. If it were no more than such a reaction, it would only confirm the colonialist thesis held by Europeans that in pre-colonial Africa there was no African jurisprudence. Moreover, it would obscure the objective that motivates anti-colonial and de-colonizing processes. The objective is not implanted in the African by Europeans. What lies behind these processes and what is the telos of these processes is inherent in Africans as Africans. It is already found in pre-colonial Africa in Africans. It is a part of what constitutes the substance of African jurisprudence. It is self-affirmation and the self-constitution of the African people. It is precisely such an affirmation that colonialism sought to erase or deny, and it is precisely what anti-colonial and de-colonizing processes seek to re-affirm and protect. What must also be taken into account is that by self-affirmation, it is not meant the affirmation of an isolated self. Such a self can only be an expression of a mad person or of a person who is not conscious of his or her personhood. In Africa, and not only in Africa, personhood is social. African jurisprudence is a part of African social anthropology. The view that jurisprudence takes a person in her or his social situation is precisely the same view that the Ancient Greeks expressed when they claimed that man is a social and political animal. And it is not only the Ancient Greeks who thought of personhood this way. Asians, Native Americans and other peoples held the same view. Apart from social and political contexts, jurisprudence, African or non-African, is without meaning. As indicated, these contexts are the contexts of what is human. What is human from an African perspective is what the proper province of African jurisprudence is. Indeed, it is what is proper for all genuine provinces of jurisprudence. It is precisely for this reason that the conventional modern Western literature on jurisprudence does not fully address what is at stake in jurisprudence. For the most part, jurisprudence in this literature concerns itself with the nature of law, the source or the sources of law, the hermeneutics of law, the administration of law, types of law, and so on. All these concerns with law fall under the concept of the rule of law. Jurisprudence, therefore, turns out to be an investigation of the nature of the rule of law in its substantial and procedural contexts. This conception of jurisprudence is derivative. What is elemental in every jurisprudence is the conception of being human that is presupposed. It is precisely for this reason that it is herein claimed that African jurisprudence is what is at stake in being human for Africans. If jurisprudence is to be understood as a science, in its African context, it is to be understood as a science of being human as understood by Africans. African jurisprudence is an African sociology. In this regard, African jurisprudence does not stand alone. All jurisprudence is sociological.

As indicated above, African jurisprudence takes human beings in their social setting. Such a setting, contrary to the claims of Western modernity, is not a social construction. Human beings are not social beings because they socialize with one another. They socialize with one another because they are social beings. This is an elemental form of sociality—an organic society that European modernity denies. The claim that human beings are social beings is not to be taken as denying individuality. That is, it is not to be taken as denying so-called individual rights or individual autonomy. Individual rights or individual autonomy in a social vacuum are theoretical constructions that are removed from human reality. In Africa, legality is not a social construction. It is a natural social setting in which the African has her or his being. This setting should not necessarily be linked with social tyranny. It should not be necessarily linked to communistic or totalitarian social regimes. It is not an expression of an essentialism that dispenses with historicity or with temporality of being human. It is a dimension in which a human being is a human being. The projection of the precolonial African societies as societies in which individual rights or individual autonomy were suppressed is a misconception of these societies. This is not to deny that there were instances of such suppressions. There is no society that is totally immune from such suppressions. The overcoming of such suppressions, however, should not lead to a situation where human society is reduced to a mere aggregate of individuals. Such an aggregation can only lead to a situation where the individual is alienated from his or her humanness. Instead of construing these suppressions as deprivations of the individual's autonomy, they are instruments of securing the humanity of the individual.

When it is asked what is African about jurisprudence, one must look at Africans. One must look at the way Africans view themselves. Moreover, since they do not exhaust the class of human beings, the way they view themselves has a bearing on the way they view other human beings. After all, an African is an African in the context of other Africans, and as a human being he or she is a human being in the context of other human beings. What African jurisprudence calls for is a dialogue among Africans on being human, a dialogue that of necessity leads to the dialogue with other human beings. This dialogue is not an end in itself. It is a dialogue with an existential implication. It aims at living in accordance with what one is. Although one is what one is, what one is, is dialogical. To be dialogical is necessarily to engage others and leaves what one is open and calls for dwelling in this openness. The other is not just the living other. The other is also the departed (the ancestor), and is also the one who is to come. Moreover, the other is not solely the human other. It is also all that is animate and that which is inanimate. In other words, African jurisprudence is not only a humanism. A human being for the African is more than a human being. She or he is a part of what is. What is is perhaps what the Greeks named *physis*, and it may have a bearing on what the Chinese call Tao. What Europeans have termed superstitious in Africa may yet throw light on what matters not only in African jurisprudence but also in that location where the provinces of jurisprudence intersect, an area where Europeans too have their being. In Africa, what matters is expressed cryptically. What is said cryptically has its own clarity. If what has been said herein has been said uncryptically, it should be heard cryptically. In Africa, jurisprudence is more than a formal science. It is also a science of the occult. The ancestors are the guardians of the occult. At an age where African ancestrology has been projected as anachronistic, African jurisprudence is likely to suffer the same fate. In this fate, the soul and life of the African is at stake.

We live at a time when Euro-American jurisprudence has taken a global dictatorial grip on thinking about jurisprudence. That is, anyone who expects to get any credibility in thinking about jurisprudence must pass through the gates of thinking guarded by Western thinking police. The Euro-American jurisprudence that prevails is remarkable in being one dimensional. It encourages a one dimension thinking that suppresses or inhibits alternative and oppositional thinking—a thinking that would expose its one dimensionality. It has not only ignored the socialist/communist jurisprudence but also has sought to discredit it. The collapse of the Soviet Union, the compromising of Chinese communism and the concerted attack on socialist nations by the West has had a remarkable toll on socialist/communist jurisprudence. Within the Western world, Marxist jurisprudence has suffered institutional censorship. It has thoroughly been discredited. Western left-leaning legal scholars—a minority in Western legal scholarship—have operated in the margins of legal education. They have either been ignored, or have been tolerated to give the impression that, in the legal academy, there is freedom of speech. The same fate has befallen both Western feminist jurisprudence and the race-based-jurisprudence. Despite their oppositional stance, left-leaning jurisprudence, feminist jurisprudence, and race-based jurisprudence (espoused by critical race theory theoreticians) largely remain manifestations of liberalized Western jurisprudence. They remain within the ambit of Western jurisprudence, and are to be construed as essential weapons of the Western empire in its effort to secure and promote its global hegemony. In this effort, Western jurisprudence acts in concert with or as an embodiment of Western politics, economics, and culture generally. It is in this context that one is to understand the task of those who have embarked on the task of thinking through African jurisprudence. It is a task in which the humanity of the African as exemplified in his/her culture is at stake. It is a task that involves more that analytical jurisprudence. That is, it is more than undertaking an analysis and clarification of the basic concepts of law. It has to secure, defend, and promote the dignity of Africans in all spheres of social existence. By dignity, it is not meant the inner dimension of Africans or a metaphysical state of being African. Inwardness is a modern construction of Western European culture, and has one of its roots in Christian religion. It is foreign to African culture, and where it is found, it is usually a result of Western European Christian missionary activity. This does not mean that, for the African, dignity lies in outwardness, if by outwardness it is meant what is the opposite of inwardness. For the African, human dignity lies in the sensuous, in the lived-space. Moreover, for the African, dignity is not to be thought of as a rational nature that each of us has, and that sets us apart from the rest of the animals, and from things. For the African, dignity lies in the *Ubuntu,* a term that does not readily render itself to translation in other languages. It is what makes a human being a human being without cutting him or her off from the rest of the animals or from anything else. It is a practice in being human, a practice that intrinsically links human beings with all beings. It is in this domain that African jurisprudence is to be placed. Thinking about law in Africa, the practice of law in Africa, legal education in Africa, thereby receive inspiration. It is not a matter of having an approach to jurisprudence that isolates Africans from other human beings. It is a matter of setting up the criteria for defining the relations that African are to have with other human beings, and a matter of setting the parameters within which Africans are to interact with one another and with other human beings.

In Ubuntuism lies what is authentic about the African, hence what is authentic about African jurisprudence. It is precisely this point that Ramose Mogobe of South Africa attempts to articulate in his studies on Ubuntuism.[35] It is what circumscribes the province of African jurisprudence. Circumscription demarcates the borders of this jurisprudence, the province of this jurisprudence. These borders are life borders; they are borders of African life. As such they are living borders. They blend into other living borders. That they do not sever the African from other human beings, and from everything else that lives, should not therefore come as a surprise.

Regardless of how fragmentary the human community is, each sector of the human community is what it is by being a part of the whole human community. Any well-being of one sector that is pursued at the expense of the well-being of any other sector is not well-being. To be sure, this does not mean that a given sector cannot behave otherwise. However, if it behaves otherwise, the behavior may be a result of the ignorance of what constitutes one's well-being. Ultimately, it is an attack on oneself, and, as human beings, such an attack is an attack of us all. Given this possibility, then, what passes as legal education takes on an enormous significance. Training a lawyer is not analogous to training a dog. Training a dog does not aim at the intrinsic well-being of a dog, let alone the well-being of all dogs. We train dogs for our own benefit. We use them as a means to our well-being. Training a lawyer ought to be qualitatively different. It is the educating of a human being for human well-being. We may not know what human well-being is, in which case, training a lawyer should be a part of the quest for what constitutes human well-being. To be sure, it may appear as if this is asking too much of legal education. To be sure, there is also a possibility of asking too little of legal education. Although it is difficult to determine what is asking too much or too little of legal education, it should be a central mission of legal education to question itself.

To the extent that law is the focus of jurisprudence, law must be construed as the gateway to and a place where being human or where the well-being of being human is made manifest. In this case, jurisprudence is anthropology, but as the word *Ubuntu* suggests, it is not anthropologism or a humanism that seeks to sever being human from other modes of being, or to sever human well-being from the well-being of everything else. If this is not the sort of jurisprudence that is practiced in other traditions, it does not follow that the African has to abandon it. At the core of African jurisprudence must be the exposition of the Africanness of the African—an exposition that is inevitably linked to the quest for the well-being of the African. It is an act of the highest irresponsibility to train African young men and women to think like lawyers without placing this training in this framework. The uncritical importation of other frameworks for the legal training of African lawyers may compromise the Africanness of the African and may be detrimental to the well-being of Africans. Thus, the issue of thinking like an African lawyer is one that has to be brought to the forefront of African legal education. It would be an error for non-Africans to assume that African jurisprudence lies out there as an object of inquiry. The path to it does not lead away from a non-African. He or she is implicated in this inquiry in the sense that his self or her self is also thereby inquired into. Similarly, African jurisprudence does not lie within the African. An African does not have an inside where anything could be. This is not because he or she is an African. It is because he or she is a human being. A human being is a public being. The African is not privileged in the inquiry into the nature of African jurisprudence.

There was once a man who was driven into insanity by excessive fear. In this state, he often complained that there was a man who constantly followed him during the day when the sun was shining, and often disappeared when the sun stopped shining. When asked by a passerby how he knew that someone was following him, he said that he could see his shadow but when he turned around to see who was casting a shadow, he saw no one, and the shadow also disappeared. The passerby told him that the shadow he saw was his own shadow, and the fear he had was the fear of himself. He denied that this was the case, and told the passerby that it was he—the passerby—who trailed him. During this exchange the sun had unnoticeably disappeared in the horizon. To avoid any injurious confrontation, the passerby walked away. The insane man walked away too, at this time, without the fear of being followed. This does not mean that the insane man was cured of insanity or that the passerby passed by. This is the way of man and, as the way of man, it is the way of African jurisprudence. One is not quite sure about what one is getting into as one enters the world of African jurisprudence. The study of this jurisprudence is a riddle.

In the light of what has been said so far, it should be evident that there is a crisis in African legal education. When African students enter into law school, their objective is primarily to practice law after graduation. Their teachers prepare them to meet their objective. Generally, in the curriculum there is no place for African jurisprudence. Such a course is likely to be perceived as a luxury. It is indeed correct to point out that the aim of legal education in other countries is similar to the aim of legal education in Africa. However, it is worth pointing out that the practice of law does not take place in a social vacuum. African students have a lesson to learn from the practice of law during the colonial period and during the Apartheid period. For the most part, in both situations, the practice of law legitimized and reinforced the oppression of Africans. The practice of law in the Americas during the enslavement of their cousins served the same objectives: legitimization and reinforcement of the enslavement of Africans. What the study of African jurisprudence can do or ought to do is sensitize Africans to the type of society in which they will practice law—the type of society that their practice will legitimize or reinforce. It is particularly important that the law curriculum include legal history in Africa so that they can see what has been done in the name of law. Inescapably, such legal history will be a political legal history. It will demonstrate the lie of approaching the study of law apolitically. It will demonstrate the lie of distinguishing the rule of law from the rule of man. The rule of law is the rule of man, and who man is matters.

Chapter 3
Thinking Like an African Lawyer

> If you think that you can think about a thing inextricably attached to something else without thinking of the thing it is attached to, then you have a legal mind.
> -Thomas R. Powell[36]

Much dialectical work needs to be done to illuminate what is at work in thinking like an African lawyer. We launch a reflection on the above observation to prepare the way for such work. Before the commencement of a journey, it is advisable to prepare oneself. Such preparation is not an easy undertaking. There is a saying in Africa that states, "Haraka haraka haina baraka", translated as "Hurry, hurry has no blessing". How one commences a journey matters in a very significant way, for it contributes to the overall success of the journey. It is especially important to recognize that the journey, in part, is directed by the goal it seeks. Where, in part, the goal is in question, as is the case with every philosophical goal, how one prepares oneself is problematic. Moreover, since one cannot definitively predict what may happen in the course of the journey, it may happen that one is not as prepared as one thought. Then, preparation becomes an ongoing process. It has to be this way in order to be appropriate for the goal to be attained. It should also not be forgotten that a philosophical journey, in so far as it is truly philosophical, begins at home and ends at home. Philosophical reflection on what it is to think like an African lawyer must be taken in this spirit. One's thinking must a priori be a part of this thinking to think it.

What can be inferred from the observation by Powell is that the legal mind is not what it appears to be. It is obfuscated and it obfuscates. It is dislocated where it is located, and is located where it is dislocated. Consequently, the thinking it engages in is equally dislocated where it is located, and is located where it is dislocated. Although it appears that the author is speaking about the universal aspect legal mind and, consequently, about the universal aspect of thinking like a lawyer, he is speaking about a particular legal mind and about a particular aspect of legal thinking. He has in mind the modern European conception of legal mind, and has in mind a modern European conception of thinking like a lawyer. Failure to recognize this is not accidental and, clearly, it is not solely a deliberate effort by a particular individual or a group of individuals to bring it about. It is an institutionalized way of thinking about legal mind as well as an institutionalized way of thinking about legal thinking. It is the work of the modern European mind—a mind that not only obscures its modern European context in so far as it is claimed to be universal, but also that obscures the context of the legal thinking it engages in. This contextual obfuscation is currently in the process of being institutionalized globally. Resistance to this process is an integral aspect of thinking like an African lawyer. The success of this resistance depends on an understanding of what is being resisted. The resistance removes obscurity from obscurity so that it can be seen in the very way it is. An inquiry into what Powell has in mind may pave the way for the disclosure of what is at work in thinking like an African lawyer.

A better understanding of what Powell claims, and the implication I am drawing from this claim, calls for a broader and deeper investigation. The legal mind he has in mind and the thinking that flows from it is likely to make more sense if one recognizes that neither exists in a historical or cultural vacuum. What is required is an entrance into the legalist psychology that is the source of this thinking. Such a psychology is not exclusively legalistic, although it may be appear as such. It is essentially a modern Western European psychology—a psychology that is deeply shaped by Western European history and culture. Among Europeans, there are those who appear to have excelled as students of this psychology. Such students include the German philosopher, Friedrich Nietzsche. Looking deep into the European mind, he notes that,

> The intellect, as a means for the preservation of the individual, unfolds its chief powers in simulation; for this is the means by which the weaker, less robust individuals preserve themselves, since they are denied the chance of waging the struggle for existence with norms or the fangs of the beast of prey, in man this art of simulation reaches its peak; here deception, flatter, lying and cheating, talking behind the back, posing, living in borrowed splendor, being masked, the disguise of convention, acting a role before others and before oneself—in short, the constant fluttering around the single flame of vanity is so much the rule and the law that almost nothing is more incomprehensible than how an honest and pure urge for truth could make its appearance among men.[37]

The intellect that he speaks about is the intellect that has given us the European legal mind, a mind that obfuscates itself, and that obfuscates what it does.

Among multiple modern European inventions must be counted the European mind—the mind that has given birth to the European legal mind, and to the legal thinking associated with it. This legal mind is one among other minds that have been given birth to by European intellectual imagination. The birth of this mind has been paradoxical in the sense that it has, in turn, given birth to the parent—the European. The European legal mind itself has been transformed into a resource of validating and providing legitimacy to the European mind and to European identity. Perhaps, to refer to these processes as paradoxical is to mystify them. These processes are processes of obfuscation. Nietzsche deserves credit for shedding light on this obfuscation. He was talking of the European mind or intellect when he said,

> There have been eternities when it did not exist, and when it is done for again, nothing will have happened. For this intellect has no further mission that would lead beyond human life. It is human, rather, and only its owner and producer gives it such importance, as if the world pivoted around it. But if we could communicate with the mosquito, then we would learn that it floats through the air with the same self-importance, feeling within itself the flying center of the world.[38]

Lack of historical awareness may be a hindrance to the recognition that Europe is a creature of history. There was a time when there was no Europe and without a Europe there was no European or a European mind.

The modern European mind has created a world and has also created itself into an axis around which the world it has created rotates. It uses legality to secure and give legitimacy to itself. African and other non-Europeans have paid dearly for the hubris and self-delusion in which it has shrouded itself. The theater of the operation of the European intellect has not been confined and still is not confined within the boundaries of Europe, or within the colonies of European descendants. Its boundaries are like the boundaries of venereal disease. It knows no territorial boundaries. It has sought and seeks to trespass all territories. Its spatiality is polymorphously perverse. What it has not been able to digest, it destroys. This has been the course of European modernity. Africa has fallen under its regime and continues to languish under it. Its tyranny has concretely been experienced by Africans in the form of slavery, colonialism, neo-colonialism, and apartheid. These heinous institutions were embodiments of European legalism. They were given legitimacy by the European legal mind. It was a criminal offense to challenge slavery, colonialism, neo-colonialism, and to challenge apartheid. The desire to be free of oppression and exploitation was viewed as evidence for criminal intent. Under the European legal regime, what Africans experienced was the gun man situation writ large.[39] This is how the European sense of legal mind and thinking like a European lawyer came across to the African. It should be borne in mind that contemporary African nation states are not only creations of the European mind but equally the case is the fact

African legal minds themselves creations of the European legal mind. Moreover, intra-African legal jurisdictions have been put in place by European juridical criteria. Intra-African international law is dependent on legal parameters established by the European legal mind during the colonial phase of African history. Moreover, outside of Africa, African international law operates on premises established by the European legal mind. The so-called law of nations has a European foundation. It is the European mind that has given rise to the idea of African national identity. Clearly, it is not in the interest of thinking like an African lawyer to think in a way that deprives Africans of agency in shaping their destiny. The recovery and affirmation of this agency is central to thinking like an African lawyer.

It was a part of the conclusion of the European thinking that Africans were devoid of intellect, or if they possessed one, it was of an inferior sort, primitive, or severely underdeveloped. The European mind declared that Africans were mindless and, consequently, it would have been absurd to speak of the African mind, or to speak of the indigenous legal mind in Africa. Accordingly, in European eyes, thinking like a lawyer was foreign to Africans. Apparently, Africans were living in a lawless world, and had to sense no law.[40] Having created this void and, of course, denying that they had created it, Europeans set out to fill it up. This became the task of European legal missionaries. Africans were projected by the European mind as being incapable of understanding and managing their own legal affairs. Having no legal mind of their own they could not think like a lawyer on their own. They needed a European legal mind to think for them and to place their lives under the law. The need was not indigenous to Africans. It was a creation of the European mind and was a major modern European invention. It was a need that only they (Europeans) could meet. In line with the mystification of European intellect, this mind was projected not as European but as mind in itself, and the legal aspect of it was equally presented not as European but as a legal mind in itself, as a thing in itself. Having deceived themselves about themselves, Europeans set out to have Africans deceive themselves about themselves.

The deception about legal mind and, consequently, about thinking like a lawyer, was a part of the overall historic deception that characterizes Western European modernity. This particular form of deception is closely tied to the Western European Christian religious deception and, most likely, rooted in it. Nietzsche, a noted European student of the European Christian religion, has noted,

> perhaps there even exists an order of rank about these burnt children, these born artists who can find the enjoyment of life only in the intention of falsifying its image (as if it were a longwinded revenge on life): the degree to which life has been spoiled for them might be inferred from the degree to which they wish to see its image falsified, thinned down, transcendentalized, deified—the *homines religiosi* might be included among artists, as their highest rank.[41]

Christianity in Europe radically transformed the indigenous inhabitants of Europe into a self-denying people and beautified this denial to the point at which instead of appearing as what it was—self-denial—it appeared as self-affirmation in the most intoxicating splendor. The transformation brought about a religious interpretation of existence that was not native to the European mind. It was a product of Christian psychology—a psychology that rested on the erasure of native European psychology. European scholars have spoken eloquently about the contribution that Roman law made in the formation of the European legal mind, but have not equally recognized the contribution the Romans made to the formation of the European religious mind—a mind that was instrumental in the creation of the European legal mind.

The rise of the European religious mind and, hence, the rise of the European legal thinking can be traced to the Roman conquest of what we today regard as Europe. The conquest had a historic tragic effect on the inhabitants of Europe. It is a tragedy the Romans had themselves suffered when they were converted to Christianity. Initially, the Romans resisted the worship and the practices of Christianity and prosecuted Christians. This remarkably changed in the course of time. Constantine, the Roman Emperor, was converted to Christianity. He liberalized religious space and unwisely made room for Christianity. The Edict of Milan (313 AD) brought an end to the oppression and persecution of Christians. Toleration of Christian worship and practices was officially allowed in the Empire. In the reign of Emperor Theodosius, Christianity was unwisely made the legal religion of the Empire. Once Christianity became the legal religion of the Empire, gradually, as if it were revenge against their erstwhile persecutors, Christians became intolerant of the followers of other religions. The followers of other religions were persecuted. For the Christian believers, there was only one true God, and that God was their God. There was only one true religion, and that religion was their religion—Christianity. True law became Christian Divine law, the Christian Church law. The Christian God was taken to be the Supreme Law Maker, the Supreme Judge, and the Supreme Executor of His Law. In the light of this understanding of law, the autonomy of the indigenous Roman law has no place. It was either incorporated in the Christian ideas of law or it was eradicated. Roman law was interpreted in a way that supported Christian irrational and superstitious beliefs and practices. Reason itself, in its Hellenic sense, was baptized and lost its pagan nature, and was used to provide legitimacy and validity to Christian beliefs and practices. The study of law was ultimately transformed into a Christian theological study since, strictly speaking, law was the law of the Christian God. There developed a legal mind that was essentially a Christian mind. This is essentially the message that comes across in St. Augustine's jurisprudence and in St. Thomas Aquinas' jurisprudence. Neither jurisprudence can be intelligible if the Christian God is left out. For these students of law, legal thinking led inevitably to thinking about God; it is theological thinking.

The conversion of the Romans into Christians led to the eradication and disappearance of the Roman chthonic gods and goddesses and to the religions associated with them. Hellenic gods and goddesses and the attendant religious worship and practices met the same fate since, like their Roman counterparts, they were chthonic. Many Roman and Hellenic religious shrines were destroyed and the sites where they were transformed into sites for the construction of Christian churches. These sites lost their earthly grounding, and the loss resulted in the uprooting of man from the earth and made man homeless on earth. The earth itself received a new status, a status in which it was perceived to be inferior to Heaven. What died when the Roman Gods and Goddesses and their attendant religions died was the death of Roman self. The way that the Romans understood themselves perished. This is the same fate that happened to the Greek Gods, goddesses, and their attendant religions. The Greek sense of who they were as Greeks perished as a result of the triumph of Christianity.

Under the Roman Christendom native European Gods and their attendant religions met the same fate as the Roman and the Greek Gods and Goddesses and their attendant religions. They were systematically destroyed and replaced by Christianity. But what happened to the Romans at the hands of Christians was nothing compared to what happened to the inhabitants of what we today call Europe. The tragedy here was deeper and more pronounced. At least, the Romans and the Greeks were able to retain some aspects of their indigenous chthonic roots. The inhabitants of Europe were hit by a religious tsunami, and instead of reclaiming what they had lost, they celebrated and continue to celebrate the loss. An ontological void in the self-consciousness of the European man was created by Christianity. It was a void that could only be filled by Christianity. The fanaticism of these new Christian converts is unmatched by what happened to the Romans when they were Christianized. In mass, the inhabitants of Europe joined that Christianity Salvation Army to conquer the world for Christ. Amnesia set in. Their Gods and the religions associated with them disappeared from history. They became a people without a past. They later tried to fill this void by claiming the Gods, the Goddesses, and the religions of the Romans and the Greeks as their own—hence, the fascination of Europeans with the Roman and Greek Classics. These classics fill a void created by the triumph of Christianity. The fascination however was skin-deep, for a total embrace would contradict Christian faith. Despite the triumphant spirit of the European mind, beneath it there lies unfathomable existential angst. It is precisely this angst that Europeans have attempted to create in the African.

In Christianized Europe, as had been the case with the Christianized Roman world, law became the instrument of dislocating the Romans from earthly life, of turning them to the "Other world". The conversion initiated a gradual erasure of earthly life and believers were gradually oriented towards the "Other world". Europeans lost their earthly leaning and turned heavenwards. Law was instrumental to this revolution—a revolution that is just as important as the Copernican Revolution. When Christianized European turned to Africa and sought the conversion of Africans into the Christian faith, Africans were dislodged from the earth and like Europeans and the Romans earlier were turned heavenwards, to the "Other world". Christian missionaries told Africans that they had to be born again—born again and take up citizenship in the "Other world". The birth could not take place as long as they held on to their heathen Gods and Goddesses, as long as they held on to the religions associated with them, as long as they held onto their culture, and as long as they held on to their indigenous sense of who they are. Africans are yet to fully acknowledge the cost of being Christian. What the Christian missionaries were asking of Africans, they themselves did not undergo when they became Christians. They had not become so by having their cultural grounding destroyed by foreign missionaries, by foreign cultural imperialists. They had not been attacked as heathens and savages by another people who had invaded their country to civilize them. They were not subjected to a racist imperialism like the one to which Africans were subjected by European imperialism.

It is Christianity that has taught us the virtue of the "Other World", and that has discouraged us from laying our treasures in "this world"—a world it deems worthless. Here, in "this world" mind is out of place. It is homeless. Its true home is in the "Other World." In "this world" it is deprived of its true nature. Its own work, the work of thinking, attains its truthfulness only if it disengages itself from "this world" and focuses attention on the "other World". It is this thinking that lies at the foundation of Modern European humanity. It is what renders Rene Descartes intelligible. One of his remarkable accomplishments is disengaging the mind from what it cannot be disengaged from: the human body. In his essays titled Meditations on the First Philosophy, he attempted to demonstrate not only that mind exists separately from the body but also to demonstrate that mind does not need the body to do what it essentially does: to think. He sought to establish the credibility of the incredible. It should not take much gumption to recognize how this way of thinking could set the stage for the purported existence of the legal mind that Powell speaks about. Descartes is not normally understood as a major contributor to modern European jurisprudence, but as one of the founding fathers of modern European thought he set the stage on which the drama of a detached legal mind could play out. He is to be accorded a place among the founders of modern European legal consciousness. Moreover, since his egology is unintelligible without Christian theology, legal consciousness would equally be unintelligible outside the context of this theology.

Let us briefly summarize what has been said previously. The legal mind Powell has in mind is not an invention of lawyers or of European legal scholars. It is an invention of European Christian theologians. It is an invention of the imagination of the Western European mind—a mind that is deeply rooted in Christian imagination. Since Descartes, through our modernity the ideas of a mind detached from what it cannot be detached from has been thoroughly institutionalized in the West, and neither the materialism of classical science or secularization has been able to dislodge this mind from a state of detachment. It has become a central part of modern Western religious secularism. It is also one of the major building blocks of Western European identity, and as such, it is a historic error to mistake this identity for the universal human identity or to mistake the European concept of legal identity for a universal human identity, if indeed there is such an identity. Unfortunately, it is the mistake that has ruled most of the modern world, and that continues to rule the world today. The world continues to suffer from the hubris of European humanism and from the legalism that is secreted by this humanism.

The brief account of the rise of the historical and the nature of the ideas of legal mind that Powell speaks about can easily and readily be taken as a digression or as irrelevant to what it is to think like an African lawyer. Taking this position, however, misses a major point. What is undeniable is that millions of Africans have been converted into Christianity by European Christian missionaries and, in the course of this conversion, some Africans have been recruited to this missionary undertaking. Africans have also been recipients of the aid provided by the Western missionaries of law, and equally undeniable is the fact that there are some Africans who have been recruited to join this aspect of Western missionary activity. Missionarism does not allow for a meaningful dialogue. The missionary is in possession of truth and his or her victim is not. He or she requires the victim to accept what is said by faith. But what is in the heart and the mind of the missionary is not just a religious sentiment. It is an understanding of what it is to be a human being. When the Romans were converted into Christianity, they were converted to a particular understanding of what it is to be a human being, and similarly when the inhabitants of Europe were converted into Christianity they were thereby converted to a particular understanding of what it is to be a human being—to a Christian anthropology. What Africans were converted into is the Christian understanding of what it is to be a human being. The detached legal mind that has been accepted by Europeans has been used to impregnate the African mind so that it can give birth to a similar birth. In the light of slavery and colonialism, neo-colonialism and apartheid this impregnation is an act of violence, an act of rape. This is precisely what happened to the Romans and it is what happened to the inhabitants of Europe. A concerted effort was made to make the rape "lawful". One is not paranoid in being suspicious of what passes under the notions of law, legal mind, and thinking like a lawyer in European discourse.

It should be noted that a fuller understanding of what is at stake in thinking like an African lawyer is not possible unless one understands what it is to think like a European lawyer and, conversely, one cannot have a fuller understanding of what it is to think like a European lawyer without an understanding of what it is to think like an African lawyer today. To the extent that Western European legal philosophy is silent on African legal philosophy, it is in part silent about itself and, conversely, an African legal philosophy that is silent about European philosophy is, in part, silent about itself. The same holds of the relation between African legal philosophy and Islamic philosophy. Such a relationship does not hold between African legal philosophy and Chinese or Indian legal philosophy. A deeper adverse relationship exists between Africans and Europeans. What Europeans have done to Africans reflects their understanding of law, and most of what passes as African philosophy of law is, in part, a reflection of the reaction to what has happened to Africans under the European regime of law.

The content of the perennial song sung in the West about spreading democracy in Africa and in the rest of what used to be referred to as the Third World is engulfed in a thick mist. Equally and similarly engulfed is the notion of the rule of law that is assumed to be the engine that drives democracy. The rule of law, it appears, knows no national, cultural, or historical barriers. Rule of law is rule of law everywhere. It has become an imperial rule par excellence unmatched by any other empire in the past, but this is an empire that is veiled, an empire whose inside is concealed. Africans have become parties to this concealment as they blindly call for the reign of the rule of law in Africa. Nobody dares speak against the rule of law out of fear that one may be branded as an outlaw, as someone courting lawlessness. To think we have to think the same, and an African who dares to make a case for thinking like an African lawyer is likely to be portrayed as a fool or as insane. After all, such an African is likely to be depicted as an obstacle to the current globalization of thinking like a lawyer.

Let us keep in view the fact that, in the West, the rule of law is usually distinguished from the rule of man—the rule that is an obstacle to the rule of law. Accordingly, having a legal mind—that is thinking like a lawyer—is projected as if it is immunized from this obstacle. From Powell's view, which to me is an unassailable characterization of the legal mind as widely understood in the West, it appears that this is a delusion or an outright falsehood. It is a historic delusion and falsehood that has had and that continues to have grave consequences. It appears that to make life bearable one has to lie about it. There appears to be pre-judgment that life as it is is unbearable, and rule of law can transform life from being what it is to what it ought to be. It is such a faith that animates the thinking of Thomas Hobbes whose judgment about life in a state of nature paints life in such a way that it is depicted as a life of misery. In his view, the rule of law is intended to overcome this misery, and it is a view of the rule of law that is central to Western European thinking. It is the view that Western legal missionaries have been attempting to instill in the African.

Contrary to the prevailing orthodoxy, in the name of law, what Africans have received from the West is not law as law severed from what is attached to it. It is law inextricably bound to what it is attached to, namely, Western culture and Western society, ultimately to Western anthropology. This means that thinking like a lawyer in the Western sense is thinking like a Western lawyer. But it is presented as if it is extricated from this Western cultural anthropology and from this Western sociology. It is presented as if it stands on its own. Overtly, what it appears to be is the opposite of what it truly is. Accordingly, when an African is trained to think like a lawyer in Western legal education, he or she is trained to ignore or forget about his or her own culture. Under the guise of culture-free legal education, he or she is trained to embrace Western culture. Legal training becomes an instrument of Western cultural imperialism. The foundation for this imperialism was laid down during the colonial period. For the most part, during the post-colonial period, thinking like a lawyer rests on this foundation. If the rule of law in the West is intended to overcome the misery in which human beings find themselves in the state of nature, what Africans experience under the European rule of law is mostly the misery that Hobbes speaks about. This rule bred misery in African life.

Apparently, legal education takes place in an apparent cultural vacuum. When an African is trained to think like a lawyer he or she is trained to have a legal mind that ostensibly has nothing to do with any cultural underpinning. One is at a loss as to what is to be made of the expression thinking like an African lawyer since thinking like a lawyer is presented as the same everywhere and anywhere. The qualification of thinking like a lawyer by the word "African" can only point to a geographical location or a racial identity. Apparently, there is nothing more substantive about the word "African" in this context.

An African who seeks to free himself or herself from the delusion or the falsehood that is associated with thinking like a lawyer in a cultural vacuum encounters a formidable obstacle. He or she is likely to be isolated from the fashionable legal thinking that is projected as culture free. He or she is likely to be tagged as a demagogue and viewed as engaging in an illegitimate legal thinking. He may be viewed as ridiculous or as suffering from an inferiority complex that he or she covers up as a genuine indigenous African legal thinking. Hountondji has alerted us to the possibility that,

> The quest for originality is always bound up with a desire to show off. It has meaning only in relation to the other from whom one wishes to distinguish oneself at all costs. This is an ambiguous relationship, inasmuch as the assertion of ones's difference goes hand in hand with a passionate urge to have it recognized by the other. As this recognition is usually long in coming, the desire of the subject, caught in his own trap, grows increasingly hollow until it is completely alienated in a restless craving for the slightest gesture, the most cursory glance from the Other.[42]

It is indeed the case that some of those who undertake the quest for originality are driven by the desire to show off, and are to be found in every society. However, it does not follow that everyone who undertakes this task desires to show off. Curiosity, the simple desire to know or to understand, can be a legitimate human motive. Another possible motive is a legitimate desire to defend oneself from the charge that one is solely parasitic to others. One cannot always be sure of the motive that drives others and, perhaps, one can never be sure of one's motives. Besides, there are times when motives are so intermingled that it is difficult to disentangle them. It may be worth noting that Europeans have yet to face the issue of originality. They shield themselves from facing this issue by grafting themselves to Roman history, to Hebrew history, and to the Hellenic history, that is by turning away from Europe, from themselves.

The Other that Hountondji has in mind in the above passage is the European, the Western European man. He is speaking from the standpoint of the African, the African who is burdened with the task of showing off his own originality to the Western European man. Let us place what Hountondji is saying in the context of thinking like an African lawyer. In thinking like an African lawyer, how is the African to think in a way that avoids the trap that Hountondji calls to our attention? One possible venue is to abandon the quest for originality all together and engage in a non-original quest for thinking like an African lawyer. If the African chooses this venue, it may turn out that thinking like an African lawyer is no different from thinking like a non-African lawyer. Consequently, this may call for the rejection of the view that thinking like an African lawyer is different from thinking like a non-African lawyer. In other words, the difference must be rejected.

Another venue is to embark on the quest for originality in a manner that disregards the Other. Such a quest would disregard the recognition of the Other. In thinking like an African lawyer, the African would not be seeking recognition or approval of the other. Among the problems that the African would face were he or she to embrace this venue is that the Other is not just going to disappear. It is no longer possible for the African to isolate himself or herself from the Other. The attempt by the African to think like an African lawyer cannot be isolated from the Other's thinking like a lawyer, and conversely, in the world we live in today, the Other's thinking like a lawyer cannot be isolated from thinking like an African lawyer. This is not solely because of the ongoing globalization. Even if, in the quest for originality, the African were to disregard the Other, he would have to extract and dispel the Other's thinking from his own or her own thinking. This would be necessitated by the slave and the colonial experience that the Other has imposed on the African's thinking. That is, African thinking would have to be de-colonized if there is to be an original thinking like an African lawyer.

Whatever venue the African embraces, in thinking like an African lawyer, the African cannot avoid de-colonizing his or her own thinking. In doing so, he or she cannot seek recognition or legitimation from the colonizing Other or engage in a show off thinking. It is an essential and unavoidable task for the African to find a way of thinking that does not amount to self-alienation. Above all, it means that genuine African thinking has to be historically contextual. As Nkrumah has noted,

> Colonialism and its attitudes die hard, like the attitude of slavery, whose hangover still dominates behavior in certain parts of the Western hemisphere.[43]

There is a colonialist/neo-colonial hangover that is to be overcome if one is to think like an African lawyer. There are those who have this hangover but it is covered by a false sobriety. The distinction is not easy to make especially after a long process of being hungover, when hangover has been normalized. False self-consciousness is a feature of people whose self has suffered oppression for a long time.

Under the topic "thinking like an African lawyer", it is reasonable to expect that what is said will shed light on what it is to think like an African lawyer. A reasonable expectation calls for the recognition that the speaker does not have a monopoly in saying what ought to be said about thinking like an African lawyer. Inevitably, thinking like an African lawyer involves thinking, and in so far as all of us are thinking beings, we are implicated in thinking about what it is to think like an African lawyer. That is, none of us is a total stranger in or to this thinking. One does not have to be an African lawyer, an African, or a lawyer to think like an African lawyer. To this extent, every member of the audience has a vital role to play in bringing forth the truth of what it is to think like an African lawyer. If one is not clear as to what one's role is, hopefully, what is said will be helpful in reflecting on what this role is. It is also a part of reasonable expectation to bear in mind that thinking is socially and historically situated. Accordingly, this is true of thinking like an African lawyer. Nkrumah's quote is intended to call attention to the socio-historical situatedness of this thinking. Thinking like an African lawyer is socially and historically constituted and it is as such that it has to be understood. It does not make sense outside the context of African society or outside the history of African people.

During Nkrumah's presidency in Ghana, conventional wisdom in the West was that Nkrumah was a megalomaniac. In the name of erasing the vestiges of colonialism in Ghana, and in the process of liberating the rest of Africa from Western imperialism, it was alleged that he built himself up as a dictator and brought unbearable suffering to Ghanians. Nkrumah was not a lawyer, a magistrate, a judge, or a law professor. It is indeed true that he studied philosophy, but there is no evidence that he took interest in legal philosophy. Why then is one invoking his name in the attempt to shed light on what it is to think like an African lawyer? Isn't this a dangerous diversion? In response to these questions, let me say that what follows is not an attempt to defend the charge against him. My task is to take up the challenge raised by this charge: the challenge of coming up with thinking that illuminates what in African legal thinking could contribute to a social existence in Africa in which there is minimal oppression and exploitation of Africans. I am assuming that those who level the charge will not only have an interest in what I am trying to accomplish, but will also help out in this undertaking. Whether Nkrumah is guilty as charged, the charge makes it clear that Africans are not immunized from oppressing and exploiting fellow Africans. Where anti-colonialism is used to cover up this state of affairs, the cover should be identified and removed so that African collaborators and perpetrators of oppression and exploitation can be exposed. What I present as thinking like an African lawyer incorporates this role. That is, I see the pursuit of social justice in Africa as an integral aspect of thinking like an African lawyer. Moreover, our understanding of thinking like an African lawyer may be impoverished if we set it apart from other features of thinking like an African. Nkrumah may not have been directly involved in the legal profession, but there is no legal profession that exists in a socio-political vacuum. As the President of Ghana, and as a powerful Pan-African political leader, he contributed to the institutionalization of the framework of thinking like an African lawyer. He created an environment where thinking like an African could contribute to the erasing of colonial and neo-colonial vestiges in Africa. It must be kept in view that legal thinking was not immunized from colonialism and it is not immunized from neo-colonialism.

Bringing in the specter of colonialism is not intended to turn back the clock in Africa, or to flog a dead horse. I am calling attention to the historicity of thinking like an African lawyer. It is worth repeating that an African does not and cannot think like a lawyer in a historical vacuum. In the post-colonial period, one must not forget the colonial hangover. Moreover, one cannot fully understand the situation of thinking like an African lawyer today without an understanding of thinking like a lawyer in Africa when Africa was under European colonial domination. European colonial domination in Africa had a European jurisprudential blessing, and even what is jurisprudentially going on in Europe today continues to have an impact on thinking like an African lawyer in Africa today.

Colonialism implanted self-harming and self-destroying attitudes in African thinking in general. This implantation of self-violation was on the one hand explicitly a violent phenomenon; and on the other hand, it was disguised as harmless and constructive. One of the tasks of thinking like an African lawyer is to bring into relief this disguise, that is, to bring into the open the role that colonialist thinking like a lawyer harmed Africans, how it suppressed thinking like an African lawyer.

The European colonized the African under the guise of civilizing him. He was bringing light where darkness prevailed. One of the theaters of this drama was in education. Colonial thinking was at the core of colonial education and it had the blessing of European jurisprudence. It touched on every aspect of African thinking. Education was and remains a double-edged sword.[44] On one hand, it was and it is an ally on the human side in the course of eliminating whatever lies on the path to human self-knowledge and to human well-being. It is the kind of education that nurtures being free and that opens up paths for spiritual and material venues that lead to overall human good. On the other hand, it created, creates, and secures obstacles to these venues. During the colonial period, the education that was provided to Africans largely promoted the creation of such obstacles. Ways of thinking that fostered these obstacles were integral to colonial education. An education that would have contributed to self-knowledge and to the well-being of Africans would have been incompatible with the project of colonization. As it has been correctly noted,

> The object of education under colonialism was not as altruistic as it is often made to be. The idea of a civilizing mission, through which Africans were Christianized and taught to read and write, was first and foremost an attempt to produce Africans who would be serviceable for the project of colonialism; Africans who will acquiesce to the strategy and tactics of the colonial project.[45]

It is precisely this situation that Africans inherited on the day formal colonialism came to an end. The task facing African education leaders in the anti-colonial struggle was to annul this inheritance by instituting alternative ways of thinking. This implied a critical revisiting and reconstruction of all the areas of African thinking. It is in this context that thinking like an African lawyer today is to be understood. Essential to this thinking is the process of de-colonization. To take note of this role seriously, thinking like an African lawyer must itself be de-colonized.

In post-colonial Africa, the training of Africans to think like a lawyer testifies to a remarkable absence of liberating (de-colonizing) legal pedagogy. In part, such pedagogy calls for a re-visit of colonizing thinking. Such thinking needs to be understood. The absence of liberating pedagogy was institutionalized during the period in which Africans were under European colonialism. This was not a simple omission. Pedagogy could not contradict colonialism. It is what fueled colonialism. During this period, European colonizers held the view that Africans suffered from a biological defect that incapacitated them from distinguishing fact from fiction, a defect that rendered them incapable of grasping true causation in the realm of phenomena, and consequently, a defect that rendered them incapable of making valid inferences. In the eyes of Europeans, the African world was dominated by magical and superstitious beliefs. Europeans believed that they were products of superior genes, and did not suffer from the incapacities that were to be found in Africans. They believed that they were bearers of a scientific and rational culture, and that Africans were bearers of unscientific and irrational culture. It appeared not to have dawned on them that what they believed about themselves, as was the case with what they believed about Africans, provided evidence to demonstrate their own superstition and their own irrationalism. Since, in their eyes, Africans did not possess a fully developed scientific and rational thinking, it appears to follow that Africans were incapable of grasping and putting into practice the thinking that is required in legal thinking. What was expected of Africans is that they would obey but not question the colonial legal order. They could not participate in making law or in interpreting law. Some of them could be used in the low level enforcement of law especially the enforcement that required brutal force and blind following of colonial orders. A case in point is the way that the colonial police, colonial prison guards, colonial chiefs, and headmen treated Africans. The whip, the baton, the gun, and the fear of going to jail or to prison were essential instruments in the colonial governing of Africans. It could accurately be said that legal power came through the barrel of a gun. An effort was made to integrate customary local African legislation and adjudication into the colonial legal order. This effort was not undertaken out of respect for African customary law but to facilitate the institutionalization and promotion of the colonial social order. The staff for the administration of the local customary law was selected on the basis of loyalty to the colonial legal order.

Post-colonial legal educators inherited a colonial legal training that was thoroughly integrated into a general colonial education designed to legitimize, to preserve, and to promote the colonizer's world-view. Since, in the eyes of Africans, colonialism was a regime of injustice, legal education under it was in the service of injustice. The justice that prevailed was indistinguishable from the injustice of colonialism. Post-colonial legal education did not fully address the injustice of colonialism. The establishment of formal legal education for Africans was not a genuine break with colonialist-oriented legal education. Neo-colonial legal education was established under the guise of independent African legal education. Neo-colonial law was instituted to serve the neo-colonial African social order. It was interpreted in a way that reinforced and promoted the neo-colonial African social order.

It is historically evident that in the early days of the independence of African states there were very few African lawyers, and practically no African law schools to train African lawyers. Africans were deemed to be too stupid to participate intelligently in lawyering, and clearly, colonial leadership would not condone putting Africans in a position where colonial injustices would be exposed, and where the possibility that the culprits would risk being arrested, tried and punished. It is undeniable that the colonialists were guilty of crimes against humanity.[46] The gravity of this criminality is yet to be fully studied. The exclusion and legal disenfranchisement of Africans was often portrayed as evidence to show that Africans were not ready for self-government. Under these circumstances, critical legal education for Africans was a liability in the colonial rulers except when they were called upon to help with the administration of colonial legal and social order.

In the post-colonial phase of African history, legal education was provided to Africans to serve neo-colonialism. Efforts to Africanize legal thinking were similar to the efforts at Africanizing European Christian missionary activity in Africa. Church leadership and Christian evangelism would be taken over by Africans without change in substance. It was simply a matter of replacing "white" bodies with "black" bodies. The crusade against African culture (the culture that was manifested in indigenous African religions) would continue under the directorship of Africans. In matters pertaining to law, de-

Africanization of African culture would continue under the direction of neo-colonial African agents of law. "Black" bodies would replace "White" bodies on the bench, and would wear the same black robes that were previously exclusively worn by "White" bodies. The colonial regime of law would substantively remain unchanged. On the surface, it appeared to be a new regime whose aim was to secure and promote African well-being, but underneath, it was a continuation of the old colonial regime under the guise of a new regime. It should not come as a surprise the court architecture has remained the same (one is reminded of walking into a church when one walks into African courtrooms); judicial regalia has remained the same (with European medieval judicial regalia still visible in African courtrooms); and underneath it all, lies European cultural anthropological imperialism. The regime of the European sense of being human continues to be the bedrock of judicial thinking in Africa and the bedrock of thinking like a lawyer. Walking into a decolonized African courtroom one should have a sense that one is truly walking into an African courtroom and not a European courtroom. The attire of the judges and other officers of a decolonized courtroom should convey a sense of a decolonized African judicial culture. The architectural layout of courtrooms has remained largely European. Decolonization of the courtroom architecture is yet to fully enter into the consciousness of African courtroom architects. Thinking like an African lawyer cannot be isolated from the ecological context in which it takes place.

An African and, indeed, anyone who embarks on thinking like an African lawyer, or who seeks to understand what it is to think like an African lawyer, must bear in mind the impact that colonialism and neo-colonialism have had on African thinking not only in regard to thinking like a lawyer, but also to thinking like an African in general. To be authentic, thinking like an African lawyer must be an instantiation of thinking like an African. As an instantiation of thinking like an African, it bears the entire weight of the consciousness of being African. Without consciousness of being African there cannot be consciousness of thinking like an African lawyer. To be truly what it is, thinking like an African lawyer manifests and must manifest what it is to be African. If a human being is a thinking being, every aspect of thinking that a human being engages in exhibits what it is to be human. It is for this reason that thinking like an African lawyer is legitimately expected to exhibit not only what it means to think like an African, but also what it is to think like a human being. If legal thinking is thinking that sets human beings apart from other beings, then Africans could appropriately engage in this thinking to the extent that their thinking exhibited what it is to be human.

Africa was portrayed by European colonizers as a lawless continent. Accordingly, her inhabitants not only lived lawlessly, but also had no sense of what law is. According to the colonizers, legal thinking had not evolved in Africans, and it was the task of colonial agents to instill and nurture the sense of legality, primarily to make Africans good colonial subjects. Since it required a civilized mind to understand legality, and Africans were deemed to be uncivilized, it would require violence to instill and nurture legality in them. As Frantz Fanon has amply demonstrated, colonialism was and is a form of violence.[47] Colonialism violated the humanity of the African. As a thinking being, his or her thinking was violated. Thinking like an African lawyer had no immunity to this violation. It was detrimentally affected by colonialism.

Who is and what is an African lawyer? Can it be determined what it is to think like an African lawyer, if it is not first determined who or what an African lawyer is? Clearly, there are those among us who consider this latter question frivolous if not nonsensical. Can an African mistake herself or himself for a Chinese or for a European, or can anyone else for that matter mistake her or him as such? With rare exceptions, we are likely to question the sanity of anyone who makes such an obvious mistake. The conventional wisdom is that Africans are natives of Africa, just as Chinese are natives of China, and just as Europeans are natives of Europe. Now, the word native in this context suggests the place of one's birth. It appears evident that Africans who are born out of Africa continue to be viewed as Africans, just as Chinese who are born outside China continue to be viewed as Chinese, and just as Europeans who are born out of Europe continue to be viewed as Europeans. In either of these cases, it seems that it does not matter where one is born, as long as one's ancestors are born in a country that bears one's identity. But if the criterion of one's identity is the birthplace of one's ancestors, the issue of one's identity still remains problematic.

If one supposes that all human beings originally came from Africa, as it is claimed sometimes, does this mean that all human beings are Africans? And since today, it can readily be conceded that not everyone is African, when did some human beings cease to be African so that they can take on new identities? If the change occurred due to migration of Africans, clearly, a case can be made for the migration of human identity; that is, for migration as an identity-generating process. Those who are African today may not be Africans tomorrow. Geographical determination of who or what an African is has relative fixity. As who or what an African is changes, so does what it means to think like an African lawyer. Thinking like an African lawyer today will not be identical with thinking like an African lawyer tomorrow because the African of today may not be the African of tomorrow. The African of today may cease being African tomorrow. If it is location that establishes one's identity, change of location may bring about the change of identity. Moreover, since change is temporal, one's identity is bound to time. More generally, history is to be taken into account in the construction and knowledge of identity. Thus, thinking like an African lawyer will depend on the historical period in which this thinking is taking place. It may also depend on the historical period in which the investigator of this thinking is situated.

Making who or what is African depend on geography, and consequently, making what is thinking like an African lawyer depend on geography, may raise another complication. The dependency may lead to uncritical reliance on geography in the determination of who and what an African is, and consequently, in the determination of what it is to think like an African lawyer. It is precisely this uncritical reliance on geography that leads Hountondji, an African philosopher from Benin, to offer an unsatisfactory conception of African philosophy. It is his view that "The Africanness of our philosophy will not reside in its themes but will depend above all on the geographical origin of those who produce it and their intellectual coming together."[48] If geography is taken as the sole criterion of what African philosophy is, then the same criterion applies to what an African philosopher is. The Africanness of a philosopher will depend on the geographical origin of the philosopher. But to fully understand what is claimed here one must understand the geographicity of origin. One must understand the geographicity of geography.

To Hountondji, Africa appears to be nothing more than a physical territory among other physical territories, and when the word Africa is used to qualify philosophy, it expresses nothing more than a location of philosophy in such a territory. Similarly, one could imagine Hountondji claiming that the Africanness of an African lawyer, as is the case with the Africanness of African jurisprudence, will depend on geographical origin. By viewing Africa as being nothing more than a geographical territory, Hountondji fails to grasp the multiple senses of the word Africa, just as he fails to grasp the multiple senses of the word geography.

Africa is not merely a landmass, bounded by the Atlantic Ocean, the Indian Ocean, the Red Sea, and the Mediterranean Sea, or a landmass that is largely taken to be the indigenous home of the African people. It is more than the home base of the so-called dark-skinned people. It is more than the location of some of the largest game reserves in the world, and it is more than the location of the great Sahara and the Kalahari Deserts.

Africa is significant. It is a sign whose meaning varies depending on who is doing the deciphering. At one time, for the European, it was a Dark Continent, a continent where savagery, barbarism, and heathenism flourished. As such, it was a fertile ground for planting Christian seeds, and also, for planting the seeds of European civilization. At that time, such an Africa was unknown to Africans, and the Africans that Europeans purported to see in it were equally unknown to Africans. Clearly, the Ancient Greeks who went to study in Africa did not go to study in such an Africa, or to study with the inhabitants of such an Africa. In short, the Africa that Europeans have had in mind for centuries was a creature of their own imagination, and so are the Africans they had in mind. The Africa that was a lawless jungle was one of historic fictitious inventions of the European mind. There is an Africa for Africans—an Africa that is a construction of Africans, and there are Africans for Africans—Africans who are constructions of Africans. Thus, to present Africa as if it is nothing more than a physical territory is to misconstrue it, or at least, to opt for the erroneous view that Africa has only one meaning. Equally, this holds true when an African is depicted as being nothing more than an inhabitant of an Africa so presented. A human being does not inhabit the same way that a thing is in place. Strictly speaking a thing does not inhabit a place. Human habitation is a significant habitation. It is so culturally. But, from the human standpoint, things themselves are culturally situated and, in this sense, they, too, may share human habitation not in their own right but on the account of other human beings. This is in part evidenced by the fact that they are owned by other human beings. Things are significant. Law of property recognizes this significance.

The word African, as is the case with the word Africa, is a multiple signifier. It has multiple senses. The determination of what it means to think like an African lawyer will largely depend on the type of African one has in mind. In our case, our interest lies in the African of the African, even if it must be conceded that the African of the African also has multiple senses, thereby complicating our interest. Multiplicity of sense for any given phenomenon is not a discovery of European post-modernists. It is an elemental aspect of the way that human beings experience themselves, and of the way they experience phenomena. Even those who argue that there is only one way to experience a phenomenon, must deny that there are other ways, and such denial is recognition of what is denied.

The meaning that Hountondji associates with geography is one among many meanings of geography. He appears to present the meaning of geography that has been embraced by modern science, and excludes the multiple meanings that this word has had in the course of history. He excludes the diversity of meanings it has, and that it has had in different cultures in different historical periods. It is in the context of this diversity of meanings that one can hope to adequately present the meaning or the meanings that geography has to Africans. It cannot be assumed that the concept of geography that has been generated in modern science is the only proper concept. Here, one must guard oneself from a proclivity of scientistic thinking that seeks to establish a monopoly of knowledge and understanding. Failure to guard ourselves may render us vulnerable to a conceptual imperialism that robs us of the perception of conceptual diversity that we need in order to adequately understand geography. To the extent that the earth is what geography concerns itself with, the earth could have a spiritual or religious meaning; it could have a poetic meaning, or it could have a scientific meaning. Any one of these meanings could be culture-specific. Given the heterogeneity of human cultures, it is not inconceivable that the earth could have multiple meanings. To construe the earth as having one and only one meaning is to adopt a dogmatic opinion that is likely to lead to cultural imperialism. If it is conceded that the earth may have more than one meaning, perhaps, it may be the case that there is nothing absurd to claim that the earth is a tabula rasa, upon which meaning may be inscribed. Thus, even if it were to be conceded that an African is to be defined geographically, one would know little if anything at all about the content of this definition unless one pays attention to what is inscribed on it. In other words, even if the African is to be defined geographically, she or he is what she or he makes out of geography.

The difficulty in attempting to define who or what is an African using a geographical criterion may tempt one to abandon such a criterion. This temptation should be resisted. It would not make sense to abandon it all together. It is senseless to deny that the African is geographically situated, just as it would be senseless to deny that any other human being is geographically situated. The African is a *mwananchi* (a child of the earth), and so is every other human being. All human beings are earth-bound and earth-born despite the attempt by some to divorce themselves from their earthly nativity, despite the seduction of otherworldliness. What is to be recognized or understood is that there is no pure or virgin geography—a geography that is not charged with socio-cultural significance. There is no immaculate conception of geography. All geography is a lived-geography. At the very outset, it is inscribed with human meanings. Inevitably, geographers impregnate the earth with meaning. Thus, if thinking like an African lawyer is given a geographical contour, such a contour already has a socio-cultural signification. To think of an African lawyer as geographically situated is to think of him or her in his or her socio-cultural situation. That is, to conceive and attend to what it means to think like an African lawyer, one must do so in an African socio-cultural context, bearing in mind that what is African about the socio-cultural context is a matter of socio-cultural construction. In the attempt to present law as a science, modern Western legal scholars obscure socio-cultural construction of legal thinking and nowhere is this state of affairs more pronounced than it is in their conception of the rule of law. They have led themselves to believe that their own legal thinking is freed from the demands of their own social cultural environment. They appear to be insensitive to the imperial aspect of the legal thinking they promoted globally. Being African, they appear to believe is inessential to what it is to think like a lawyer.

Another tempting opinion in the course of determining who or what an African is comes by the way of biology. The conventional wisdom is that what sets the African apart from other human beings, or conversely, what sets other human beings apart from the African is biological constitution. Such biological determination gives an African a specific bio-physical appearance. In the contemporary world, the governing term here appears to be blackness, a term that has been constructed by and that has gained prominence in the Euro-Western global conceptual regime. In this line of thinking, thinking like an African lawyer is synonymous with thinking like a black lawyer. African jurisprudence, it would appear, is synonymous with Black jurisprudence. An African lawyer is synonymous with a Black lawyer. Despite its general acceptance, this synonymity conceals more than it reveals, and the concealment is not fully grasped if it is not seen in the context of cultural imperialism, and more specifically, in the context of a racist industry of concepts. How thinking like an African lawyer is to be found in the African genetic constitution remains a mystery, but a mystery that is a concoction of a racist biology.

It is not the case that everyone who is supposedly black is African. There are many Arabs who are so-called black. There are millions of Asians who are supposedly "black" but they are not taken to be Africans. Millions of them are Indians of India. To say that some of them are Indians of India should remind us of a problem of identity that has been imposed on Africans by Europeans. The Caribbean Islands were transformed into West Indies and the Africans who were settled there by Europeans were transformed from being Africans into being West Indians. The natives of America were transformed from their indigenous identities into American Indians. Indianization of the Americas and the contiguous islands created a new identity for the Africans who were brought into this part of the world. These transformations are a part of the achievements of European modernity. Thus, in addition to Indians of India, apparently there are Indians of other parts of the world. To speak of the Indians of India suggests that there are other categories of Indians. But there are no Indians who are not Indian. The so-called West Indians and American Indians are concoctions of European ignorance, despite a wide acceptance of the label Indian by some Native Americans and by many non-Indians. It is a part of the European ideology of Indianism—an Indianism that must be resisted not only by Africans but also by all those who have been Indianized.

Africans who were brought to the Caribbean and who still live there were not and are not West Indians. They may be so in the eyes of Euro-westerners, but they are not Indians. They were and are Africans. Similarly, the so-called American Indians are not Indians, and one can argue they are not Americans, for Americans are creations of Europeans just as America is a creation of Europeans. Before the creation of America and the creation of Americans there were people inhabiting the land that Europeans called America. These people did not refer to themselves as Indians or as Americans. They had names for self-reference that should be used when one is referring to them, unless one wants to arrogate onto oneself the right to determine how other people are to determine themselves. Like Africans in the so-called New World, they suffered from the subversion of self-reference. The idea of extending the Indian identity to people who are not Indians is violative of people upon whom this extension is imposed.

The exportation of European racism in Asia has forced some Asians to flee from their appearance, and adopt an opinion about their appearance that is favorable to Europeans. Many Indians who are "black" deny they are "black", and would rather be classified as white to enjoy the privilege of being white. Perhaps, some of them feel that by being called black, they are likely to be associated with Africans, and since, in the European mind, Africa is associated with negative connotations, they would rather be associated with being white. Equating Africans with the so-called dark people breeds conceptual confusion and does not help us in the quest for a clear distinction between who is and who is not African. Even if one were to accept dark-complexion as a criterion of who is African, some Africans would be ruled out as Africans since not all Africans are dark-complexioned, and since not all dark-complexioned individuals are Africans. Being classified on the basis of the complexion of one's skin has had grave and still has grave implications. In a racist world, it results in the assignment of legal liabilities, capacities, immunities and privileges. Dark complexion embodies liabilities. Being of white complexion embodies capacities, immunities, and privileges that being non-white lacks.

The Euro-Western engineered flight from what one is has had a tragic effect on Africans. It is no longer a secret that there are Africans in Africa and in the African diaspora who have embraced the flight from being African, a flight they understand as a flight from being black. The project of transforming the African from being African into being Black exemplifies such a flight. Although this project is to be found throughout the African world, it is, perhaps, pursued with a greater vigor in the United States where the pressure and the means of self-denial are more sophisticated and more abundant. Here, one finds almost a near total acceptance of black identity among the Africans who were forced into slavery in the United States. After a period of resistance to being called African, being called a Negro became fashionable, and when being called a Negro became unacceptable, being called Black became acceptable. Now, the term African American is fashionable and today it is widely accepted as being synonymous with the term Black American.

The flight by Africans from being African has implication on what it is to think like an African lawyer. Africans who flee from themselves flee from thinking like African lawyers. But often they do not think of themselves as being in flight. They are comfortable in de-Africanizing law since, for them, Africanization of thinking like a lawyer robs thinking like a lawyer of its essence. This false comfort, however, makes sense when it is put into a historical context.

During slavery being African was associated with what was lawless, savage, barbaric, heathen, beastly, mindless, dirty, and sickly to the point where some Africans did not want to face and embrace their Africanness or to embrace Africa—their ancestral home. Africans were socialized into being ashamed of being African and into being ashamed of their ancestral home. In an address to fellow African Americans Malcolm X observed,

> You know yourself that we have been a people who hated our African characteristics. We hated our heads, we hated the shape of our nose, we wanted one of those long dog-like noses, you know; we hated the color of our skin, hated the blood of Africa that was in our veins. And in hating our features and our skin and our blood, why we had to end up hating ourselves. And we hated ourselves. Our color became to us a chain—we felt that it was holding us back; our color became to us like a prison which we felt was keeping us confined, not letting us go this way or that way. We felt that all of these restrictions were based solely upon our color, and the psychological reaction to that would have to be that as

> long as we felt imprisoned or chained or trapped by black skin, black features and black blood, that kin and those features and that blood holding us back automatically had to become hateful to us. And it became hateful to us.[49]

Africans succumbed to being de-Africanized, to being negrified or to being blackened. The resistance to being African was institutionalized. It is partly the success of this institutionalization that leads some of them today to use the terms African and Black as if they are synonymous. Any elementary school kid with some sense knows that African and Black are not synonyms. Yet, one will find fairly educated men and women using them as if they were synonyms and teaching the young to view them as if they are synonyms. Because the word African continues to bear the burden of a negative legacy, the expression Black American continues to be a favored term of self-reference among a good number of the descendants of Africans in the United States. It appears to be more fashionable to speak of thinking like a Black lawyer than to speak of thinking like an African lawyer. The producers of this fashion remain shielded in a mist that is secreted by racism.

The de-Africanization of the African did not take place only in the United States. It also took place throughout the African diaspora, and also in Africa. In *Black Skin White Masks*[50] , Frantz Fanon reminds us of what has happened in the Caribbean. In Latin America and in Brazil, the words Negro or negra are widely used in reference to Africans and are accepted by both Africans and non-Africans. It is not a secret that even today, there are millions of Africans who apply chemicals to their body to bleach their skins so that they can look white. There are millions of Africans who straighten their hair so that they can look white. Standards of beauty continue to be overwhelmingly white. There are millions of Africans who have changed their names to European names to avoid the African names that would tie them to the so-called black skin. These undertakings are indicators of what racism has done to the thinking of the African people. The way one looks has a bearing on the way that one thinks. To think like an African one must look African. The consciousness that Africans have of their bodies determines the way they think about their thinking. Thinking is corporeally rooted. To think African one must be African. If one asks what an African looks like or what it is to be African, and the question is raised seriously, it should be clear that it should not be taken for granted that looking like an African or being an African is self-evident. It is a matter of being educated as to how one is to look or to become African. Such an education is especially needed after a long period of subverting both the African look and the being of the African. To think about thinking like an African lawyer is problematic because being African is currently problematic.

Like African thinking in general, thinking like an African lawyer is yet to be fully immunized from European racist thinking. African law schools can be clinics for this immunization especially when legal education is transformed into a mere dissemination and digestion of trade skills that are needed to practice law. The immunization conceals the specificity of socio-cultural substance that makes up law, and also the manner in which power is deployed in society. The subversion of what it is to think like an African lawyer is deeply and widely institutionalized, and its uprooting will take a long time.

The process of de-Africanization of the African has been given legal legitimacy. Under the slave and the colonial regimes, any African who resisted this transformation was accused of undermining law and order. Anything that reminded Africans of their Africanness was banned during the slave period, for it was not possible to succeed in the enslavement of Africans if the African's self-consciousness as African was not eradicated. In Africa too, there was a systematic attempt to degrade African culture and the African body. There was the glorification of the European body at the expense of the African body. The European impressed on the African the angelic aspect of the European body and the diabolical aspect of the African body. It was impressed on Africans that the European body was divine and that the African body was diabolical. God was White, and Satan was Black. God was European and Satan was African. God (the European) was rational, and Satan (the African) was irrational. European theocratic jurisprudence relegated the African to the realm of lawlessness on account of color. The lawlessness that Satan embodied came to be embodied in the African. The African has to be saved from himself by the European. This salvation called for the African to be anti-himself or anti-herself. The architects of the slave and colonial psychology created a psychology for Africans in which Africans were forced into fleeing what or who they were. The process affected not only the way Africans thought about themselves; it also affected the way they thought about the world. The transformation of Africans into Negroes or into Blacks and the forcing of Africans to flee their Africanness is the work of European racism. Negroism and Blackism are productions of Euro-American cultural industry. When an African in Africa or in the African diaspora accepts being referred to as black, he or she accepts a designation imposed on him by a racist Euro-American culture. It forces the African to embrace fixation on skin color, a fixation that is occasioned by the Euro-American skin fixation. The former is parasitic to the latter. It is an acceptance of racism by the victim of racism.

The word "black" in such expressions as black legal scholarship, black lawyer, black law firm, black law professor, black law journal, black law school is symptomatic of racism, despite the fact that this does not appear to be the case. The fact that the word "black" is widely accepted and used illustrates the degree to which the internalization of the effects of racism has succeeded. One of the ways in which Europeans have distinguished themselves is by what may appropriately be referred to as skin fixation. Just as Freud laid the foundation of psychoanalysis on genital fixation, European racism has its foundation on skin fixation. A student of American society has pointed out that,

> When you lift the rock of American society and look under it, you almost always see race. It's at the dark heart of our conflicted nature. We are in a sense a schizophrenic people. I do not mean that we have a split identity, but we have a deeply conflicted, self-cancelling identity. We are at war with ourselves. And this explains , I think why we so often march off to war against others—as horrific as foreign wars are, they are much easier for us at home than it would be to face the internal battle of being at war within ourselves. Anything to avoid the war within ourselves that is still actively forging our identity, a war whose outcome hasn't been decided yet; and until it is, we won't really know who we are.[51]

What Banks, the author, says is not only true of the America that Europeans created. It is also true of the modern world that European created. He echoes the words of W.E.B. Du Bois, an African American, who at the dawn of the Twentieth Century observed that "The problem of the Twentieth Century is the problem of the color-line—the relation of the darker to the lighter races of men in Asia and Africa, in America and the islands of the sea."[52]

Thinking about thinking like an African lawyer, of necessity, must think about the race factor. But there is much mist that shrouds this factor. There are those who think that the problem of race vanishes when there is integration, desegregation, assimilation, when civil rights and political rights have been legally affirmed, and when all doors of opportunity have opened up to all races. This has been generally the case in the US and in other societies where racism has been a problem. Unfortunately, the problem of race is deeper and calls for a deeper solution. It is an ontological problem. The thinking like a lawyer that prevails in the United States and in the rest of the European-created world does not take the study of racism as a central factor in the study of legal thinking in this sense. The same applies to the study of thinking like a lawyer in Africa. Thinking of the rule of law as nothing more than the rule of law obscures the rule of law. It obscures the nature of what law is. This obscurity is best expressed in the orthodox belief that law is law and nothing else.

Eurocentric legal consciousness has been arrested at the level of race fixation and much of the attendant psycho-pathology cannot adequately be understood if this fixation is not taken into account. For Africans to embrace a black identity as a term of self-reference or as the cornerstone of thinking like an African lawyer is to embrace a crippling mental illness. It is, however, difficult to take note of such a state of affairs where illness has been transformed into health, and where health has been transformed into illness. It is precisely for this reason that it is not problematic for African American legal scholars to think of themselves as Black American legal scholars. Those among them who see themselves as occupying the "left" sector of the legal scholarship have embraced what has come to be known as the Critical Race Theory.[53] The advocates of the Critical Race Theory conceive of it as being synonymous with Critical Black Theory. It is unfortunate that, in the literature of Critical Race Theory, one finds a pervasive use of the word "Black" as a word of self-reference among African Americans. In the Sixties, it may have been fashionable for Africans in the Americas to highlight their blackness and shed off Negroness, but one could imagine Africans in Spanish- or Portuguese-speaking territories who would find no problem using the word "negro" since it is what the English word black translates into either of these languages. The point here is that whether the word "black" or "negro" is used, it is in reference to the skin of one's color. As long as Africans continue to refer to themselves on the basis of skin color the references will be conditioned by racism. New meanings cannot erase the stigma of the old names. New identities require new names. Africans are Africans. A de-enslaved or decolonized African returns to his or her African identity. The return enables an African to think like an African lawyer.

To characterize African American legal philosophy as Black legal philosophy is to reinforce racism in America. The attempt by African American legal scholars to carve an oppositional space for African American legal philosophy fails, in part, because they have yet to come to terms with the problematic aspect of their identity in American legal philosophy. To make skin pigmentation the bedrock of African American legal philosophy is to strengthen racism in American legal philosophy. For the most part, in America, America equals Europe, or in racist terms, American equals white. The so-called diversity of races in America is largely immaterial. This is likely to happen if the word "African" as a qualifier of American legal philosophy means nothing more than "Black". Such meaning robs the word "African" of its non-racist cultural richness and creates an obstacle in inter-cultural dialogue on legal philosophy. Thinking like an African lawyer is a Pan-African thinking. What is taken as legal thinking in the African American world has a direct bearing on what is taken to be thinking like a lawyer in Africa and wherever Africans reside. Conversely, what is taken as legal thinking in Africa or wherever Africans resided has a direct bearing on what is taken as thinking like a lawyer in the Americas and in the Islands.

Generally, in the United States legal philosophy suffers from skin fixation, and by embracing black identity, African Americans reinforce this fixation. It is a part of thinking like an African lawyer whether in America or in Africa to think in a way that undermines this reinforcement. Black legal philosophy, which is essentially melanin philosophy—a philosophy that leads to black jurisprudence, is not only a bogus philosophy or bogus jurisprudence; it is also a philosophy and jurisprudence that empowers racist legal philosophy and racist jurisprudence. It obscures African legal philosophy as well as African jurisprudence and gives life to racist legal thinking. Although there is enormous pressure to join those who insist that African legal thinking should have a skin fixation, African legal thinking should not be thinking that is skin-based. It should be a legal thinking that is founded on the African. About such thinking we will learn nothing from the skin, or from biology.

Construing Africans as black is a part of the racial categorization of human beings. The classification of human beings on the basis of such categorization is not only a difficult task; it is also racist classification. If it was undertaken in the interest of science, this undertaking was inseparable from the racist culture of those who undertook the undertaking. Although, it is possible to make a successful counter-claim to this contention, nothing much would be gained since being black is not without socio-cultural signification. The human body, whether it is an African body or a non-African body, is not given as nothing more than a sense datum. It is not a *tabula rasa*. It is significant. Deciphering its significance is a clue to what it is. Moreover, the significance that it has is not eternally embedded in it. It is specific to phases of history and its significance is socio-culturally rooted. Thus, what we said previously about geography applies to human biology and to human physiognomy.

There is no pure or virgin biology or physiognomy. Neither of them is immaculately conceived. Initially, each is already charged with human meaning. To claim that Africans are black is to impose a meaning on their body. It is to violate the African body. It is to invade it and subject it to a meaning that is not inherent in it, and with a meaning that obscures who and what Africans are. Regardless of how absurd it may appear Africans are not black. This does not mean they are brown or any other skin pigmentation. It does not mean that they are men and women of color. Human beings are not colored. Africans are Africans. There is a qualitative difference between being African and being Black. A name or naming matters. How one is named, or how one names oneself matters. Naming could be a source of empowerment, or of disempowerment. One only needs to look at the history of naming and its consequence on Africans. In the so-called New World, violent erasure of African names was a part of reducing Africans to the state of slavery. In colonial Africa, the Christianization of Africans, and the subjection of Africans to "modern" education was accompanied by the erasure of African names. To be Christian, Europeans do not have to change their European names to African names or to Chinese names. At one time, Africans expected and were forced to get rid of African names and adopt European names as a condition for being Christians. They were led to believe that Europeans names were Christian names and Christian names were European names. An African could not be a Christian and retain an African name. This is what was at stake in the ritual of baptism. There is an analog in this in legal language, where Africans are expected to embrace European legal language as a condition of attaining legal legitimacy. African legal language was construed by Europeans as having no legal legitimacy. The language of law had to be a European language.

Thinking like an African lawyer is not the same as thinking like a Black lawyer. When an African lawyer thinks like an African lawyer she or he thinks in such a way as to make this difference apparent. Her or his task in thinking like an African lawyer is not only to think in such a way as to reveal what it is to think like an African lawyer, it is also to think in such a way as to reveal the

Africanness of her or his thinking. To do this successfully, it is important to free herself or himself from the trappings of a one dimensional biology or physiognomy. The Africanness of the African does not reside in African genes, and because it does not reside there, it is in vain that one can trace thinking like an African lawyer to African genes. There are no African genes. If there were, they would be nothing more than inventions of bogus genetics, whose inventions are self-serving most likely in a racist sense. An African gene, a gene that embodies thinking like an African, is one of the historic inventions by Europeans. Of course, this does not mean that the African is to flee her or his body to be what she or he is. It does not mean that thinking like an African lawyer is not embodied. Contrary to Cartesian belief, the African is his or her body just as any other human being is his or her body. And contrary to what Cartesianists may believe, thinking like a lawyer, or thinking like anyone is not an outer body experience. If the African is his or her body, such a body is not solely that body that modern science embraces. It is a lived-body in which social and cultural meanings are inscribed. It is to such a body that one is to turn to make sense of what it means for an African to be African and to which we must turn to decipher what it is to think like an African lawyer.

The fact that, on one side there are Africans who believe that thinking like an African lawyer is synonymous with thinking like a Black lawyer and, on the other side, there are Africans who believe that thinking like an African lawyer is not synonymous with thinking like a Black lawyer points to a difference in the understanding of what it is to be African. In a racist world, such difference is not harmless. It may be symptomatic of a deeply rooted racism in the construction of what it is to be African. The racism that is directed towards the African may be so internalized by the African to the extent that it loses its negativity and becomes a positive feature by which the African comes to define himself or herself. Where this state of affairs is the case, thinking like an African lawyer calls for a psycho/existential analysis that exposes and eradicates intra-African racism. Black psycho/existential analysis inhibits such exposure and reinforces African psycho-existential pathology (racism). Blackness is the negation of Africanness. It is cancerous. It is a cancer that results from the cancer of whiteness. It cannot be cured and it will never be cured unless and until the cancer of whiteness is cured. It is foolish to believe that this is an easy task. Many of the people who call themselves white have worked themselves into the ignorance of their own illness. Being white is just as sickly and sickening as being black. The two have an ontological bond. They are parasitic to each other. Neither can be eradicated without the eradication of the other. To think of this illness that affects the so-called black and the so-called white people exclusively as somatic is to misunderstand it. It is psychosomatic. Frantz Fanon, the psychoanalyst of the colonized psyche, tells us that "The attitude of the black man toward the white, or toward his own race, often duplicates almost completely a constellation of delirium, frequently bordering on the region of the pathological".[54] The inescapable corollary of this observation is "The attitude of the white man toward the black, towards his own race, often duplicates almost completely a constellation of delirium, frequently bordering on the region of the pathological". At the time Fanon wrote *Black Skin White Masks*, he had not yet attained a psychoanalytic insight that would have called his attention to the fact that the use of the words "black" and "white" reflect a deeply rooted pathology, and that the elimination of this pathology called for the abandonment of these words never occurred to him. Even today, many of us continue to use these words, a usage that reinforces the illness that they signify. Those of us who are committed to the diagnosing and the curing of this illness continue to undermine our effort if we persist in using these words. The persistence reinforces what we want to cure. In other words, it matters whether Africans are to be referred to as Africans or as Blacks. The shift from the latter to the former is a revolutionary move that is psychotherapeutic. African legal philosophy and African jurisprudence should be a part of this move, and it is a move that should inform what is genuine about thinking like an African lawyer. Thinking like an African lawyer should have a psychiatrical component, a component that allows the African to recover his or her body and also to recover his or her perception; in short, it should aim at the recovering of the African's lived-body. Existential psychiatry and existential psychoanalysis should be a part of the education in thinking like an African lawyer.

Psychological disturbances reveal themselves in multiple ways. They can reveal themselves somatically. They can also reveal themselves on the domain of language. What reveals itself on the domain of language reveals itself on the domain of thinking. It is in language that our thinking is revealed. Embracing "negro", "black", or "colored" identity to the point of accepting the word negro/black/colored as a word of self-reference is symptomatic of an existential/psychological disturbance; it is symptomatic of a diseased thinking. The disease may be so advanced that one who is victimized by it ceases to think of it as a disease, and comes to think of it as if it were a sign of health. Diseased thinking is mistaken for healthy thinking. To the extent that such a mistake has taken place in the African, thinking like an African lawyer must of necessity be psychoanalytical and psychotherapeutical. It must be dialectical. It must be diagnostic, and must be carried out in such a way as to reveal the condition in which the African finds himself or herself today. It must also clear the way for the construction of healthy Africanness—a clearing that must also open the way for the investigation of what would constitute healthy Africanness. In other words, the thinking that is at stake in thinking like an African lawyer matters. If it matters, the language of this thinking equally matters. Calling oneself an African lawyer matters. Calling oneself African, as opposed to calling oneself Negro, Black, or Colored, matters. Fanon reminds us that "a man who has language possesses the world expressed and implied by that language. What we are getting at becomes plain: Mastery of language affords remarkable power. Paul Valery knew this for he called language "the god gone astray in flesh".[55] As Ngugi wa Thiong'o has pointed out,

> Language carries the cultural universe of the community and in that universe also resides the entire body of values held by that community. Every community of humans with a given particularity has notions of what is right and wrong, of the bad and the good, of the ugly and the beautiful, in short a system of ethics and aesthetics the entirety of which, with associated feelings, emotions and attitudes forms the basis of their identity or their being for themselves.[56]

Clearly language matters. Negro, Black, and Colored are words that are radically different in meaning from the word African. To name thinking like an African lawyer is to invoke an African world. It is to raise on the level of language such a world. It is to endow thinking and the language that expresses it a power of renaissance; it is to bring into being that African world that has been desecrated by Europeans, and that remains forgotten, for the most part, in contemporary Africa. As long as this is a living thinking and the language of this thinking is a living language, this bringing into being is not exclusively an archeology. It is thinking and language that is creative. The African world is not complete. Like any other human world, it is always in the process of being constituted. It is the psychoanalytical and psychotherapeutic objective of thinking like an African lawyer to preserve and promote this process. And this thinking can bring about a realization of this objective by being a part of this process. As a part of this process, it is itself a part of the unfinished task. It is itself by being ahead of itself. It is what it is by continuously being itself.

At this age of the globalization of thinking—a process in which Euro-American thinking like a lawyer is being globalized—an African who has set out to think like an African lawyer faces a formidable obstacle. She or he must think in such a way that she or he does not contribute to the flight of Africans from being African, thereby contributing to the crime against the humanity of Africans. In thinking properly like an African lawyer, she or he must think in such a way as to define, preserve, and promote liberated African socio-cultural existence. Not only must she or he face the intra-African difficulty in this undertaking, she or he must also address the non-African anti-African obstacle that has been erected along the path of his or her thinking like an African lawyer. A part of the work of thinking like an African lawyer is the work of working out what is to constitute being African. This working out is and can be on the way to being successful if it remains rooted in what it is aiming at. It must originate from the African and aim at the African.

Although it is rarely explicit, a part of what is at stake in thinking like a lawyer involves the constitution or conservation of self. Thus, thinking like a Roman lawyer involves the constitution or preservation of a Roman self, thinking like a German lawyer involves the constitution or preservation of a German self, and thinking like an American lawyer involves the constitution or preservation of an American self. An African lawyer who thinks like an African lawyer has the same task: to constitute and preserve an African self. In part, it is this task that is to direct her or his thinking. It is precisely for this reason that one cannot blindly be educated to think like a lawyer. Legal education is autobiographical. Jurisprudence is autobiographical. Being trained to think like a lawyer is being trained to think autobiographically. To be sure this is not always the case. In Anglo-American jurisprudence, for example, jurisprudence as autobiography of the Anglo-American is suppressed. The study of the nature of law is not explicitly presented as the study of being Anglo-American. The study of law as a study of a special type of rule or rules is not explicitly presented as the rule or the rules of one's being. The study of the source or the sources of laws or the study of the validity of laws is not presented as the study of the validity of one's being or the sources of one's being. The often touted "rule of law" that is contrasted to "the rule of men" in the Anglo-American world is a legal fiction that obscures the rule of Anglo-Americans.

The rule of law, the way it has been exported to Africa from the West, is a Trojan horse. In it, there is what threatens thinking like an African lawyer. It fosters thinking like a non-African lawyer. It sweetens the non-African thinking and camouflages anti-Africanness. As John Hasnas has observed,

> People who believe they live under "a government of laws and not people" tend to view their nation's legal system as objective and impartial. They tend to see the rules under which they must live not as expressions of human will, but as embodiments of neutral principles of justice, i.e., as natural features of the social world. Once they believe that they are being commanded by an impersonal law rather than other human beings, they view their obedience to political authority as public-spirited acceptance of the requirements of social life rather than mere acquiesce to superior power. In this way, the concept of the rule of law functions much like the use of the passive voice by the politicians who describe a delict on his or her part with the assertion "mistakes were made". It allows people to hide the agency of power behind a facade of words; to believe that it is the law which compels their compliance, not self-aggrandizing politicians, of highly capitalized special interests, or wealthy white Anglo-Saxon Protestant males, or (fill in your favorite culprit).
>
> But the myth of the rule of law does more than render the people submissive to state authority; it also turns them into the state's accomplices in the exercise of its power. For people who would ordinarily consider it a great evil to deprive individuals of their rights or oppress politically powerless minority groups will respond with patriotic fervor when these same actions are described as upholding the rule of law.[57]

What the author of the above passage says has significant African nuances. Thinking like a lawyer is expected to enshrine the rule of law and, in turn, the rule of law is expected to provide space where thinking like a lawyer shines brilliantly, and where it is best understood. The belief in the rule of law has been introduced in Africa as if it were a religious dogma. Africans are expected not to question it in the same way that they are expected not to question Christian faith. Its ideological dimension is mystified. To resist it is to resist enlightenment; it is to court lawlessness and savagery. On the political level, it is projected as the engine of democracy. Hence, to oppose it is to think counter democracy; it is to pave the way for dangerous anti-democratic forces. If one is pro-democracy one has to be pro-rule of law. But, what precisely is the rule of law? How can one who thinks like an African lawyer answer this question? Here, it is worth recalling that one of the justifications of the oppressive racist European colonialism in Africa is that colonialism sought to institute law where lawlessness prevailed. Subjugation and oppression of Africans was consistent with the rule of law as it was understood by the colonialists. If the rule of law was the engine of democracy—democracy as the government of the people, by the people, and for the people, the democracy that was advocated was a democracy of the colonizers, by the colonizers, and for the colonizers. The concept of people was exhaustively populated by colonizers and Africans were non-people, resources for the people. There was no democracy by Africans for Africans.

Clearly, in post-colonial Africa, the mystification of the thinking about the rule of law has not been cleared. It has become complicated. The colonialist officers of the rule of law have been replaced by Africans, and none of the post-colonial African officers of the rule of law have declared themselves to be the enemies of the rule of law or as enemies of democracy. But, again, one can ask, what is the post-colonial rule of law? If the rule of law is the engine of democracy, who are the people in this democracy? Who are the people who are being served by the rule of law? It is tempting to say that the post-colonial rule of law in Africa is the African rule of law, and people who are served by this rule are Africans. What people are being served by African legal thinking? Here there is no mystery. The people who are being served are the people in power. The people are the people in power. As was the case during the colonial days, in post-colonial Africa, the masses of the African people are left out in the cold. They are not only non-people; they are anti-people. The rule of law is the rule of the elite, and the people who are served by this rule are the elite. Law has become inaccessible to the masses of Africans and has become forbiddingly expensive for ordinary people, and for them, the rule of law is not their rule. It is what rules them. Moreover, instead of this rule being a rule of a particular group of people, it is presented as if it were an impersonal and impartial rule. David Luban hits the nail right on the head when he says

> Laws do not rule, and the "rule of law not of men" is actually a specific form of rule by men (including, nowadays, a few women). These rulers are not slaves to anything. Furthermore, the construction of the slogan—rule and not rule of men—has unfortunate connotations. It suggests that the personal qualities of the human rulers required to secure the rule of law are nothing more than forbearance and disinterestedness—a resolution to stay out of the law's way.[58]

Inevitably, thinking like an African lawyer will remain mystified until the class or the elite dimension of the thinking about the rule of law or thinking like a lawyer becomes translucent and reveals what lies under the camouflage.

In contemporary African society, thinking like an African lawyer has been transformed into an economic resource, and this resource is being exploited in the African capitalist political economy with the blessing of the World Bank, International Monetary fund and by other international financial institutions that are controlled by the West. Following the footsteps established in the West, in Africa, legal profession has been transformed or rather has taken the shape of a business profession. It primarily serves individual interest. Professional legal life has been transformed into a business enterprise, and legal thinking has been tailored to this enterprise. Demystified, legal thinking has been transformed into the thinking that is practiced by business people. For the most part, a pecuniary motive is the driving force. Pursuit of justice has been rendered incidental.

The rule of law will never be the rule of law. It will always remain the rule of the men or the rule of men and women securing and promoting the interest of a particular segment of society. Differently stated, the rule of law will always remain the rule of men. A truthful understanding of the rule of law will inevitably reveal the men and women who rule and the interest that they serve and promote. It will also bring into the open what is concealed by such notions as "divine law" or "natural law". These notions are nothing more than ingenious ways by which men conceal their rule. There never was and there will never be divine law or natural law. Both of these conceptions of law are nothing more than human law masquerading as other than what it is. "Rule of law" is essentially the rule of man, not man in abstract, but real empirical man. There is no general man. There are only men. Similarly, the "rule of law" as the rule of "state" or as the rule of "government" is a subterfuge. The "state" or the "government" represents the will or the interest of a particular group of people. Piercing the veil of the "state" or the veil of "government" can help recognize who makes up this group. Doing so is an essential task of those who have committed themselves into thinking like genuine African lawyers.

Other than being prohibitively expensive, legal service has become professionalized, and is largely construed and administered by legal professionals. It is these professionals who think for the masses in matters that pertain to law. They have insisted on monopolizing thinking like a lawyer. For the most part, the language of law is barely understood by non-lawyers Most of it is in non-African languages, and it is only the professionals who have the ability to read, write and understand these languages. These professional languages are mostly European languages—the languages of former colonial masters. The implication here is that, today, thinking like an African lawyer largely amounts to thinking in a non-African language which is more or less thinking like a non-African thinker; in this case it is like thinking like a Western European thinker. The language of law, as is the case with thinking like a lawyer, becomes abstracted from a socio-cultural context, and this abstraction becomes a cover-up of the process by which the African socio-cultural context is undermined and in which a Euro-social context is institutionalized and promoted as being other than what it is. Law becomes law irrespective or the socio-cultural context and thinking like a lawyer becomes a thinking that is what it is irrespective of the socio-cultural context.

We are now in a position to recognize how the students of African legal philosophy or the students of African jurisprudence run the risk of erroneously studying other people's legal philosophy and other people's jurisprudence as if it were their own. Such erroneous studying may be at work when legal philosophy or jurisprudence is de-contextualized, when, for example, legal philosophy or jurisprudence is presented as the universal philosophy of law or as universal jurisprudence. When legal education is projected as education in legal "science", the impression is that legal education can take place in an autobiographical void. One does not think like a lawyer in an autobiographical void. To think like a lawyer is to think in a way that implicates one's being. To consciously do so is to render explicit what one is. It is in the context that one is to see and understand what it is to think like an African lawyer.

Critical pedagogy in legal education is especially appropriate in this phase of human history when being African is under assault from multiple sides. An African student of law must especially guard herself or himself from the Western missionaries of legal education. In the work of re-constructing and constructing her or his identity as an African, she or he faces no greater threat than the threat that emanates from the West. In fending off this threat, an African student of law must not be oblivious of the danger from within. He or she may have internalized or may be internalizing anti-African values in the education he or she has gotten or that he or she is getting. In the name of legal science, he or she should avoid mistaking what is thinking like a lawyer in a non-African tradition for thinking like a lawyer in his or her own tradition. The pressure to appropriate the Other, and create oneself in his or her image, is tremendous. One cannot always be sure that one is aware of all the sources of this pressure. Hence, constant vigilance is a virtue in the study of legal thinking.

Being African, as is the case with any other mode of being human, is being embodied. As indicated previously being African does not take on a black embodiment. It takes on an African embodiment. That is, the African's body is not black; it is African. An African takes on the body of an African, and it is as such that he or she engages African jurisprudence. An African who thinks like an African lawyer is an African who inhabits an African body. Such a body is not simply a body that is projected by biological and physical science. It is a lived-body that takes on socio-cultural significance. Given the historical desecration and degradation of the African body by Europeans, it is the task of the African lawyer to think of herself or of himself in a way that rescues the African body from such desecration and degradation. It is not enough to say that my body is not an object, an assemblage of parts, or a conjunction of physiological systems. As a lived-body, the African body must be a body in revolt, a body that subsumes and is subsumed by a revolutionary process. It is only in this context that the African lawyer can truly think like an African lawyer. For an African, to teach African jurisprudence, to study African jurisprudence, or to practice law is to do so in this context.

In teaching, studying African legal philosophy or African jurisprudence, or in practicing law, the African is not *a res cogitans*, divorced from the body in a Cartesian fashion. It is only as an Africanly embodied being that he or she can undertake these activities. There is a corporeal imperative that binds any African who has self-consciously embarked on the task of investigating or constituting African jurisprudence, or who self-consciously embarks on practicing African-centered law. Truly thinking like an African lawyer requires that thinking be corporeally rooted in an African body, and such thinking is what it is by reflecting that upon which it is rooted. It is a corporeal thinking. Differently stated, for an African, thinking like an African lawyer requires an embodied consciousness of himself or herself as African.

In the preceding reflection, we have been looking into or feeling our way into what it is to be an African legal thinker. As indicated earlier, it cannot be determined what it is to think like an African lawyer if it is not determined who and what an African is. In the course of this determination we have pointed out the inadequacy of using mere geography and mere biology as criteria for who and what an African is. What then would be a more adequate determination of who and what an African is? It has been pointed out that African thinking when properly understood is a means of determining who and what an African is. The next logical question is what does authentic African legal thinking tell us about what it is to be African? In answer to this question, an important avenue lies in thinking like an African lawyer. That is, we are to turn to the kind of thinking that an African lawyer engages in, in such a way as to reveal what is at stake in being African. It is the task of the African who thinks like an African lawyer to think in such a way as to make explicit what is involved in being African. This has already been anticipated, for example, in positing an African as a being whose being is caught up in an emancipatory process, a process that entails a constitution of the African self. Let us now turn to and explore further what is involved in thinking like an African lawyer. In so doing, we pursue further the course of determining who and what an African is.

Part II

Attention has been paid to the sense of what is to be understood as "African" in the expression "thinking like an African lawyer". It is now time to focus more attention to the thinking that is involved in thinking like an African lawyer. If an African is thinking like a lawyer, it is to be assumed that he or she is a thinking being. A being that thinks exhibits what it is in thinking. Thus, it should be expected that in thinking like an African lawyer, an African will think in a manner that exhibits what she or he is. Now, defining a human being as a thinking being is precisely what modern Western man has thought of as the essence of what it is to be human since Descartes. It is Descartes, who, in his metaphysical investigation of what is essential about man, apparently discovered that man is essentially a thinking being. It is one of the modern European discoveries, and perhaps, more appropriately, one of the modern inventions of modern Europeans. The thing that thinks discovered itself as a thinking thing, or more appropriately invented itself as a thinking being. It is not made clear what it was before it discovered or invented itself. If it was nothing, then it came into being out of nothing, and therefore, strictly speaking, it cannot be said to have discovered or invented itself, for it would have to be before it was. Like his fellow Christian believers, Descartes got rid of the enigma by postulating the existence of God who created the thing that thinks out of nothing. Thus, Descartes' claim that "I think therefore I am" is intelligible only from a Christian theological standpoint. In other words, for him, thinking is theologically based. Without theology, it is unintelligible.

The "I" that Descartes had in mind is an isolated individual that would become the fundamental building block of society in late European modernity.[59] Modern European society is thoroughly individualized, and this individualization founds the modern European view of thinking. One thinks as an individual, and when one enters into a thinking relation with others, one enters into it as an individual in relation to others as individuals. This conception of being human and its attendant thinking has no equivalence in African thinking since an isolated individual, an individual who is cut off from social reality, would be unthinkable. In speaking about the concept of individuality in African societies, John Mbiti correctly observes,

> In traditional life the individual does not and cannot exist alone except corporately. He owes his existence to other people, including those of past generations and his contemporaries. He is simply a part of the whole. The community must therefore make, create or produce the individual; for the individual depends on the corporate group. Physical birth is not enough: the child must go through rites of incorporation so that it comes fully integrated into the entire society. These rites continue through the physical life of a person, during which the individual passes from one stage of corporate existence to another. The final stage is reached when he dies and even then he is ritually incorporated into

> the wider family of the dead and the living...Whatever happens to the individual happens to the whole group and whatever happens to the whole group happens to the individual. The individual can only say: "I am, because we are; and since we are, therefore I am".[60]

Eugene Cotran, a British student of African law, has also noted that,

> It is undoubtedly true that African law is essentially a law of groups or communities rather than of individuals. This characteristic expresses itself in almost every branch of law. In the law of marriage, the marriage contract was not so much a union of two individuals as an alliance between two family groups and divorce was only possible through the group. In the law of property, right to land was vested in a political or social group and an individual's right was subjected to that of the group. The law of succession often involved succession by families or groups rather than individuals. In the law relating to injuries or wrongs, the damages were often payable by one family or clan to another and not by one person to another.[61]

The observations that Mbiti and Cotran make should not lead to the belief that individuality has no place in African thinking or in African life and existence. It is precisely this erroneous belief that Paulin Hountondji exposes in *African Philosophy Myth and Reality*. Hountondji, however, errs on the opposite side. He is paranoid about any trans-individual African self-consciousness. In his eyes, trans-individual thinking is a product of ethno-anthropology, and is a European generated fiction. In defense against the charge that Africans are unanimists, he posits Africans as monads; that is, as existing independent of one another. In this position, he is clearly wrong. The kind of individuality he talks about does not exist in Africa, and it is inconceivable that it can exist anywhere else despite the pretensions of European modernity. The trans-individual consciousness is not to be mistaken for the bogus ethno-philosophical consciousness that Hountondji rejects as being nothing more than a product of European fictional work. It is not the unanimist or the unconscious consciousness. It is the consciousness that one must embody and that one must be conscious of in order to be human. Being human is the consciousness of being human, and such consciousness is essentially communal since no one can be human in isolation from other human beings.

That an African is an individual in the context of corporate existence is not only uniquely an African phenomenon. To be conscious of oneself as a human being is to be conscious of oneself as belonging to the community of other human beings. Thinking, as is the case with language, is a social event. To think of oneself as a human being is to think of oneself in the community of human beings. Descartes could not have been possibly right in thinking that he could think as a monad. If he could do so, he would not be able to communicate with us, and no other human being could communicate with him. He could not be conscious of himself as a human being.

To the extent that Descartes has been instrumental in erecting the foundation of liberal social theory and its attendant legal theory, it should be clear that both the social and the legal theory that arise from his conception of being human do not have analogues in the African social existence and could ultimately not have an analogue in any human existence. One must indeed question the view of being human that it presupposes. The cult of individualism that is unleashed by European modernity fails not only to do justice to African legal philosophy jurisprudence but also to any truly human legal philosophy. If Europeans are at a loss as to who they are, Africans do an injustice to themselves if they convert to this cult. Furthermore, by converting, they reinforce European self-alienation, which, in turn, reinforces African self-alienation. At this age when Africans readily go for any fashion that is produced in the European world, there lies a danger in that the fashions that they are adopting will further estrange them from who and what they are. The legal philosophy and jurisprudence emanating from the European world pose such a threat. In our rush to "modernize" and "develop" there is great likelihood that we Africans will opt for a legal thinking that is going to tear apart our corporate existence, destroy our social existence, alienate us from one another, and render us strangers not only to ourselves but also to the other members of the human community.

To return to Cartesian metaphysics, the thing that thinks, a thing Descartes called mind, is radically separate from the body. The essence of this thing lies in thinking. If Descartes had to write a treatise on thinking like a lawyer, the lawyer would not be anyone that we can see or touch, since he or she would be disembodied. Indeed, we would not be able to tell whether the lawyer is a man or a woman. The words "man" and "woman" would not be applicable to this thing that would be a lawyer. In a Cartesian world, one would be hard pressed to make sense of feminist jurisprudence. The claim that feminists make about feminist jurisprudence would be meaningless since the concept of the feminine would be empty. To use Kantian language, there would be no content to intuit.[62] There would not be patriarchal or masculinist jurisprudence for the feminist thinker to challenge. Provided that an African is a human being, there would be nothing distinctly corporeal that would set him or her apart from the European or from an Asian. I say provided, for Europeans have had some doubts concerning the humanity of Africans. This should not come as a surprise with someone who is familiar with the stories that Europeans have told themselves about Africans. Levy Bruhl, for example, has a book titled the *Mind of the Primitive* where he portrays Africans as having a pre-logical mind, a mind that is incapable of grasping the subtleties of European thought.[63] A reference has already been made to Montesquieu who thought it absurd that God, a supremely wise Being, would think of placing a soul in the body of an African. Obviously, he did not take note of the superstition of himself as having a soul, or of believing that his fellow Europeans had such superstitious entities in their bodies. Perhaps the same can be said about Descartes. This thing that he calls mind whose essence is to think may be nothing more than a species of superstition that Gilbert Ryle, a fellow Westerner, referred to as the ghost in the machine.[64] What is even more superstitious is to have Africans embody European superstitions in order to think of themselves as human. Without embodiment an African is not, and indeed, no one is. As Achille Mbembe has pointed out,

> It is now widely acknowledged that Africa as an idea, a concept, has historically served and continues to serve as a polemical argument for the West's desperate desire to assert its difference from the rest of the world.[65]

What is said about Africa by the West applies to the West's idea or concept of the African. Unlike the Western man who is distinguished as the thing that thinks, in the eyes of the Western man, the African is apparently distinguished by his or her body—by the thing that does not think, or if this thing thinks, it thinks in an undeveloped, or infantile way. If the Western man has a body, it is a body that is furthest removed from the body of the African. Again, as Mbembe has pointed out,

> The theoretical and practical recognition of the body of "the stranger" as flesh and body just like mine, the idea of a common human nature, a humanity shared with others, long posed and still poses a problem for Western consciousness.[66]

The prominence of dualistic understanding of a human being in the West, and the association of thinking with a disembodied being has undermined the integrity of a human being as a thinking being. Thinking is corporeally rooted and it is only as such that a human being can think. Whether incorporeal beings (if there be such beings) can think is up to such beings if they exist. It is not up to us. When the Westerner sees the African, he sees the body—the body that is devoid of thinking. To him, this seeing is thinking. When he sees himself, he sees the thing that thinks. He thinks what he sees of himself. After all he is Descartes' heir. His proclivity to thinking as an abstract incorporeal activity is not an accident. It is how he has defined and understood himself. He will take notice of legal thinking only if it is a formal science, if it is responsive to logic. Legal or Jurisprudential thinking must not be bound by space and time. It must be global, global in the way he understands it. It is only in this way that jurisprudential thinking can be the foundation of a scientific study of law. Thinking like an African lawyer in this context is a diversion and an obfuscation of what it is to think like a lawyer. Being African does not matter when thinking like a lawyer is at stake. But perhaps this is itself an obfuscation of thinking like a lawyer, and more particularly, an obfuscation of thinking like an African lawyer. We must return to body-thinking for we are body-thinkers. The human body thinks—not that body that is a product of abstract or theoretical thinking, or a body that is an assembly of parts or an assembly of physiological systems, but that lived body that makes each of us a human being. It is this thinking that is likely to be fruitful in jurisprudential thinking.

Thinking like an African lawyer is a corporeal thinking—a thinking that exemplifies a lived-body that is both historical and socio-cultural, a thinking in which the corporeal African is autographed. It is a corporeal thinking that is pan-African. Even in its particularity, the African body incorporates all Africans wherever they are. It is the pan-African body that embodies the thinking in which the African inscribes his or her identity. Because he or she is rooted in and embodies Pan-Africanity, in thinking like an African lawyer, he or she has to think in a way that exemplifies this mode of being. He or she does not have to think outside of himself or herself, because outsideness and insideness are spatial categories that are not proper to him or to her. To be is to be with other Africans. This is what it means to call oneself African, and it is precisely this mode of being that the liberalism of the West has sought to undermine by imposing subjectivism or individualism on the African. It is also the basis of legal thinking that Western legal thinking has sought and seeks to banish as anachronistic. To think like an African lawyer is to bear the entire weight of what makes one African. The jurisdiction of thinking like an African lawyer is Continent-wide, and more than this, it encompasses Africans wherever they are scattered throughout the world. Given the division of the African Continent into nation-states, this jurisdiction may readily strike one as fantastic, but the line between what is fantastic and what is not, in this case, remains problematic. It is only in so doing that one can truly think in a way that essentially implicates all other human beings. The humanity of one African is not foreign to the humanity of any other African, and the humanity of the African is not inessential to the humanity of any other human being.

Conventional wisdom in the West has it that a particular type of thinking qualifies a lawyer as a lawyer. It is this thinking that is the staple diet of students in Western law schools, especially in North America. What then is this type of thinking that establishes a lawyer's identity as a lawyer? Is thinking like a lawyer a mode of thinking that is universal; that is, a thinking that all lawyers must exhibit irrespective of their social, cultural, or historical situation, or is it specific to a situation? Assuming that these questions are raised in a philosophical context, as is the case here, is the philosophical thinking that is implicated in raising and trying to answer these questions universal or is it situationally determined? The raising of this latter question is not a digression. A philosopher's conception of philosophical thinking is exhibited in whatever a philosopher picks up as his or her subject of inquiry. It should not be assumed that when a lawyer thinks about thinking like a lawyer, he or she thinks the same way as a philosopher when a philosopher thinks about thinking like a lawyer. If one takes the view that philosophical thinking is universal, then philosophical thinking about thinking like a lawyer is universal regardless of whether thinking like a lawyer takes place in Africa, in the United States, in China, or in any other place. Other than being an expression of a geographical demarcation, thinking like a lawyer in Africa or in the United States would be indistinguishable from thinking like a lawyer in any other place. Other than the geographical sense, as a branch of African philosophy, thinking like a lawyer in African jurisprudence would be indistinguishable from thinking like a lawyer in any other philosophical jurisprudence. On the other hand, if philosophical thinking is not universal, then thinking philosophically about thinking like a lawyer will depend on the situation within which one is thinking. Thus, thinking like a lawyer in Africa will entail more than placing this thinking in a geographical context. Seen from the standpoint of African philosophy, it will require that such a philosophy be placed in an extra-geographical context. In this regard, determining what it is to think like a lawyer in Africa is inseparable from thinking what it is to think philosophically in Africa. Whereas it may be the case that when a lawyer determines what it is to think like a lawyer he or she can do so without raising the question as to what it is to think philosophically, a philosopher who sets out to determine what it is to think like a lawyer cannot do so without at the same time determining what it is to think philosophically.

As indicated previously, Paulin Hountondji has claimed that it is geography rather than content that determines the Africanness of philosophy.[67] In the light of this assertion, he would claim that, other than the geographical context, the philosophical determination of what thinking like a lawyer is in Africa is indistinguishable from thinking like a lawyer anywhere else. To him, those who think like lawyers are fungible regardless of where they are. Hountondji appears to be of the opinion that it is as senseless to think of the Africanness of African philosophy being other than a geographical demarcation of philosophy as to think of the Africanness of African chemistry other than a geographical demarcation of chemistry. For him, philosophical thinking is a scientific undertaking, and such thinking is inevitably universal. In short, Hountondji embraces and propagates the spirit of scientism. By pushing the view that African philosophy must be what it is by being scientific, he hopes, thereby, to rescue African philosophy from what he calls ethnophilosophy.[68] By placing philosophy in the bondage of science, he adopts an unphilosophical view about philosophy. He fails to be a good servant of philosophy, and also fails to be a good servant of science by importing to it what does not belong to it. A good scientist minds his or her business and does not confuse what he or she does in science with what a philosopher qua philosopher does. A good servant of philosophy is one who truly guards philosophy from the capture and enslavement by scientism or by any other creed. In its imperial sense, scientism is a transgression from the proper domain of science to other domains, whereby these other domains are forced to succumb to the imperative of science. It exemplifies the spirit of reductionism, and is averse to heterotopia. It stands for one-dimensional thinking. A good servant of philosophy resists the transgression of scientism and seeks to preserve heterotopia whereby each domain has its respective place. He or she resists the spirit of reductionism, and preserves the openness in which each domain can be what it is without interference from other domains. It is in this sense that philosophy, in principle, has no quarrel with science. But when an imperialist move is made in the name of science, science is thereby discredited. When this happens, it is a part of the task of the good servant of philosophy to point this out.

One can understand what appears to motivate Hountondji in his crusade to scientize African philosophy, his crusade to reduce philosophical thinking to scientific thinking. He has embraced one of the Western European views about philosophy, in which philosophy is projected as a scientific activity. In its classical sense, this view promotes the spirit of empirical science under the name of positivism. It is a rejection of a metaphysics that rejects a phenomenal world in favor of a transcendent world. It is a phase in the continuing struggle about the nature of philosophy in Western/European history. As an African, Hountondji, in his early thinking, forgets his own history and crusades for Western/European history. In effect, he has enrolled in the Western/European evangelical crusade. He has become a convert in the Western/European mission in Africa. Nothing should be construed here as implying that the science of positivistic thinking is intrinsically or exclusively Western/European. Science and positivism are possibilities available to all human beings. The issue is whether or not these possibilities are to be taken up and made the only views of thinking about reality or thinking about the world. It has been assumed that these are the only legitimate views. This has been the case with Logical Positivists. It has been assumed that these views are exclusively European or Western to the extent that if an African thinks scientifically, he or she is said to be thinking like a European or like a Westerner. This view is not only erroneous. It is a part of European or Western ideology to further the subjugation of non-Europeans and to integrate them into a Western regime of thinking. It is the failure to grasp this state of affairs that leads Hountondji to construe philosophy as if it were a science.

In so far as legal thinking in Africa is derived from the West, it displaces Africans from their African identity and promotes a Western view of man in Africa. Herein lies the danger of the view that thinking like a lawyer is the same regardless of time and place. Under this conception of thinking like a lawyer, a particular view of thinking like a lawyer is imposed on everyone everywhere. By adopting this view the African, unwittingly, becomes an agent of the Western/European ideology of thinking like a lawyer. The conception of the rule of law in the Western/European world conceals this state of affairs. Let us note what is involved in training someone to think like a lawyer in this world. We will single out what it takes to be trained to think like a lawyer in the United States as an illustration.

In some law schools, if not all law schools, first year students are in one way or other informed that they are there to be trained to think like lawyers. For the most part, this implies that they are to abandon other ways of thinking if they are going to master the skills that are required of them in their chosen profession.[69] It is not rare that the name of Socrates is invoked. Socratic thinking is projected as the paradigm of thinking like a lawyer. Lest it appear as if this thinking is foreign, Socrates has been construed as a Westerner and his thinking is embraced as if it were Western. The history of Western philosophy has already institutionalized the embrace. Little matters about how Socrates thought about his identity or how he characterized his thinking. The fact that Socrates thought of himself as a philosopher and not as a lawyer is rarely if ever brought to the attention of students. The fact that Socrates exemplifies thinking like a philosopher rather than thinking like a lawyer is rarely if ever mentioned. If it is granted that this is the case, then, most likely, it would appear that the Socratic thinking that one hears mentioned in modern legal education has little to do with genuine Socratic thinking. This is precisely the point made by William C. Hefferman[70]. He accurately traces the forerunner of the Socratic thinking of the law schools not to Socrates but to Protagoras, the sophist. He further notes possible conflict between genuine Socratic thinking and the Socratic thinking that is the staple of the law schools.

> If law professors were to employ the education methods of Socrates, then they would violate the fundamental norms of their profession. However strong the current interests in moral issues surrounding professional responsibility may be, law professors are not permitted to use their classrooms to carry out direct moral instruction of their students. Furthermore even if the ethical purpose underlying Socratic method were to be discounted, it must be remembered that law professors do not, as a rule, set aside textual criticism in favor of the pursuit of abstract definition of basic concepts of law. The term "Socratic method" may therefore serve as a flattering conceit for professors of law, but it bears little similarity to the method of Socrates.

The presentation of Socratic thinking in law schools as if it were the genuine Socratic thinking is revelatory of the kind of thinking that largely goes on in legal education not only in American law schools but also in Western/European law schools. It is a part of what it means to be trained to think like a lawyer. It is an art of chicanery that the ancient Greek sophists instituted and perfected. It was a part of the trade of the sophists to master the skill of intentionally presenting what was the case as if it were not the case and vice versa. They advocated whatever they were paid to advocate. What drove them was the desire to gain the attention and the praise of the public by doing whatever it took to be victorious in whatever they argued for. If it meant bending the truth they would not hesitate to do so, and if it meant telling the truth would ensure their victory they would tell the truth. Because of their chameleon-like nature, it was difficult to distinguish them from philosophers, and this difficulty is not one they wanted to get rid of because it served them in their of art of disguise. They were not men of principle, although this does not mean that they would not attempt to present themselves as men of principle. They sought to impress the audience by any means and reap the honor that the public bestowed on the victors. Even more important, they sought to be remunerated for their victory. Socrates, the philosopher, sought to distinguish himself from them by pursuing truth and telling truth to the extent that he knew what it was, and not simply tell the audience what it wanted to hear. Moreover, the truth he was seeking, or the truth he would tell, was not an end in itself. It was a truth that would enable him and his fellow Athenians to lead a virtuous life (what today we inadequately think of as a moral life). In other words, genuine Socratic thinking was not an embodiment of clever thinking, or clever use of language to attain self-serving ends. It was not a means to accumulate wealth or a means of pursuing fame or honor at the expense of virtue. It was a means of nurturing virtue among fellow citizens. It was an invitation to fellow citizens to engage in a thinking that would generate political virtue—a virtue that was needed for good life. If we bear in mind that justice was one of the key features in being virtuous, concern with justice was integral to Socrates' conception of thinking as a philosopher. To Socrates, philosophical thinking aimed not at the betterment of an isolated individual or an isolated segment of the polis but for political betterment—betterment of the whole, the whole in which the individual had his being and in which any segment of the polis had its being. Sophistical thinking ignored the betterment of the whole, and catered to the betterment of the individual. It did not take into consideration the individual's political betterment. It marginalized the question regarding the betterment of the whole. In a sense, it is the forerunner of modern individualism or construed the betterment of the whole as a betterment of an aggregate of individuals.

The separation of legal thinking from the concern with virtue has taken many forms. One of them is the separation of law from morality. The separation has been advocated by legal thinkers who are associated with legal positivism. Legal positivists have claimed that if law is not separated from morality there will be confusion of legal matters with moral matters, and the former will be mistaken for the latter. That is, law as it is should be separated from law as it ought to be. It appears that the way law ought to be is a moral concern and should be strictly separated from the law as it is. Differently stated, if rules and principles that are strictly legal are not clearly distinguished from rules and principles that are strictly moral, the former will be confused with and will be mistaken for the latter, and, conversely, the latter will confused with and mistaken for the former. The confusion and the mistaken identity that ensue compromise both the integrity of the concept of law and the concept of morality. Hart, a latter day legal positivist, has observed that,

> What Bentham and Austin were anxious to assert were following two simple things: first, in the absence of an expressed constitutional or legal provision, it could not follow from the mere fact that a rule violated standards of morality it was not a rule of law: and conversely, it could not follow from the mere fact that a rule was morally desirable that it was a rule of law.[71]

According to Hart, the original framers of the separation of law from morality had the intention of avoiding two dangers that would occur if law and morality were not separated. The first danger was that "law and its authority may be dissolved in man's conception of what law ought to be" and the second was "that existing law may supplant morality as the final test of conduct and so escape criticism".[72] Since it is assumed that what is moral is in the eyes of the beholder subjective judgments prevail in the moral realm. Subjective judgments compromise objectivity and impartiality—features that are projected as essential to the concept of legality. Thus, those who are trained to be lawyers are socialized into believing that thinking like a lawyer requires an abandonment of moral values as well as other subjective considerations in legal deliberations. In legal practice, they are not to concern themselves with whether their clients acted or act in moral or immoral ways, but rather, whether their actions are legal or illegal. They are members of the legal bar and not the moral bar. The practice of law is an amoral activity. The judiciary should not be a moral forum where officers of the court legislate on moral matters or where they pass moral judgments on those who enter into the precincts of the court. This view is reinforced by holding up the study of law as a scientific study. It must be recalled that the study of law as an academic subject is a recent phenomenon. One became a lawyer by apprenticing oneself. Once the study of law was introduced into the academy it had to struggle to attain academic respectability. One way of doing this was to give it an aura of scientificity. The orthodox view of science is that science deals with facts. It dispenses with values since they compromise scientific truth. Scientific truth does not rest on moral, social, political, religious, racial, sexual, or gender considerations. What is true is universally true.

In the case of Hart, perhaps, the primary concern is not with the legitimization of the study of law as a scientific study. It seems that he is driven by a craving for logical clarity. If law is law it must be law and not something else. If morality is morality, it must be morality and not something else. If he is attracted to the Austinian jurisprudence, it is precisely because Austin, despite his shortcomings, sought to establish such clarity. His attraction to both Austin and Bentham is exemplified in the observation he makes, namely that both "constantly insisted on the need to distinguish, firmly and with maximum clarity law as it is and law as it ought to be".[73] In addition to this concern with logical clarity, there is also the concern with epistemological clarity. Something is known if it is what it is and not something else. That is, something is clearly known if it can be clearly distinguished from things that are not what it is. Armed with such knowledge then one can intelligently act in the light of one rather than the other. For example, when one is legally adjudicating, one is legally adjudicating and not doing some other type of adjudicating. Similarly, when one is under the obligation to obey the law, one is under the obligation to obey the law and not to obey something else. Indeed, there is no equivocation as to how Hart would construe the proper functions of the three powers that make up the government: the legislative branch would make laws, the judicial branch would interpret laws and adjudicate the disputes that would be brought into the court, and the executive would execute and administer the laws made as determined and interpreted by the courts. The demarcation of the three branches would be firmly and clearly established to avoid any confusion in the performance of duties. In its capacity to make laws, the legislative branch would make any law regardless of how repressive and morally offensive it is without the interference of the other branches of government.

Despite Hart's modification of Austin, law making would be an exclusive function of the uncommanded commander. In the performance of its duties, the judiciary would not interfere with the making or the administration of the laws regardless of how repressive or morally offensive they are. Under the guidance of a subservient judiciary, the administrative organs of the government would faithfully enforce the laws regardless of how repressive or morally offensive they are. It seems to me that it is precisely this kind of thinking that made judicial legitimization of the enslavement and the colonization of Africans possible. It is also the kind of thinking that made the judicial legitimization of apartheid possible. From the standpoint of law, judges, policemen, the armed forces, and administrators could readily absolve themselves of any responsibility in enforcing repressive and inhumane laws. If challenged, they could easily say that they were merely carrying out their legal duties, and, in carrying out their duties, it was not their function to determine whether the laws were moral or immoral, human or inhumane. If those who hired themselves out to carry out these legal duties were themselves victims of these repressive and inhumane laws, it is difficult to imagine that they would zealously carry out these duties. For the most part, they were beneficiaries of these laws. If Hart were an African living under the apartheid regime, or as an African living under colonialism, if, as a Jew, he were living in Nazi Germany instead of Britain, or if he were an African enslaved in European plantations in the Americas, one would have reason to seriously question his sanity. In an assessment of Hartian view, Dugard, a legal scholar from South Africa, has accurately observed that "This view, with the greatest respect, is itself extremely naive and could be advanced only by a legal philosopher who has spent his life in a liberal democracy where the harshness of positivism is tempered by the utilitarian philosophy".[74] Under slavery or colonialism, or as victims of apartheid or as victims of the contemporary authoritarian regimes in Africa today, it would be tragically absurd for Africans to embrace this kind of thinking.

It is frightening to think of the enormous influence that Hart has had especially in the English-speaking world. The influence attests to the enormous insensitivity of those who uphold fidelity to the dominant legal thinking in the English-speaking world—thinking that has been constructed within a European liberal tradition that flourished precisely at a time when Europeans were constructing hell for Africans, to thinking that pays little or no attention to the inhumane world of those who have suffered at the hands of the English and other Europeans and the descendants of Europeans. It also attests to the existence of an enormous gap between dominant legal thinking in the English-speaking world and the emancipatory legal thinking which ought to be the appropriate legal thinking in the African world. It is essential that Africans free themselves from the dominating legal thinking that emanates from the English-speaking world. In the course of such liberation there may arise a possibility of reminding Hart and his fellow devotees that Western legalism as captured in Western legal thinking is not fully intelligible if an African perspective on it is not taken into account. In substituting liberalist legal thinking for Austinian jurisprudence, it appears that Hart forgets that the humanism that is courted by Western liberal legal thinking is,

> a humanism of comprehension—a few mount guard around the treasure of Western culture; the rest are subservient. It would mean that Western humanism, like the Hegelian State, subordinates empirical humanity to a certain idea of man and is uprooting institutions. It would imply that at the end Western Humanism has nothing in common with a humanism in extension, which acknowledged in every man a power more precious than his productive capacity, not by virtue of being an organism endowed with such and such a talent, but as a being capable of self-determination and of situating himself in the world. In its own eyes Western humanism appears as the love of humanity, but for the rest of men it is only the custom and institutions of a group of men, their password and occasionally their battle cry.[75]

It is not totally absurd or erroneous to claim that ink that has been expended in the writing of jurisprudence in the West has concealed much of the workings of Western legal thinking. With all the due respect of Dugard, especially in his commendable effort to expose the shortcomings of the Hartian legal positivism in general and the Hartian version in particular, he too fails to diagnose an essential shortcoming. He sees himself as defending the legal values of Western society which are,

> the well-being and free-development of the individual... freedom from arbitrary arrest and detention without trial; freedom from cruel and unusual punishment, the right to legal representation when the individual's liberty is at stake, the right to be heard in one's own defense before one's liberty is curtailed; equality before the law; freedom of speech and literary expression; freedom of the press; freedom of assembly; and freedom of movement.[76]

These values may have been exemplified in the way that Westerners treat one another, but historically, it is clear that, for centuries, they have had no bearing on the way that Westerners have generally treated Non-Westerners, especially the way that they have treated Africans. Moreover, one cannot help but sense a streak of hubris in Dugard. Instead of recognizing that the values that he believes are Western are essentially human, he appears to see them as essentially Western. It is not a surprise that when Africans and other non-western people affirm these values, Westerners appear to believe that they are becoming Westernized. Here one cannot fail to suspect a paternalist attitude on the part of the Westerners. It is as if, if a non-Westerner wants to assert himself or herself, if he or she seeks self-determination, if he or she wants to affirm his or her liberty, he or she wants to become Western. Even more to the point, if he or she wants to affirm his or her humanity, he or she wants to become Western. This is an attitude that is proper to those who seek to dehumanize other human beings. Aime Cesaire calls our attention to the offensiveness of the humanism practiced by Europeans in Africa during the colonial period.[77] The humanism of apartheid, the humanism of the Nazis, the humanism of the colonizers and slave holders like the humanism of the Idi Amins, Mobutus, and Mugabes is an insult to humanity.

Even if it is granted that law is separate from morality, it does not follow that what law is, is so self-evident that it allows no ambiguity or vagueness. One of the functions of judges is to determine what the law is. In determining what the law is, judges do not merely state what the law is; that is, they do not merely repeat what the legislators have legislated or re-state what the legislators have stated. They occasionally interpret what the law is. Given the fact that on occasion, judges disagree on the interpretation of what law is, surely there is an element of discretion in stating what the law is. With such discretion, there is bound to be a disagreement on what law is and what law ought to be. In other words, firm and maximum clarity on what the law is, is an elusive and, perhaps, a deceptive ideal. Law as it is and law as it ought to be collapse into each other. Instead of blindly maintaining that there is a difference between law as it is and law as it ought to be, the preservation of the integrity of law may necessitate a recognition that law as it ought to be is inherent in law as it is. This will enable those who concern themselves with law to be ever vigilant in construing and interpreting law. It also makes those who overtly concern themselves with law accountable to those who covertly concern themselves with the law. It will serve as a reminder that law is an expression of the condition of being human, a condition in which there is little that is ever definitive. Such a reminder may also expose the futility and the error of attempting to divorce law from other spheres of human existence. The belief that what is should be distinguished from what ought to be may be beneficial to those who are pursuing logical clarity or those who are pursuing some epistemic objectives, but surely one does not want to confuse logical clarity or narrowly tailored epistemic clarity with existential clarity. Moreover, the distinction between what is and what ought to be may be in a sense culture-specific, and it is not without some metaphysical assumption. Metaphysically, there are cultures in which what is, is what is and it is distinguishable from what ought to be. In a different culture, the distinction may be metaphysically meaningless, especially if it happens that what is, is indistinguishable from what ought to be because what is, is constantly in the course of becoming.

Logic, especially in the traditional sense, tends to favor the lifeless, the formal, the immobile, the unchanging, the eternal. Its sphere is in the mechanical. It operates within the realm of the ossified. What is historical or temporal is irrelevant to it. It is precisely in the historical and the temporal that thinking about law takes place, unless of course one has in mind Divine or Natural law. But the Divine and the Natural are culture-specific, and as such, they, too, are bound to the historical and to the temporal. Thinking about law in a non-historical or non-temporal manner will most likely lead to a conservative view about the prevailing social order. Conservativeness may be important for the stability of a legal order, but there are times when a new order is called for, and this will necessitate destabilizing the existing legal order. But, it is also important not to banish logic, since the formal sphere of thinking has role to play in the general spectrum of human thinking. It is another thing, however, to force all human thinking within the framework of logic. It is precisely this illicit move that Hart appears to embrace in his version of legal thinking. It appears that he is forcing legal thinking into the mold of an early phase of analytic philosophy.

The quest for clarity in jurisprudence is a part of the overall quest for clarity that was initially sought by logical analysts and logical positivists. These philosophers, or more accurately, these logicians, construed philosophy exclusively as logical analysis of language. In service to logical clarity, it was their mission to purge language of all misleading and meaningless statements. Those who associated themselves with the analytic movement sought to establish a sharp distinction between statements of fact and non-factual statements. Statements of fact were statements that were in principle subject to empirical verification. Non-factual statements were not subject to verification or to empirical falsifiability. These included moral statements and statements on aesthetics. Statements of logic were not subject to this criterion. Their meaningfulness, truthfulness, or falsehood, could be determined solely by conceptual analysis. Moreover, they did not make substantive claims. They were exclusively of a formal character. Their truth or falsity was merely formal. Hart is to be credited for introducing analytic philosophy in legal thinking. In the context of analytic philosophy, a context in which Hart places statements on the nature of law, the question is whether these statements are factual or non-factual. Austin, the father of legal positivism, believed that they were factual. They were neither formal statements nor moral statements. The sole substance of these statements was nothing more than what the sovereign commanded, and the command could empirically be found out. Hart did not disagree with this statement. He merely modified it to make it clearer. He did this by introducing the rule of recognition that would distinguish a legal command from any other command, especially the command of a gunman. His disagreement with Austin's claim was that law as the command of the sovereign could not be distinguished clearly from the gunman situation writ large. His distinction between having an obligation, such as an obligation that is created by legal command, and being obliged when, for example, an armed robber asks for your money and threatens to shoot you if you do not was intended to sharpen this distinction. The rule of recognition, which according to Hart is a key element in a fully developed concept of law is among other things, intended to render explicit who is and who is not authorized to issue a legal command. It is with this ammunition provided by analytic philosophers that Hart turned to jurisprudence. He hoped thereby to rid jurisprudential language of all ambiguity. Hence his attraction to Bentham and Austin's view that what law is and what law ought to be should be firmly and clearly distinguished.

A fully developed critique of Hartian jurisprudential thinking entails a critique of analytic philosophy. The introduction of logical analysis in jurisprudence de-historicized jurisprudence, and precludes alternative ways of construing jurisprudence. Morton Horwitz has already noted this state of affairs in his critique of Anglo-American jurisprudence titled appropriately "Why Is Anglo-American Jurisprudence Unhistorical".[78] Horwitz correctly points out that "Hart's definition of the province of jurisprudence is designed to reinforce clear boundaries; especially the boundaries between law and morals, law and custom, and, most important of all, law and politics".[79] The separation of law as it is from law as it ought to be, or the separation of law from morality, shielded this separation from its moral and political context. Judges and those who are called upon to administer or enforce law can always put themselves beyond moral and political criticism by claiming that they are only doing what law obligates them to do. It may be immoral, unjust, ungodly or inhumane but they are only doing what is expected of them as officers of the law. Legal education is appropriately carried out when students are trained to focus attention only on what law is and not on what law ought to be.

One cannot by fiat dismiss moral or political consideration from the definition of law, unless one dogmatically opts for the Austinian/Hartian view that law is law. This dogmatism stifles critical thinking, and banishes philosophical thinking from the province of jurisprudence. Such dogmatism may benefit those who are benefiting from the prevailing version of legal order, but for those who are suffering from the prevailing legal order it only secures and promotes the suffering. This way of thinking about law can breed a psychology that is amenable to totalitarianism and gives comfort to those who derive satisfaction from oppressing other human beings. And it is easily understandable why those who are committed to analytic jurisprudence would have an aversion to critical jurisprudence. At least one of their objectives appears to be a simple universe where everything is what it is and not something else. Law as it is as opposed to what it ought to be fits into such a universe. But regardless of how seductive such a universe is, questions about it still linger, even if raising them calls for a less simplified world. For example, if the non-distinction between law as it is and law as it ought to be compromises the integrity of law, the law whose integrity is compromised may be but one conception of law among other conceptions of law. Why must it be assumed that this conception of law is the only conception of law? Why can't there be another conception of law that calls for a non-distinction between what law is and what law ought to be, a conception of law which would not compromise the integrity of law? Making it appear as if there is only one conception of law may render the concept of law obscure, thereby running counter to the assumed pursuit of clarity which is the forte of the legal positivists. But the more important issue here is not the lack of conceptual clarity in what legal positivists are after. It is the material implication of their conceptual project. It gives legitimacy to an oppressive social universe, if only by making law irrelevant to the project of liberation in such a universe. If the oppressed in such a universe were to embrace legal positivism they would be acquiescing to a legal discourse that is indifferent to their suffering. As an oppressed people Africans would be acquiescing to their own oppression if they were to embrace legal positivism. It is especially important for Africans, at this phase of their history, not to embrace the separation of law from morality or the separation of law from politics.

In indigenous African society, moral or ethical matters were essential features of the political landscape. Law was a central aspect of this landscape. Hence, the severance of morality from law de-politicizes law. It fosters the separation of law from politics. The positivistic conception of law encourages such separation. Politics is projected as too partisan, and thereby threatens the integrity of law, since one of the law's virtues is impartiality. It is said that one of the central features of the rule of law is the equal treatment of everyone under the law.[80] Hence those who are trained to think like lawyers are encouraged to divorce their thinking about law from political concerns. The judiciary is not the proper domain of politics. The proper domain of politics is in the political body, the legislature. The would-be lawyers are encouraged to think apolitically. It is precisely this kind of thinking that leads to the abandonment or to the trivialization of justice in the training of lawyers. The training encourages the divorce of law from justice. A law may be unjust but it is still a law. A law is not necessarily just. Hence, those who study law need not necessarily concern themselves with justice. Those who are asked to uphold the law should do so whether it is or it is not just. It is ironic that those who are trained to be indifferent or to be hostile to justice are called upon to ensure that justice prevails in society. Instead of having ministries of justice or departments of justice, we should be having ministries of law and departments of law since those who staff them have been trained in law and not in justice, unless of course being trained in law is the same as being trained in justice, which amounts to an anathema to those who are obsessed with linguistic clarity.

It is precisely this hostility to justice that the sophists exemplified, and it is what provoked a counter hostility from philosophy. Socrates, the philosopher, argued that the viability of the polis depended on the presence of justice in the polis. Instead of recognizing Socrates as the benefactor of the polis, his accusers, among whom were sophists, portrayed him as the enemy of the polis. The portrayal persuaded the majority of those who sat in judgment of Socrates, and he was found guilty and put to death. When thinking like a lawyer takes the form of sophistical thinking, injustice is likely to prevail, or put differently, justice is likely to be compromised. Injustice is likely to pass for justice. Of course, this does not disturb the conscience of a lawyer. He or she has been trained to be insensitive to the collusion of opposites. It is a part of his or her trade. Being trained to think like a lawyer is being socialized into this insensitivity. Being socialized into this insensitivity is not only a threat to the polis, it is also a threat to society. Justice is what holds the polis or society together, short of force or fear. The thinking that is a threat to society is presented as if it is not a threat to society, and the thinking that is not a threat to society is presented as if it is a threat to society. It is this mystification of thinking that the sophists thrived in, and it is the deceptive aspect of this presentation Socrates sought to expose. In African law schools we have generated and continue to generate men and women who are desensitized to the claims of justice, and we complain when they are indifferent to justice. Our law schools continue to imitate European and American law schools. In this condition, we cannot expect the graduates to be nothing more than mostly imitations of their European and American counterparts, and our societies are being transformed to inferior imitations of European and American societies. Our governments subsidize this transformation and law professors are servicing this transformation. In this transformation, the governments are subsidized for non-African governments and by international organizations. As Robert C.Gordon has pointed out in matters of law making,

> Frequently the law in question is made by foreigners drafting constitutions and codes or regulatory laws that must be adopted wholesale as a condition of receiving multilateral assistance. [81]

When foreigners make constitutions and codes or when they provide assistance in making them, they also end up assisting in interpreting them. The economic situation of most of the African nations as it is the case in every nation is woven into an economic fabric, and the captains of economics end up being the captains of law. The linkage of law with economics is not an innovation of the University of Chicago. In the nineteenth century Marx had already pointed out this linkage. He illuminated how legal thinking had been transformed into an engine of capitalism. The African experience of law under the European oppressive regimes provides unquestionable evidence for this linkage. Slavery, colonialism, apartheid, and neo-colonialism were both legal and economic institutions that worked hand in hand.

Thinking like a lawyer does not exist in a social vacuum. It does not exist apart from or in opposition to other types of thinking in society. It reinforces or is reinforced by other types of thinking in society. It is a reflection of a society at a given historical period. Thinking like a lawyer in Western/European societies is a reflection of these societies. It reinforces them. Sophistry is an important feature in them. One sees it in economic life, a life that is distinguished by cutthroat competition—a competition that is judged in terms of economic success and not in terms of virtue. A clamor for economic justice is projected as a threat to these societies. If there is justice it is more or less a camouflaged injustice. In educating economists, there is not even the pretense of teaching moral philosophy or ethics. The study of justice is not a part of the economics curriculum. This is the state of affairs that the West has introduced in Africa.

Let us now imagine what it would be like to train Africans to think like a lawyer. Let us assume that the training is done by Westerners/Europeans. Let us think of the Westerners/Europeans as purveyors of legal education. Since they come into a world where they assume that there is no jurisprudence, they will inculcate sophistical reasoning in African students. Students will be trained to disassociate concern with virtue from what it means to think like a lawyer. As practitioners of law, they will be insensitive to the moral demands of their society and they will compete for clients by displaying the intellectual debates either in the courtroom or outside the courtroom. Like their Western/European counterparts, they will insist that the practice of law be limited to those who are trained the way they are trained. Indeed, they will have it declared illegal for anyone who practices law without the kind of training they have received. The apparent justification in this declaration is the protection of citizens from harms that are likely to be incurred if those who are not trained in law are allowed to practice law. The real reason may lie in preventing citizens from recognizing the effort by those who are trained in law to monopolize legal practice for their personal gain. What they resist is democratization of legal practice.

It does not take much gumption to recognize that the law they practice in post-colonial Africa is similar in many ways to the law that was practiced in colonial Africa. In colonial Africa, colonialist lawyers (who were mainly drawn from the colonizer community) were insensitive to the colonial injustices to which Africans were subjected. The judiciary during the colonial period was a colonialist instrument that European colonizers used to subjugate and repress Africans. In the part of Africa colonized by the British, judicial officers were under His or Her Majesty's Service. They greased the British colonial machinery so that it could operate more effectively. Raising moral questions about the colonial project would not have been in line with the legal profession. It was up to missionaries and other moralizers to raise moral questions. Colonial administrators would not have tolerated missionaries or moralizers who raised moral issues about legal thinking in the colonial project.

The separation of governmental powers may be understood as a product of sophistry. Its truth can be established only after de-mystification. The separation of the legislature from the judiciary is partly intended to provide the judiciary with the authority to curb the tyrannical and oppressive tendencies of the legislature, and to provide the legislature the authority to curb the tyrannical and oppressive tendencies of the judiciary. The legislature is charged with making laws and not adjudicating, interpreting or enforcing the laws. The judiciary is restricted to adjudicating, interpreting, and enforcing the laws. Its task is not to make laws. In its activities it is restricted to the laws that have been enacted by the legislature. The legal profession makes a mockery out of this separation without acknowledging that it is doing so. In adjudicating and interpreting law, the judiciary determines what the law is. Whoever determines what the law is, is the one who truly makes the law. If the judiciary is given the authority to determine what law is, one must wonder whether the legislators know what it is that they make when they make law. The ignorance of law on the part of the legislators provides members of the judiciary with an opportunity to merge interpreting law with making law, and this merger is merged with making law. This merger process is reinforced by other means. In the course of law making, lawmakers draft legal bills with dominant assistance from the members of the legal profession. Before bills are enacted into law, they are presented to legislators for debate, and lawyers (the real drafters of the bill) figure prominently in these debates as advisors to the legislators. In other words, for the most part, the work of the legislature is taken over by the judiciary. In other words, adjudicating becomes legislating. In their chameleon-like nature, members of the judiciary subvert what they are supposed to be doing and also subvert what the legislature is supposed to be doing. Members of the judiciary not only usurp the authority of the legislature. They also invade executive authority. Since the executive branch of government is charged with executing the laws, and the laws are laws as interpreted and determined by the judiciary, the executive branch executes laws that are determined to be laws by the judiciary. By so doing, the judiciary becomes the real executor of the laws. The separation of judicial and executive powers collapses. The police power of the executive branch of government is effectively at the hands of the judiciary. The usurpation of the authority of the legislative by the judiciary and the usurpation of the executive power by the judiciary are concealed under the guise of the doctrine of the separation of powers. Since lawyers are fed with a diet of sophistical thinking, and are thus, not men or women of principle, the usurpation is not in principle offensive. It is a part of thinking like a lawyer. If the notion of the separation of powers is retained in this thinking, it is retained as a mask. It covers the politics of the judiciary, and also the personal politics and values of the judicial members. Under the cover of the judiciary—a branch of government that is supposed to be apolitical lawyers and judges can pursue their political agendas.

The construction of legal thinking as sophistical thinking in the Western world has led to the institutionalization of an adversarial system of law. This is especially the case in the Anglo-American world of law. The life of law is depicted as the life of combat. The courtroom is a battleground between two opposing adversaries. The object is to win for one's client by any means necessary within the bounds of law—bounds that are determined by lawyers. He or she must be an advocate for his or her client and do so zealously. Perhaps, the best depiction of an advocate was illustrated in Lord Henry Brougham's defense of Queen Caroline. He stated,

> An Advocate, in the discharge of his duty, knows but one person in all the world, and that person is his client. To save that client by all means and expedients, and at all hazards and costs to other persons, and amongst them, to himself, is his first and only duty; and in performing this duty he must not regard the alarm, the torments, the destruction which he may bring upon others. Separating the duty of a patriot from that of an advocate, he must go on reckless of consequences, though it should be his unhappy fate to involve his country in confusion.[82]

An advocate who would follow Lord Brougham's recommendation may be driven by a Jesus complex, especially if one is willing to face any consequence for advocating for one's client. It requires a selflessness or lack of self-regard that is rare among mortals. Perhaps, Jesus could open himself to persecution unto death because he was god, or at least the son of God, and as such, he knew he would not truly die, since God is immortal. But for a mere mortal to sacrifice oneself at any cost may either be a result of madness or foolishness. Whereas, an advocate may presume to have a right to self-sacrifice in defense of his or her client, it is another thing all together for him or her to defend his or her client regardless of the consequences to society. In more recent legal thinking Luban has projected legal adversarism as an embodiment of what he calls neutral partisanship. He says,

> Neutral partisanship sees lawyers as hired guns, whose duty of loyalty to their clients means they must, if necessary, do everything the law permits to advance their client's interests—regardless of whether those interests are worthy or base, and regardless of how much collateral damage the lawyer inflicts on third parties.[83]

One cannot ignore the significance of the phrase "everything the law permits". The determination of everything the law permits under "the rule of law" is made by lawyers and is subject to an adversarial thinking. It is likely to embody the evils of adversarism among which is the tyranny of lawyers—a tyranny that is imposed on society at large by the legal profession. The tyranny is likely to be sugarcoated in a way that makes it tolerable to non-lawyers. One cannot expect the lawyers to police themselves. In doing so they are likely to serve their own interests which may be anti-thetical to the interests of society. Legal ethics cannot exclusively be a concern of lawyers or of Professors of Legal Ethics. It is primarily a concern of all citizens. Because lawyers monopolize authority in legal thinking, the majority of citizens play a marginal role as agents of this concern.

Anyone who is familiar with African societies knows that the individual has a sense of being in society, and without society he or she is not. Hence, the protection of the interest of society is paramount. But, it must be observed that this paramouncy is not at the expense of the individual. There is no society without individuals, and there are no individuals without society. The fact that there are societies that repress individuals does not call for the elimination of society all together to end the repression. Regardless of the extent of the individual repression, he or she remains a social being. Westerners may trace their social and political consciousness to the Ancient Greeks, but it is obvious that Broughamian thinking, a thinking that is later embraced by liberal social theory, does not fully demonstrate that Westerners have fully digested the Ancient Greek understanding of what it is to be human, which means that they do not fully understand who they are. If they cannot digest the Hellenic understanding or fully understand who they are as human beings it is not likely that they will understand Africans or the way in which Africans understand themselves.

One possible consequence of such an extreme advocacy is disintegration of society. Monroe Freedman has suggested that,

> the adversary system proceeds on the assumption that the best way to ascertain truth is to present to an impartial judge or jury confrontation between the proponents of conflicting views, assigning to each the task of marshaling and presenting evidence for its side in as thorough and persuasive a way as possible.[84]

Another virtue of the adversary system is said to be that it is the best way to safeguard the interests of the individual against an undue encroachment by the government. Again, as Freedman points out, "Before we will permit the state to deprive any person of life, liberty, or property, we require that certain processes which ensure regard for the dignity of the individual be followed, irrespective of their impact on the determination of truth". It should be noted that truth is not the highest value in the adversary system. It may be sacrificed or deliberately suppressed if a competing value is deemed to be more important. In the case of Brougham, for example, saving the life and the dignity of Queen Caroline was more important than saving national honor or the Royalty. When a lawyer is hired, he or she is expected to exhibit complete loyalty to his or her client. Not to do so is to fail his or her duty as an advocate of his or her client. The truth that the adversary system is expected to midwife is of secondary importance. As an observer of the adversary system in the United States, Susan Estrich has pointed out,

> The adversary system is not the most efficient route to truth; it does not pretend to be. The defendant has the right to remain silent, even when he knows the truth; the right to plead not guilty, even if he is guilty; the right to challenge evidence, even if it is reliable and probative. He has right to counsel, who will tell

> him not to confess, not to answer questions, not to help prosecutors make the case against him.[85]

To be sure, an advocate cannot operate in a vacuum. He or she has to operate within the bounds of law. But it must not be forgotten that the bounds of law are subject to legal determination. Given the sophistical nature of legal reasoning, the determination is sophistical. There is no objective way of setting the bounds. The only semi-objective way of setting them is to find a way that will not compromise the sophistical way of legal reasoning. The legal profession is a monopoly and non-lawyers are excluded by law from interfering with legal matters. Setting the bounds of legal boundaries is a preserve of lawyers. It is a part of the independence of the judiciary. It must be emphasized that no judiciary exists in a socio-cultural vacuum. It is shaped by the socio-cultural context in which it exists. But it is not merely a passive institution; it preserves and promotes a specific socio-cultural existence. Those who constitute membership in it are agents who carry out these functions. For African members of the African judiciary, the issue is whether they are consciously preserving what ought to be preserved in African socio-cultural existence and whether they are promoting what should not to be promoted in African socio-cultural existence. They cannot preserve what ought to be preserved or promoted unless they know what ought to be preserved and what ought to be promoted. Such knowledge cannot be assumed. It must be acquired in law schools. Law schools must be staffed by instructors who have this knowledge and who keep on augmenting it through scholarship. Staffing is a political matter—not in the vulgar sense, but in a sense that recognizes societal ideals. The material that is used for courses must contain information that provides students with an opportunity to think about and participate in the production of this kind of knowledge. Are there such schools in Africa today? Are there instructors in African law schools who are initiating students into this kind of knowledge and into this kind of thinking?

The elemental questions that make up the core of thinking like an African lawyer remain buried in the spirit of pragmatism and practicalness that inform contemporary legal thinking. The zealousness with which legal education pursues the legal practice as an end trumps any interest in legal-social theory—an interest that ought to be taken into consideration in legal practice. In contemporary legal thinking legal education is parceled out into areas of law: public law, private law, law of contract, criminal law, civil procedure law of evidence, constitutional law, law of property, etc. Construing the world of legal education as being nothing more than an aggregate of studies in these areas conceals the irreducible social/cultural whole that informs these areas and that renders them intelligible. It encourages thinking about law that obscures the ideological underpinnings of legal education. Thinking like an African lawyer is guided by African ideological underpinnings of African legal education. In other words, thinking like an African lawyer involves thinking in ways that exemplify commitment to the goals of African well-being. Moreover it fosters a continuous reflection of what constitutes this well-being.

It should be evident that what has been said about thinking like an African lawyer goes beyond the empirical description of what this thinking is. This going beyond is not an aberration or a matter of forgetting what ought not to be forgotten. It is not a failure to distinguish what is from what ought to be. I consciously and intentionally do not want to separate what is from what ought to be. Consequently, an attempt to subject what has been said to an empirical test to determine its correctness or incorrectness misses the substance of what has been said. What ought to be is fundamentally what is. If it is conceded that this is an inappropriate test, it may seem reasonable to ask, what then is the appropriate test? How is one to tell when one is thinking like an African lawyer? These questions do not have easy answers. Thinking like an African lawyer, as is the case with any other kind of thinking like a lawyer, focuses attention on thinking and on how thinking bears on law. Until it is determined what thinking is, it cannot adequately be determined what law is or what being African is. What law is is a matter of thinking about what law is, and what being African is is a matter of thinking about what being African is. Here, it is thinking that is the common denominator. Moreover, thinking in a more fundamental sense is not an activity for the mind, and what is at stake here is not simply a matter of drawing inferences. What is at stake is not the activity that falls under the regime of logic. What then is to be understood as thinking? Differently put, how are we to think of thinking in a way that illuminates what it is?

The path to what thinking is runs into many obstacles. One can only hope that thinking itself will draw us onto itself. One of the major obstacles is the modern Western European metaphysics of thinking. This metaphysics has its early modern roots in Cartesian thinking. I will not go into the Cartesian methodical procedure except to note that for Descartes the first product of the procedure is the discovery of mind—the thinking thing. This thinking thing is what a human being is. It is thinking that guarantees human existence. To be unable to think is to be unable to be human. Thinking like a lawyer is possible because a human being is a thinking being. In other words thinking like a lawyer leads us to the being that thinks, namely a human being. It would appear, then, thinking like an African lawyer should lead us to the African as a human being. This conclusion, however, is precisely the conclusion that modern Europeans rejected. They translated this rejection to the enslavement and colonization of Africans. Modern Europeans took thinking to be a European birthright and birthmark. To think is to think like a European. In Hegelian thinking, for example, Africans are yet to emerge from non-thinking nature, and, consequently, to the extent that legal thinking is possible only for thinking beings, thinking like an African lawyer is identical with thinking like nothing. It is the same as not thinking. Within the modern European ideology of thinking, the question is not only whether there is such a thing as autonomous African thinking like a lawyer; it is whether the African can think at all.

The opinion that what defines a human being is thinking and that a human being is only human to the extent that he is thinking is a half of the Cartesian understanding of thinking and a half of the Cartesian understanding of a human being. Descartes sees the necessity of the existence of God as a guarantee of the truth of human existence, and hence, as a guarantee of human thinking. As a Christian, the God he has in mind is the Christian God. Let us then say Descartes has a theological understanding of human being and a theological understanding of thinking. It would also follow that he has a theological understanding of what it is to think like a lawyer. Moreover, like other Christians, God is the ultimate Law Maker, the ultimate Judge, and the Chief Executive of Law. Given the Christianization of Europe, therefore, it is understandable why Europeans would take a missionary attitude towards Africans. Because Africans are not Christians they do not understand who they are. They have to surrender to the teaching of European missionaries to get a genuine sense of who they are. And because thinking more properly pertains to man, if Africans are to think they can do so only to the extent that they embrace Christian humanism. To think like a lawyer they have to think like a Christian lawyer. Here, according to Christians, the qualification of thinking like a lawyer is superfluous, since it is only a Christian who can think like a lawyer.

For the African, thinking like a lawyer has the above formidable obstacle to overcome. Such thinking calls for de-Europeanization, and hence, de-Christianization. It calls for de-Europeanization and de-Christianization of thinking, and also de-Europeanization and de-Christianization of the African's humanity. The two processes are internally connected for what has happened to African thinking is mirrored in what has happened to African humanity. This spirit of critical negation in both processes may be experienced as taking away oxygen from African life, for, to many Africans, Christianity provides the core meaning of life, the core meaning of existence. To the extent that, for the most part, Christianity in Africa has found its way to the African in the course of Europeanization of Africa, de-Europeanization as de-Christianization may equally be experienced in the same way. To de-Europeanize Africans may be experienced as depriving African life of meaning. If it is borne in mind that Christianity has played a major role in the formation of European modernity, de-Europeanization of Africans may be experienced as a negation of European modernity, a negation that is likely to be experienced as robbing African life of its meaning, or as a revival of the European Africa that was portrayed as the Heart of Darkness. Such a revival, it appears, removes Africa from the project of Enlightenment—a project that is a product of European modernity.

The spirit of critical negation is not exclusively African. It is also to be found in the heart of Western European life and existence. Nietzsche, a European student of the European Christian interpretation of existence, has observed,

> It is the profound suspicious fear of an incurable pessimism which compels whole millennia to cling with their teeth to a religious interpretation of existence: the fear born of that instinct which senses that one might get hold of the truth too soon, before mankind was sufficiently strong, sufficiently hard, sufficient of an artist ...Piety , the "life in God', would, viewed in this light, appear as the subtlest and ultimate product of the fear of truth, as the artist's worship of an intoxication before the most consistent of all falsification, as the will to the inversion of truth, to untruth at any price. Perhaps there has up till now been no finer way of making man himself more beautiful than piety: through piety man can become to so great a degree art, surface, play of colors, goodness, that one no longer suffers at the sight of him.[86]

He further says,

> Perhaps the most solemn concepts which have occasioned the most strife and suffering, the concepts 'God' and 'sin' will one day seem to us of no more importance than a child's toy and a child's troubles seem to an old man—and perhaps 'old man' will then have need of another toy and other troubles—still enough of a child, an eternal child![87]

When Africans embrace the Christian interpretation of existence, they embrace this incurable pessimism regardless of how euphoric this embrace may appear. Beneath the aestheticism that this interpretation embodies there lies what is poisonous to African life. The Christian missionaries projected themselves to Africans as the beacons of civilization, but this was a civilizing mission that was deadly and that continues to be deadly to Africans.

Nietzsche's critique of the Christian interpretation of the interpretation of existence is yet to register in African thinking. African thinking remains in a state of paralysis. In part, this paralysis has come about because the brand of Christianity that European Christian missionaries brought to Africa—evangelical and fundamentalist Christianity—suppressed and repressed the kind of thinking that would expose the fatalistic and pessimistic thinking that Christianity sought to foster. This was accomplished partly by instilling in the African a fundamental fear of eternally living in 'Hell' if he was not 'saved', and by painting a rosy picture of 'Heaven' where the 'saved' Africans would live with other 'saved' ones in eternal bliss in company with angels and God. The suppression and repression of African thinking softened Africans and prepared them for the blind acceptance of the Christian theological interpretation of legal thinking, and also for blind acceptance of the modern European interpretation of legal thinking—the secular expression of the Christian interpretation of jurisprudence. The infestation of African legal thinking by Christianity must be recognized and cured if authentic African thinking is to come into relief. If this does not take place, thinking like an African lawyer will remain nothing more than a terrible dream. Being African for the African will thereby remain nothing more than a terrible dream.

The mystification of European thinking by Christianity has given rise to Western European philosophical thoughtlessness. Martin Heidegger, one of the major contemporary Western European thinkers, has recognized this plight of Western European thinking. In addressing fellow Europeans, he says,

> Let us not fool ourselves. All of us, including those who think professionally, as it were, are often enough thought-poor; we all are far too easily thought-less. Thoughtlessness is an uncanny visitor who comes and goes everywhere in today's world. For nowadays we take in everything in the quickest and cheapest way only to forget it just as quickly, instantly ....The growing thoughtlessness must, therefore, spring from some process that gnaws at the very marrow of man today: man today is *in flight from thinking*. This flight-from-thought is the ground of thoughtlessness. But part of this flight is that man will neither see nor admit it. Man today will even flatly deny this flight from thinking. He will assert the opposite. He will say—and quite rightly- that there were at no time such far-reaching plans, so many inquiries in so many areas, research carried on as passionately as today. Of course. And this display of ingenuity and deliberation has its own usefulness. Such thought remains indispensable. But—it also remains true that it is thinking of special kind.[88]

The thoughtlessness that Heidegger speaks about has become planetary, and it is to be found not only in what passes as philosophical thinking but also in all provinces of thinking. This thoughtlessness is what European 'philosophers' have introduced to Africans as philosophical thinking. Evidently, Africans have not been immunized from it, and it appears that they are yet to recognize how entrenched it has become in their own thinking. It is the subversion of philosophical thinking by Christian thinking that has led Wamba dia-Wamba to ask,

> Is it just a mere accident, a mere contingent fact, that most of the African philosophers are either priests, former seminarians, or organic intellectuals of Christian and Islamic churches? Is it not necessary to examine the effects of those material conditions of emergence of our philosophers on their philosophical discourses?[89]

The proselytizing aspect of Christianity has been incorporated in Western European 'philosophical thinking' and it is primarily as a proselytized commodity that it has reached Africans. Although disguised as a rational activity, it is primarily an article of faith that is to be embraced by Africans, and should they fail to embrace it they are depicted as irrational or as pre-philosophical. Again, as Wamba dia-Wamba asks,

> Why, indeed, are hermeneutics, phenomenology, Althuserianism, logical positivism, Hegelianism, structuralism, pragmatism, dialectical materialism, Thomism, etc., all products of specific material and symbolic conditions (specific ideological struggles), understood by our African philosophers as so many cor-

> rect responses to the philosophical questions in Africa? Why do African philosophers think of these philosophical orientations as being indispensable to the effort of clarifying the mode of being or African being in the world?[90]

In addition to Western European philosophical orientations and to the thinking that is exemplified therein, we have another orientation that one finds emphasized in Western European thinking, that is, the portrayal of thinking as essentially inferential. The central feature here is the reduction of thinking activity to making inferences, and to stating the criteria for validity. The smartest or the cleverest thinker among us is one who has mastered the art of making inferences, and one who can readily detect invalid inferences and the one who is quick at identifying logical possibilities that are not readily accessible. The hegemony and the dominance of this paradigm of thinking have left little room for alternative paradigms of thinking, and for a more profound experience of thinking. There is little room to think about that being that thinks, other than thinking that such a being is a being that infers. Even what is thought in this paradigm of thinking is violated in the sense that it is compelled to give or present itself only in ways that fit this paradigm. The fecundity of that which gives or presents itself is impoverished in the way it gives or presents itself. It is in this context that law has been presented to Africans by the West.

We have allowed ourselves to be rendered oblivious of the plight of our own thinking, and even when some memory is retrieved we are tempted to embrace the specificity of the Western European recovery of their memory as if it were our own. The recovery or the constitution of our own elemental thinking is hindered by the seductiveness of the distorted Western European thinking. If we bear in mind that our destiny is tied to our thinking, the awareness of this destiny remains concealed. Ultimately, legal thinking concerns the destiny of what we are as human beings. The kind of thinking that would bring this into relief is precisely the thinking that is obscured by the reign of the prevailing legal thinking. It is this obscuring that lies at the heart of the thoughtlessness that characterizes contemporary legal thinking.

Thinking like an African lawyer has not been immunized from thoughtlessness that generally prevails in thinking today. We fail to see how thoughtlessness in one area of thinking is internally linked to other areas of thinking. Like their practicing counterparts in other areas of African scholarship, African legal scholars, appear to be lost in this or that area of law. Even more terrifying is their tendency to look to the West for guidance in legal thinking. They appear to have accepted the conventional wisdom in the West that legal thinking in Africa is either underdeveloped is developing. And, obviously, they are in a hurry to overcome underdevelopment in legal thinking so that they can catch up with the developed Western counterparts. Having Western experts in legal thinking has become a part of foreign aid which African governments gladly welcome. The very foundation of these governments, it appears, requires a constitutional legal guidance from the West. That this aid could be a Trojan horse in which there is concealed thoughtlessness barely attracts the attention of those who are called upon to provide guidance in legal thinking. But it is not only those who are called upon to provide guidance in legal thinking who are the culprits. The danger of thoughtlessness, as indicated above, is all pervasive. It has affected political thinking, economic thinking, social and cultural thinking, and even philosophical thinking. Moreover, the detection of thoughtlessness in any area of thinking is linked to the detection of thoughtlessness in every other area of thinking. The awareness of this interconnectedness, as is the case with the detection of thoughtlessness, cannot be pursued intelligently if there is not an awareness of what it is to be thoughtful. Thinking like an African lawyer is linked to thinking like an African economist, like an African politician, like an African artist, etc. The essential defect in the thinking like any one of them is linked to the essential defect in the thinking about the others. This situation allows us to think through essentially what is African in any one of them. Fundamentally understood, thoughtlessness in any area of thinking is a threat to thoughtfulness everywhere.

In an age where thoughtlessness has become entrenched and pervasive, thoughtfulness has become so rare that thoughtlessness passes as thoughtfulness. It is this transposition of opposites in a way that gives rise to the identity of opposites that is the curse of African thinking. Here, I am not beating the drum for Afropessimism. I see myself as making a modest contribution to an ongoing African interpretation of legal thinking in Africa. The growing thoughtlessness in the West poses a formidable threat to African thoughtfulness, and the African hope in countering this danger successfully calls for thoughtfulness that Africans must cultivate within themselves. The 'within' in this context does not call for a withdrawal of Africans into themselves. This is no longer possible and it was never possible. There is no inside into which Africans can withdraw. Like other human beings, Africans are what they are in relation to other human beings, just as other human beings are what they are in relation to Africans. It is in this relationality that we are what we are. Thoughtlessness may be occasioned by others, but remains as a possibility for any one of us regardless of our location in the world. Such awareness precludes us from blaming others for our own thoughtlessness and from assuming that we have a monopoly on thoughtfulness. The possibility of thoughtlessness, as is the case with the possibility of thoughtfulness, belongs to all human beings. The thinking that is embodied in the claim is embodied in thinking like an African lawyer, and this is the case to the extent that our interpretation of thinking like an African lawyer is carried out thoughtfully.

Thinking like an African lawyer can be construed as an instrument in the service of the African legal profession or as in the service of the practitioners of law. It is a resource for attaining the objectives of the African legal profession or of the individual African legal practitioner. In either case, the objectives do not exist in a societal vacuum or in a cultural vacuum and do not exist in a historical and political vacuum. In regard to the history of African people, the objectives have been the objectives of those who have politically sought to acquire the fruits of enslaving and colonizing Africans since the early phase of modern history and the fruits of neo-colonialism and the fruits of apartheid in the late phase. These fruits of African colonialism have been produced, consumed, and marketed primarily by Europeans. Under such circumstances, thinking like a lawyer has been used as a resource for facilitating the enslavement and colonization of Africans. It is consequently proper to ask: who has been the beneficiary of thinking like a lawyer in the post-colonial phase of African history?

With the end of slavery, colonialism, and apartheid, one would have hoped that thinking like a lawyer would have a transformative effect. One would have hoped that thinking like an African lawyer would have had an emancipatory effect in African society, and would facilitate decolonization, end African oppression and exploitation, and lead to the recovery of the sovereignty of Africans over themselves and also to the recovery of resources and the seeking of reparation and recovery for alienated African resources. Unfortunately, the opposite appears to have taken place. Our legal thinking nourishes self-estrangement. Our law schools and legal faculties are sites for this nourishment. It is where we cannibalize ourselves. They are our graveyards.

Authentic thinking like an African lawyer is primarily a resource for the reclamation, reconstruction, and the renaissance of the image of the African. Unfortunately, thinking like an African lawyer has largely become predatory where Africans have continued the predatory nature of Europeans in colonial Africa. Thinking like a lawyer has largely become privatized, nepotistic, and ethnicized. A socialization of thinking like a lawyer has been rejected and deemed incompatible with development of African society. It has been incorporated in the structural adjustment spearheaded by the IMF and the World Bank—institutions that are primarily the means of Western European hegemonies. African legalism must be a part of globalism and the means of assisting Africans to join the global legal economy, the instrument for security, giving legitimacy and promoting neo-liberalist ends. African legal education institutions have been transformed into the laboratories for producing predators and the Judiciary has been used as the instrument for validating or legitimizing legal predatoriness.

Thinking about thinking like an African lawyer as an African resource runs the risk of feeding a modern resource-intensive empire. It is extremely important to recognize how during the slavery, colonial, neo-colonial, and apartheid phases of African history, Africans were used as resources for building and developing the Western European Empire. It was not only natural resources that were exploited, stolen or taken by force by the agents of this empire. Africans themselves were taken as resources—not just their labor, but their humanity, their Africanness. Today, thinking like an African lawyer runs the risk of being expropriated and used in the construction of a global economy—an economy that is not controlled by Africans and where Africans exist as parasites. There are legal ramifications to the conditionality that donors require to provide assistance. The legal aspects of the conditionality are not set by Africans. They are set by non-African donors who might as well be anti-African donors. Global economy requires global legal thinking, and this thinking is one in which African legal thinkers are legal inferiors. The latter benefit from what trickles down. It should not be forgotten that slavery, colonialism, neo-colonialism, and apartheid attained relative success because some Africans contributed to their success. Thinking like a lawyer can be hazardous to Africans. The question here is: how is an African to engage in legal thinking that does not amount to the digging of a grave for Africans? To fully understand what is entailed by this question, and by the answer entailed by it, it is not enough to acquire conventional legal education, or to practice law in a traditional way. It calls for an in-depth reflection on what is at stake in legal thinking in Africa. Such thinking is not provided in prevailing legal education in Africa, and, consequently, legal practice falls short of what it ought to be.

The path to what African legal thinking ought to be calls for staying away from legal thinking that is detached from what it cannot be detached from. African legal thinking is integral to general African thinking. It is a part of African political thinking. It is a part of African social thinking. It is a part of African economic thinking. It is a part of African cultural thinking. It is a part of literary African thinking. It is a part of African religious spiritual thinking. It is a part of African philosophical thinking. In short, it has to be a holistic thinking. Thinking of it this way calls attention to how alienated African law schools are, how alienating legal education is, how alienated African law professors are. How alienating contemporary African legal literature is. How alienating contemporary African legal thinking is. It calls attention to the danger posed by foreign and domestic missionaries of law in Africa. What is at stake in African legal thinking is the humanity of Africans, and humanity is not what one human being can entrust to another human being. Even in our cooperate humanity—in Ubuntu, we cannot live on borrowed humanity. Prevailing globalist thinking like a lawyer is a cover up of the extension of man's inhumanity to man. The goal here is not to enter into a shell where thinking like an African lawyer is to be confined—where he or she can only communicate with fellow Africans. It is to open a space where the longstanding domination and degradation of the African can be contested and where Africans join non-Africans in the joint undertaking to bring about the affirmation of our common human dignity. It is also important to recognize today the talk of common human dignity is a minefield. In legal thinking the talk includes the talk about human rights, and a talk that also has a place in the minefield. One is better off putting the talk on common human dignity and the attendant talk on human rights into a historical context. One should be legitimately paranoid about the legal context of the context for a dialogue about common human dignity or common human rights. It should not be designated by Western European legal missionaries. These missionaries are either consciously or unconsciously under the influence of Christian thinking. By definition, missionaries do not engage in an open dialogue with Others. They profess to have the monopoly of truth. They are out to convert others. Secularism is a camouflage. Africans have had a long history of adverse relation with the Westerners. The deception of the Westerners is unparalleled in human history. Africans should especially be wary of the injection of democracy in the creation of a context for genuine dialogue. It is W.E.B. Du Bois, an African American, who observed that "Western Europe did not and does not want democracy, never believed in it, never practiced it and never without fundamental and basic revolution will".

It is undeniable that the leaders of the global crusade for democracy are primarily from the West. The rule of law, as understood in the West, is the engine of democracy. The favored way of thinking like a lawyer is a way that is deeply rooted in the democratic spirit. If Du Bois is right, Africans are in deep trouble. Thinking like an African lawyer is an unenviable uphill undertaking, an undertaking that verges on criminality in the eyes of those who are in charge of the prevailing empire of law. But it may be worth recalling that the Africans who fought against colonialism and apartheid were depicted as harbingers of darkness. In the Americas those who fought against slavery, those who fought for liberty, were hanged. It is ironic that among the enemies of emancipatory legal thinking are fellow Africans. Without fundamental and revolutionary change, they too will never accept it.

Our post-colonial legal culture and the general culture within which it is embedded are set against this thinking. We will die at our hands and complete what European modernity set in motion. A genuine home security calls for more than ferocious dogs, for more than hiring Securicor or surrounding our residences with barbed and electric fences. Amassing personal property, acquiring more advanced degrees and seeking personal political empowerment especially at the expense of our fellow citizens will not bring about vital security. What we desperately need is ontological security, existential security. We need legal thinking that responds to this vital need. Currently, the need for bare survival is what commands our attention and such attention is indeed warranted, for without meeting basic demands of living there is no place for derivative needs. But if this is all one has to live for, one might as well accept the life of a beast. The colonial powers wanted nothing more for us other than animal existence, and our indigenous dictators want nothing more for us. We said no to the colonialists. We have to say no to the indigenous dictators. We have to say no to the life of a beast. We need African legal thinking that is supportive of this no.

Chapter 4
African Legal Interpretation

Legal interpretation qualifies interpretation. Evidently, there are other interpretations. For example, one can think of a religious interpretation, an economic interpretation, a political interpretation, or a scientific interpretation. There is what one may call a forest of interpretations. It is in this forest that one must seek out a legal interpretation. The seeking must be guided by a pre-understanding of what a legal interpretation is; otherwise, when one encounters it, one will be unable to recognize it, and may mistake it for what it is not. Similarly, if one is seeking an African legal interpretation, one must have a pre-understanding of what one is seeking; otherwise, one will be unable to recognize it, or one may mistake it for what it is not. Navigating in the forest of interpretations is not an easy undertaking since each interpretation is necessarily entangled with other interpretations. It is this entanglement that makes it be what it is. If this were not the case, it would not be a member of the forest that renders it intelligible. The forest of interpretations is the womb of interpretation. It gives birth to them, and it is also in it where they have to reside if they are to be what they are. Let us also note that neither pre-understanding of a legal interpretation nor a pre-understanding of an African legal interpretation is self-evident. Either requires interpretation to render it intelligible. This requirement calls for a reflection on the kind of thinking that is to animate our thinking about African legal interpretation.

Some undisciplined thinkers and writers, among whom I include myself, become victims of unclarity and incomprehension. Lack of discipline makes it difficult to sustain attention to what is presented and creates obstacles to understanding. To avoid these pitfalls, I often make an effort to discipline my thinking and writing. Constant lack of success in these areas has led me to rationalize indisciplineness. I have tried to do so by claiming that most of what I think about or write about is not subject to disciplining. Moreover, to lighten my burden, I like to share it generously with the audience. I insist that members of the audience must learn to cultivate and nurture patience and seek to overcome indisciplineness in themselves as they listen to or read what is presented to them. Impatience is not a philosophical virtue. As they attempt to overcome indisciplineness in themselves, members of the audience should also be open to the possibility that such attempt may fail. The failure may have a positive effect by calling attention to the possibility that thinking is basically indisciplinable. Under the pressure to discipline thinking, embracing indisciplinality is not an easy undertaking. This is especially the case when what is at stake is philosophical thinking—a thinking that appears to be obsessed with the desire to discipline every aspect of thinking.

In philosophy one does not listen or read passively. However, in attentively listening to and reading philosophical work, one finds oneself in the midst of a hydratic experience. In its multiple claims, the unexpected intrudes, and one is never fully successful in blocking off these actual or anticipated intrusions. One's imaginative, dialectical, and creative powers are invoked and exercised in philosophizing, and this process necessarily violates the canons of disciplinarity. Presenters, listeners, and readers come face to face with what is amorphous or with what is in disarray. In Hellenic philosophical experience, for example, this is precisely what Platonic dialogues make prominent. Inescapably, every character that is captured in the Socratic dragnet is compelled to bear the weight of inconclusive generation of the truth of whatever happens to be the subject of philosophical inquiry. Apparently, even Socrates was caught up in his own dragnet as he was often forced to defend his own position. In other words, his dragnet was not his dragnet. He too was subject to dragnet as he awakened others to the subjection to dragnet that philosophy is. It is in this context that I present an African legal interpretation. Of necessity, my presentation is circumscribed by a porous boundary. It is inescapably in disarray.

Strictly speaking, I am responding to a call from African legal interpretation, and I call on you for assistance, just as Socrates solicited assistance from those who were involved in philosophical dialogues. In part, solicitation was occasioned by the ever present danger of being sidetracked from the subject under discussion. In regard to the legal philosopher, Lon L. Fuller has noted that,

> No one more than he runs the risk of forgetting what he is trying to do. In no field more than his is the thinker likely to be lured from his goal into by-paths of his own thought or fall a victim to his own metaphors and abstractions. It is a field which requires a very special effort of orientation. It demands not only that we shall philosophize about the law, but that we shall to some extent philosophize about our own philosophizing to see what it is we are ultimately aiming at.[91]

He is being overly modest. It is not only the legal philosopher who is likely to get forgetful. This is the fate of anyone who seriously dares to take up philosophical thinking in any area of philosophy. Moreover, the notion of philosophizing about our own philosophizing is central not only in legal philosophizing. It is also central in every area of philosophy. Philosophical thinking calls for dialoguing with oneself as one dialogues with others. As we philosophize about African legal interpretation, philosophizing about philosophizing is at stake, and so is philosophizing with ourselves as well as philosophizing with others. Consequently, asking for your assistance in the project at hand is central to the task I am undertaking. It is our task.

As we reflect on what is presented as African legal interpretation, it may be worth asking ourselves, why can't what is presented be presented in a way that dispenses with both interpretation and the interpreter? And more specifically, in regard to the subject matter at hand, why can't the African sense of legal interpretation be presented in a way that dispenses with interpretation and the interpreter? In these questions, there appears to be an assumption that what is presented can dispense with both interpretation and the interpreter. This assumption, however, is not immunized from interpretation or from the interpreter, for such immunization is already an interpretation, and as such it also calls for an interpreter and for interpretation. There is also the possibility that the interpretation itself is in need of interpretation, and this, in turn, is in need of interpretation. To avoid infinite regression and, hence, render understanding impossible, axiomatically, we will problematically assume that in one way or another, interpretation rests on non-interpretation. This resting is not a one-way comportment. Non-interpretation itself rests on interpretation. There is what is enigmatic in every elemental interpretation. It is worth reminding ourselves of the enigma of interpretation as we carry out the task of elucidating the African legal interpretation. It is also worth reminding ourselves that when interpretation is taken up by philosophy it becomes philosophical. It becomes so in a way that renders philosophy subject to interpretation. In this case, it can be correctly said that to philosophize is to interpret. Philosophy is interpretation.

African legal interpretation is subject to multiple interpretations, and all of them are internally related. There is African interpretation of African legal interpretation; there is a legal interpretation of the African; there is an African interpretation of law; there is an African political interpretation of African legal interpretation of law; there is an African economic interpretation of African interpretation of law; and there is an African philosophical interpretation under which an African philosopher subsumes these interpretations. To complicate matters further, each of these interpretations, including an African philosophical interpretation, is penumbral. All interpretations have horizonal margins. Each interpretation leaves space for a further constitution and disclosure of meaning. Otherwise, it would not be an interpretation. An interpretation that is wholly exhaustive contradicts itself as an interpretation, unless it is undertaken by the

Judeo-Christian God or Allah, which is unthinkable to the believers since God or Allah needs no interpretation since he absolutely understands and knows everything. He creates everything, knows fully what He has created, and understands fully what He has created.

As is the case with every other interpretation, African legal interpretation exemplifies an understanding of the nature of legal interpretation. It is an instantiation of the theory of legal interpretation. Whether one can meaningfully speak about "the" theory of legal interpretation depends on whether one can successfully ward off the claim that such a theory does not exist, and against the claim that there exists only a multiplicity of legal interpretations. The expression "African Legal Interpretation" is not intended to take a position one way or the other, if only because the two sides may not be mutually exclusive. Moreover, those to whom or for whom the interpretation of the African legal interpretation is presented are not expected to be passive. As they listen, they have an opportunity to interpret the interpretation.

If meaning is what one is after in the process of legal interpretation, it is essential to bear in mind that meaning does not lie hidden or covered up in what is interpreted, awaiting the interpreter to disclose it. What is interpreted has no inwardness where meaning is stored for possible discovery by the interpreter. One can never have a non-contextual view of interpretation. To have such a view one would have to be a bird that flies high without ever landing which, for a human being, can only be a product of imagination. One is caught up contextually in an interpretation. It is futile to try to extricate oneself from the context of one's meaning. Meaning and what is interpreted are indivisibly linked. There is no in-between where an interpreter could situate himself or herself to bring the two together. Meaning is the flesh of the interpreted, and the interpreter shares in this flesh; for it is only as such that he or she can interpret. One interprets oneself in what one interprets. Accordingly, interpretation is not a mechanical process in which meaning is mechanically extracted from what is interpreted and brought to our attention. It is not an analytical process where one marshals logical tools to break down what is interpreted. It is a meaning constituting process, a process in which the meaning of the interpreter is also constituted. Interpretation brings forth. Accordingly, a part of what is brought forth in African legal interpretation is the sense of being African.

One of the dangers in theorizing about any legal interpretation is being oblivious of the cultural underpinnings of legal interpretation. A related danger is the likelihood of being oblivious of the role that a legal interpretation plays in promoting or in constituting the culture in which it is embedded. As one thinks through African legal interpretation, one is to be mindful of these dangers, especially since the culture of the interpreter or the cultural aspect of the interpretation does not always explicitly manifest itself in the interpretation. There is always a cultural sub-text in every interpreter and in every interpretation. The interpreter who opts for an objectivist interpretation deludes himself or herself and also deludes others.

What is one to think about legal interpretation when it is qualified by the word "African"? The preceding chapter on what it is to think like an African lawyer places us on the path that can lead us to an answer. In addition, to the extent that thinking about African legal interpretation is a part of thinking like an African lawyer, thinking about African legal interpretation can provide further illumination on what it is to think like an African lawyer. Just as the preceding chapter paves a way for an understanding of what is at stake in this chapter, this chapter is itself a path to the understanding of the chapter which comes after it. This perpetual paving of the way is a part of what is essential about thinking. Here, one can benefit from paying attention to a kind of thinking that retraces itself without repeating what has already been thought, and that deepens an understanding of what has already been thought in what is being thought—a cursive/re-cursive thinking. Just as what has been thought informs what is to be thought, what is to be thought informs what has been thought.

What has been thought, as is the case with what is being thought or what is to be thought, is never thought definitively. It is not so much that the subject matter of thinking introduces indefiniteness in thinking. Indefiniteness lies at the core of thinking itself. Inevitably, what is essential about thinking becomes a central aspect of what is being thought. Moreover, indefiniteness is not necessarily an obstacle to understanding. If what is indefinite is to be understood, it can only be understood indefinitely. It testifies to the indefiniteness of thinking. It provides the rhythm of interpretation as well as what is to pass as interpretation. Differently stated, an answer that is yielded by thinking is always pregnant with further questioning. Interpretation arises out of pregnancy and impregnates what is interpreted. The birth of the previous chapter brought into being a pregnant chapter.

Although legal interpretation appears to be a preserve of those in the legal profession, their sense of legal interpretation may be final in matters that narrowly pertain to legal practice and to professional legal scholarship, but this finality is not final. This approach to legal interpretation should not be mistaken for a philosophical approach to legal interpretation—an approach that is often at odds with finality. A philosophical approach to legal interpretation embeds legal interpretation within a philosophical environment. Moreover, it is important to bear in mind that an African legal interpretation, in so far as it is a philosophical interpretation, is subsumed under African philosophy. In illuminating African legal interpretation, we will also be illuminating African philosophy. The interpretation of what is African in this interpretation is indispensable in these intertwining processes since all of them bear directly on what it is to be an African. Being African is to be understood by bringing it under the subjection of interpretation, and to do so is to bring it under the subjection of philosophy. Accordingly, what is meant by the word "African" in the expression "African legal interpretation" is to be sought by the way of philosophy. Pointing out or constituting what it means is not reserved exclusively for those in the legal profession.

From what has been said in the preceding chapter, one is off the path to the understanding of African legal interpretation if one understands the word "African" as designating nothing more than a geographical or a biological factor. Africa is more than a continent. It is also a cultural landscape that has a porous boundary. Continental demarcations are cultural demarcations. Those who reside within these confines are culturally demarcated. Accordingly, the African is more than a bio-physical entity located in empirical space. He or she is situated in a cultural landscape. He or she is a cultural inhabitant of cultural Africa. Thus, when legal interpretation is qualified by the word "African", the word "African" does not designate an abstract geographical sense. It is not a matter of cosmetics, if by cosmetics, we have in mind what covers a surface. The qualification takes us to what is substantive, and what is substantive, in this regard, is the cultural. African legal interpretation is African cultural interpretation.

Given what has transpired in modern history in Africa, the question may be raised as to whether, indeed, there is an African cultural tradition of legal interpretation within which African legal interpretation is to be interpreted and understood. Let us recall that it was a prejudice of the European colonizers that there was no law in indigenous African society, and indeed, it was the mission of the colonizers to introduce law in an otherwise lawless society. In a law-less society, there is no tradition of legal interpretation since there is no law to interpret. From the standpoint of the colonizers, African legal interpretation is the interpretation of the law that colonizers instituted in Africa. African societies may have had customs, but strictly speaking, in the eyes of the colonizers, African customs were not laws. The colonizers' sense of law and its attendant version of legal interpretation, however, do not exhaust the sense of law or the sense of legal interpretation in Africa, unless one has in mind an Africa that colonizers invented.

In Africa, the expression "African legal interpretation" has multiple senses. It could refer to a legal interpretation that has been generated in Africa since the institutionalization of colonialism, and which was in the service of colonial African regimes of law, or it could be a neo-colonial legal interpretation that is in service of neo-colonial regimes. It could also be a legal interpretation that serves authentic African interests from pre-colonial times to the present. It is the latter interpretation that is the subject of our inquiry. It is an interpretation that predates the colonization of Africa, and that runs through both the colonial and post-colonial Africa.

Contrary to what colonizers claimed, prior to the colonization of Africa, African society was not law-less and, indeed, there was an African legal interpretation. Where there is law there is legal interpretation, and equally, where there is legal interpretation there is law. What then, one may ask, is this tradition of African legal interpretation—an interpretation that is pre-colonial and that still runs through the history of African people? Is it more than a legal imaginary? What is the historical reality of the African legal interpretation? Is there an identifiable series of judicial decisions that provided evidence for the existence of a legal tradition of interpretation? Answers to these questions presuppose an understanding of legal interpretation, and how such an interpretation has played out in the history of the African people. It has much to do with the construction of legal interpretation and placing it in the context of the history of the African people—a history that itself may be a construction. As stated earlier, legal interpretation is interpretation of law. As Alexander has correctly noted, "knowing how to interpret law requires knowing what laws are".[92] One should also add that the converse is equally true: knowing what laws are requires knowing how to interpret law. Here, one should also not forget that the notion of knowing is ambiguous. There prevails in the West the view that knowing is exclusively an epistemological matter, and more precisely, a matter of cognition, cognition as what a pure mind intuits. The reduction of knowing in this case impoverishes knowing, for knowing can also be construed as imbued with cultural, social, political and historical significance. The knower, as is the case with knowing, and with what is known, exists in these and other contexts. Thus, when one enquires into African legal interpretation, these contexts are to be taken into account. The inquiry itself is embedded in them. What being African is is at issue in this inquiry.

When one asks what the African tradition of legal interpretation is, one is also asking what the African tradition of interpreting law is. Provided that these two questions are deeply heard, they compel those who hear them to pierce the veil of law. Piercing the veil of law is what is at stake in legal interpretation or in the interpretation of law. Here, one cannot but be in agreement with Savigny who observed, "Law has not existence for itself; rather its essence lies, from a certain perspective in the very life of men"[93]. In the case of law in Africa or in the case of African legal interpretation, it is the life of Africans that is at stake. Let us also bear in mind that it is in African lives that Africans define themselves. An African legal interpretation is an interpretation of African life. It is an interpretation of the manner in which Africans live, and it is itself a living phenomenon. African life is a life in the making, and to properly interpret it, the interpretation must be an interpretation in the making. It has to be a living interpretation. It is only in this way that it can reflect fidelity to African life.

A legal interpretation, as is the case with any other interpretation, is not like a mighty metaphysical sparrow that flies far above the sky freed from terrestrial cultural forces. African legal interpretation, as is the case with any other legal interpretation, is not freed from these forces. It is not only rooted in African culture; it is also a root of African culture. We are to understand a legal interpreter in a similar manner. As an interpreter, he or she does not ride on a metaphysical sparrow. He or she is culturally rooted. Thus, to speak truthfully of a legal interpretation is to situate such a speech in a particular cultural tradition. Legal interpretation is a cultural activity that reflects a particular cultural tradition. There is no legal interpretation that is not culturally rooted. Cultural anthropology is an indispensable feature of legal interpretation, and here, cultural anthropology is not to be understood as a creature of European modernity that was invented to study what Europeans projected as primitive peoples. Cultural anthropology is concerned with human domestic affairs. It is a study of human beings wherever they are, an inscription and interpretation of what it is to be a human being. African legal interpretation is not an exception to cultural claim. It comes into relief in African cultural tradition, and it is only if this tradition is taken seriously that one can have a deeper understanding of what it is. Analogously, one cannot fully understand Anglo-American legal tradition without taking into account Anglo-American culture, and neither can one fully understand legal interpretation in civil law cultures without taking into account these cultures. It is a part of the function of the African legal interpretation to constitute and illuminate African culture in its historical context. It is only in doing so that it can itself be illuminated.

The word "African" when used to qualify legal interpretation is not merely a cosmetic element that is added to legal interpretation. It gives substance to legal interpretation in a manner that substantially differentiates it from other traditions of legal interpretation. If, as said previously, African legal interpretation is rooted in African culture, it is to be seen as a process that is inescapably bound to the interpretation of African culture. What it is is bound to what African culture is. Differently stated, what African culture is concerns itself with what is African about culture. If we bear in mind that no culture is frozen in time, it would follow that as a cultural phenomenon, a legal interpretation is not frozen in time. Accordingly an African legal interpretation is fluid. It is thoroughly temporal. Freezing its meaning does injustice to it.

The difficulty in determining what is African about a legal interpretation is compounded by the difficulty of determining what constitutes a legal interpretation. How one is to distinguish legal interpretation from other interpretations is implicated in how one is to distinguish African legal interpretation from non-African legal interpretations. The latter distinction prepares the way for the illumination of the former distinction. Neither of the two distinctions can be intelligible if what is meant by law is not rendered intelligible. Rendering intelligible is moreover a part of what interpretation implies. To interpret is to attempt to render clear what is not clear. Rendering clear lays the ground for a deeper and broader perception, and for deeper and broader understanding. This rendering clear is not exclusively a passive practice. It is constitutive. What is claimed here may come across as counter intuitive. After all, common sense tells us to interpret is to interpret something. There must be something already there to be interpreted, for one does not interpret nothing. But one should not readily submit to the dictatorship of common sense. Such submission may subvert what is at stake in interpretation. There is more to interpretive thinking than solely rendering what is implicit explicit. Such thinking goes beyond what is, and it is only to this extent that it is able to be faithful to what is. Intrinsic to what is, is what is beyond what is. It is precisely for this reason that thinking is not to be held hostage to a narrow empirical way of thinking. Thinking is inspirational. Put differently, interpretive thinking is more than an analytical, formal, or mechanical activity. It does more than describe. It is constitutive. It is driven and motivated by a beyond. Along this line of thought, when the word "African" qualifies legal interpretation, the word is charged with this beyondness. It is an inspiring word that should animate those who take up African legal interpretation seriously. Here, the distinction between what it is and what it ought to be is to be suspended. Being African is a mode of being that is inspirational. Any attempt to provide a definitive empirical description of this mode of being inevitably yields a faulty definition.

If law requires interpretation, it should be evident that what it is is unclear, and that it is not fully understood. Although this is the case, it should not be implied that what is unclear or what is not fully understood is in full possession of itself waiting to be clarified or to be understood. In every interpretation there is a constitutive aspect. In conventional wisdom, it is generally assumed that it is the task of those who are schooled in law to undertake legal interpretation. Those who are so schooled make up the judiciary. The judicial branch of government makes the determination of what law is. A part of the training of the judicial members entails training in interpretation of law. Once the law-making body in society makes law, the administration of law requires an interpretive organ—the judiciary. Since lawyers make the bulk of the judicial officers, a part of thinking like a lawyer entails the mastery of legal interpretation. This mastery does not take place in a historical or in a cultural vacuum. In its African context, it must take into account African history and African culture. It is a part of African cultural industry. Moreover, whether legal or non-legal, interpretation is conditioned not only by what is interpreted, but also by the interpreter. In legal interpretation what is understood as law conditions the interpretation. It is such understanding that guides the interpreter. Such understanding is deeply rooted in the interpreter's culture. If law students are to master legal interpretation, and do so intelligently—that is, self-consciously—they must do so taking into account their own cultural rootedness as well as the cultural rootedness of the legal interpretation they seek to master. Students of African legal interpretation must be consciously cognizant of their own cultural situation as well as the cultural dimension of the legal interpretation they seek to master. This is or ought to be central to the training of African lawyers. It is and should be a part of legal education in Africa. In so far as African legal philosophers take up African legal interpretation, they must be rooted in African culture if they are to illuminate this interpretation. African legal philosophy is a feature of African culture. It inescapably falls under the regime of African cultural anthropology

In Western democracies, the regime of legal interpretation is expected to take place in the context of the rule of law. Under the rule of law, legal interpretation is expected to be objective and impartial. Apparently, this expectation relies on sticking to the rule of law as it is and not as it ought to be. Except in rare cases, the integrity of legal interpretation lies within the ambit of the precedential legal interpretation. Moreover, although the legal interpreter is implicated in the interpretation of law, he or she is not expected to add a subjective dimension in his or her interpretation. He or she is expected to put aside his or her cultural self. He or she should not add any element that is foreign to law. This is the conventional view of the conception of legal interpretation. In this view, law is a "fact", an entity out there that only needs to be identified. It is objectively out there, the same way that the data of science are traditionally assumed to be objectively out there. It is widely assumed in the Western democracies that judges discover the law. They do not make it. The assumption rests on the assumption of the principle of the separation of powers. On the basis of these assumptions, the proper interpretation of law is intended to be "scientific" or nonpartisan, that is, to be apolitical. For those who study law, as is the case with those who teach law, and as is the case with those who interpret it, law is law. The interpretation of law, as is the case with the teaching or studying of law, aims at making clear that this is indeed the case. In his work on the comparison of Chinese and Western law, Kim reinforces this view. He says, "It takes men to make laws, yet as soon as the laws are made, they become standards and lead an existence quite independently of the men who made them".[94] He attributes this virtue of law to both the Chinese and the Western senses of law. To be true to law, legal interpretation in this view must be impartial. It should exclude moral, social, cultural, political or ideological considerations. It must take itself as a science to do justice to legal interpretation strictly speaking. The belief that law is factually out there has led to the view that legal interpretation amounts to a discovery of meaning that is already embedded in law. Ultimately, the being out there of law implies the being out there of its meaning. In other words, legal interpretation is a discovery of meaning, which is analogous to what Raz has referred to as the retrieval theory of legal meaning.[95] If this were not the case, legal interpretation would lose its integrity and with this loss there would also be a loss of the integrity of law. Obviously, this does not tell us much, for one cannot blindly or dogmatically assume that what law means is inherent in law. Moreover, this claim cannot be construed as self-evident for if this were the case there would be no need for legal interpretation. Indeed, if law needs to be interpreted the implication is that what law is is not self-evident. Its being out there is problematic. Looking out there to law for guidance in interpreting what law is is unsatisfactory. It is not the only way to think of legal interpretation. One can also look at what law ought to be for guidance in interpreting what law is. It can be argued that one who is engaged in interpreting law participates in the constitution of what law is, thereby disagreeing with the conventional view that law is out there the same way that the so called data of science are apparently out there. In other words, in this view the interpreter of law is more than an interpreter of law since he or she is, at the same time, engaged in the constitution of what he or she interprets. It is precisely this predicament that is likely to be concealed in the claim that law is law, an official doctrine in legal positivism, a view that is normally associated with Hart.[96] Hart and fellow positivists want to distinguish sharply the interpretation of law from the constitution of law. They argue that one can adopt the view that looking at what law ought to be for guidance in interpreting what law is only clouds what law is. Those who look at law as it is and not as what it ought to be are likely to argue that in the latter view one introduces into law what is foreign to it. One runs the risk of confusing law with morality. To look at law not as it is but as what it ought to be subverts this scientistic view. It risks an objectivist view of legal interpretation by injecting a subjectivist view, and by this injection, law as a "fact" itself loses its facticity and becomes merely a subjective phenomenon. Law as law loses its integrity and its purity. It should be clear that the conflict in the way law is to be interpreted is, in part, rooted in the conflict in how law is to be understood and how law is to be constituted. It is a conflict that lies at the heart of jurisprudence. The issue of African legal interpretation is inevitably tied to the issue regarding the African sense of what law is. Both issues implicate each other.

Another issue that arises in the attempt to determine the nature of African legal interpretation concerns what is to constitute legal interpretation. What makes an interpretation legal? That is, how is a legal interpretation to be distinguished from other types of interpretation? For example, how is a legal interpretation to be distinguished from a moral, religious or political interpretation? The view that a legal interpretation is nothing more than a legal interpretation—a view that would be music to the ears of legal positivists—simply will not do. The chant that law is law and nothing else may be pleasant music to logicians, but it tells us nothing substantively. It is not helpful to anyone who does not know what a legal interpretation is. A part of being trained to think like a lawyer entails a mastery of the art of legal interpretation. Perhaps, the word "art" here may not accurately convey what lawyers profess to do when they interpret legal documents. The word "art" may lead non-lawyers to see what lawyers do as if it is merely subjective or arbitrary, and thereby compromise objectivity. What lawyers like to convey is that, in interpreting a legal document, they are doing so in an objective or impartial manner. It is convenient for them to believe that what they do is legal science. In interpreting what the law says in the course of adjudication, judges seek to convey the impression that they are doing so objectively and impartially. Whereas in political or in legislative processes subjective and partisan views have a legitimate place, in the liberal Euro-western tradition, the impression that is fostered is that subjective and partisan views have no place since they are contrary to the rule of law. Apparently, once a legislative body enacts law, or once it is declared law by a court of law, whatever subjective or partisan view it happens to have embodied before becoming law mysteriously vanishes. Law becomes purely law, and has to be seen and interpreted as purely law. Those who are formally charged with adjudicating become the sole custodians of law as it is. The judiciary assumes a monopoly in the way law is henceforth to be interpreted. Law acquires an aura of sanctity, and perhaps this is why in the West and increasingly in Africa and in the rest of the world judicial robes are reminiscent of European monastic or clerical regalia. The breach of this monopoly is legally proscribed. That is, if the interpretation of law is an essential part of lawyering, anyone who is not formally admitted to the bar is not legally permitted to practice law and has no authoritative legal pronouncement on what the law is.

To think of the interpretation of law as an art gives the impression that non-lawyers may legitimately participate in the interpretation of law. To reinforce the proscription of practicing law by non-lawyers, the interpretation of law is conveyed as a scientific process—a process that is apparently driven by objectivity and impartiality. The role that culture plays in interpretation is obscured or suppressed. One cannot but see a possible hand of sophistry here. What is not, is presented as what is, and what is, is presented as what is not. In this situation, what is subjective or partisan is projected as if it is objective and impartial, and what is objective or impartial is projected as if it is subjective or partisan. How to characterize the status of what legal interpretation entails is thus problematic, and a good sophistical lawyer will excel in taking advantage of this situation to maximize the interest of his or her client. In the interpretation of law, non-lawyers have a stake not only because the interpretation has an impact on them but also because they make a contribution by accepting it or by rejecting it. To reject or accept it they have to interpret the interpretation.

One way in which the mystification of legal interpretation takes place is to project what is to be interpreted—law, as if its proper domain is the written word. Today, we live under the regime of writing. The primary theater of the drama of the conflict of legal interpretation is in the written word. The documents that a judge or a lawyer is trained to interpret could be constitutions, statutes, codes, written court decisions, or other written materials. To have a better grasp of what is involved in the legal interpretation of these documents, perhaps it is more appropriate to think in terms of the art of interpreting legal documents rather than to think in terms of the art of interpreting legal documents. This is not a minor consideration, for it is not unanimously conceded that there is an objective or an impartial art of interpreting legal documents. The claim that there is an objective or an impartial art of interpreting legal documents may conceal the possibility that a subjective or partisan interpretation is being intentionally or unintentionally passed on as if it were an objective or an impartial interpretation. Relying on precedential interpretation may perpetuate a decision wrongly made. The interpretation that one adopts may be race, class, gender, social, or culture-specific while being portrayed as if it were not. Given this possibility, a critical scrutiny of interpretation is in order. Such a scrutiny may not resolve the conflict in interpretation, but it may awaken the interpreter or the consumer of an interpretation from her or his dogmatic slumber. It may also let in non-lawyers to what really takes place in the brotherhood or sisterhood of lawyers. The mystique of legal interpretation, a mystique that is legally guarded by the members of the cult of lawyering, must be laid bare if the truth of legal interpretation is to be accessible.

An understanding of the orientation that a lawyer or a judge brings to the interpretation of legal texts matters. It has a bearing on how a legal text is interpreted. At the hands of a sophist, or of someone for whom adversarial thinking is the way a lawyer is to think, a legal text will be given a sophistical or a partisan interpretation. One will not seek to find out what the text truly says, for it essentially says nothing other than what the interpreter says it says. Thus, one will seek to construct the text in a way that benefits her or his client. Interpretation may be construed simply as one of the weapons in the lawyer's arsenal that can be employed in the quest for the victory of one's client. In other words, what the text truly says is not of primary concern for the partisan advocate. What matters is to interpret the text in such a way as to maximize the chances of victory. If what the text truly says advances her or his cause, what it says will be embraced. If it does not, she or he will try to construct the text in such a way as to make it say what she or he wants it to say, while denying that such construction is taking place. She or he will try to blur the distinction between what is in the text and what is not in it, and out of this blur, she or he will use whatever rhetorical power she or he has to persuade a judge or a fact finder that her or his interpretation is the correct one. The power in her or his command will be used not necessarily to further the cause of justice, but to further a partisan cause that may have something or nothing to do with justice. In the adversarial approach to legal interpretation, what matters is ultimately not justice. It is victory. Even if it appears that justice is at issue, justice will be a matter of adversarism. To be sure, lawyers are loath of admitting, at least publicly, that justice is in the eyes of the beholder. Thinking of justice this way is the staple diet of legal practice in an adversarial legal order.

As previously observed, by definition, it appears that if there is an interpretation there has to be something there to be interpreted. A sophistical advocate, however, is not bound by this definition, although she or he may pretend to be bound by it. She or he will not hesitate to create what she or he interprets while overtly denying that she or he is doing so. One who excels in this machination in the adversarial system of law is often projected as a good lawyer. On the basis of this unprincipled practice, one can readily see the deceptive nature of the claim that the judicial branch of government is separate from the legislative branch. The art of legal interpretation may be construed in such a way as to deliberately obfuscate this distinction if it serves the interest of a lawyer's client. If the distinction serves the interest of the lawyer's client, the lawyer may insist on the distinction. Under the cover of interpreting the law as it is, a clever mischievous judge or a clever mischievous lawyer may interpret law in a way that condones an unjust law, or a way that condones an unjust effect of law. When called upon to defend himself or herself, he or she can always say, my role is to interpret law not to make law. Similarly, those who are called upon to assist in the administration of law, such as police officers or civil servants, can always make the same claim regardless of how unjust laws are. Their duty, they will claim, is to administer or enforce laws; it is not to make laws. A serious student of justice needs to rethink the distinction between making and interpreting law. Such rethinking has a bearing in the conception and in the administration of law.

We saw a perversion of justice during the enslavement of Africans in the Americas where both the judicial and administrative organs of the government supported slavery. The separation of powers that is the cornerstone of the United States system of government may have been real for white Americans, but for Africans under slavery, as was the case with Native Americans, and women generally, it was a tragic historic mystification. Africans were murdered and lynched legally. In the case of Africans, the deprivation of life, liberty and property was made legal. Native Americans were subjected to the same legal deprivation. Women were legally deprived of their civil and political rights. The interpretation of the Constitution (the fundamental law of the land) supported these deprivations. When the Declaration of Independence by the American colonists asserted that all men are created equal, the interpretation of "men" excluded enslaved Africans, Native Americans and women. Men meant white males of wealth. This meaning constituted the law of the land.

Interpreting legal documents in ways that excluded Africans in the Americas had a counterpart in Africa. When European powers colonized Africa, legal documents were drafted and interpreted in ways that legally disenfranchised Africans. Back in France, the French were boasting of the rights of man, but in Africa, they were systematically depriving Africans of these rights under the assumption that an African was not a man vested with these rights. They adopted the same attitude towards the Indo Chinese. In France, the French put together a historic document titled Declaration of the Rights of Man and Citizen where it is claimed,

> Men are born and remain free and equal in rights. Social distinction may be based only on common utility....The aim of all political associations is to preserve the natural and imprescriptible rights of man. These rights are liberty, property, security and resistance to oppression.[97]

For the meaning of what the French meant by "Man", "Citizen", or by "men" it is helpful to look at the historical operation of this document. By these words, the French had in mind the French Man, the French Citizen, and the French men. In the African regions occupied by the French, the equality, fraternity, and liberty that the French so eloquently spoke about and that they inscribed in their legal system at home had no bearing on the way the French colonial government treated Africans. The French systematically and legally deprived Africans of liberty, deprived them of equality with other human beings, deprived them of fraternity with fellow human beings, and deprived them of their property and subjected them to forced labor. It is this network of deprivations that constituted French colonialism in Africa. As colonial subjects, Africans had no role in interpreting the colonial laws that the French instituted in African colonies. To accept Africans as interpreters of the colonial laws was to accord them a legal right and a privilege would have been inconsistent with their identity as colonial subjects. Legal interpretation was carried out in such a way as to legitimate and promote colonialist interests.

What the French were doing in their colonies in Africa was similar to what the British were doing in their colonies in Africa. The British drafted and interpreted colonialist laws in ways that legitimized and promoted British colonial policy in Africa. The laws were drafted in ways that legitimized and promoted the oppression and exploitation of Africans and in ways that promoted the exploitation and appropriation of African resources. They were interpreted in ways that were detrimental to the property rights of Africans, to the African right to life, to the African right to liberty, to the African right to African labor, and to the African right to African resources. John Locke, an Englishman and a major contributor to the construction of the doctrine of social contract theory, a theory that has contributed significantly to the construction of the modern Western legal theory, asserted that the sole reason for establishing a government was for the protection of property. As Locke has observed, "The great and chief end, therefore, of men's uniting into commonwealths and putting themselves under government is the preservation of their property".[98] Britain regarded the African territories she had occupied and the African inhabitants of these territories as British property and secured it from invasion by other European powers. Governing with the consent of the governed which he espoused in his theory of government and which he thought legitimized governing in his own country had no bearing on Africans that the British ruled without their consent. Since there was no contractual relationship between the British and the Africans, it would be more appropriate to think of the relationship between the two groups in the context of the Hobbesian state of nature. From the standpoint of Africans, it was a relationship characterized by a state of lawlessness, a state in which the British were at war with Africans. In colonial Africa, the British introduced a legal system for Africans that was more fit for animals than it was for human beings. Africans had earlier known this bestial treatment by the English in the English colonies in the New world, and later, in the United States.

During the colonial period in the United States, Africans in the United States were considered to be the property of slave owners. Since it is absurd for property to own property, the purpose of the government was not to protect Africans as persons, but as the property of the European settlers. Thus, government was of the slave owners, by the slave owners, and for the slave owners. Moreover, since it is absurd to think of property as free, it would have been absurd to think of Africans as free since they were construed as property. Thus, the government was intended to protect and preserve the liberty of the free, namely, the slave owners and other European settlers. The laws of the United States were drafted and interpreted in ways that reinforced this state of affairs. The liberty that the Englishman John Stuart Mill so eloquently defended, and that the pursuit of which had earlier brought many of his countrymen to America, was not accorded to Africans. To the extent an African was considered a human being, he or she was considered three fifths of a human being. Apparently, mathematics in the United States, at that time, was so advanced that the architects of United States politics were able to figure out the fractions that must equal a full human being. Apparently, Africans fell short of the total number of fractions. It was an amazing accomplishment for the English immigrants to come up with a mathematico-legal definition of a human being. It took a civil war, a series of Amendments to the US Constitution and the struggle by Africans in the Americas to add up to being human. Up to this time, there are those who are arguing that the process of adding is yet to be complete and the humanity of Africans is yet to be fully realized. Racism played an important role not only in the formulation and understanding of law, but also in legal interpretation.

Other minor colonial powers in Africa, such as Belgium and Portugal, similarly adopted a dual system of laws in Africa. The laws they instituted in Africa, and the way they interpreted them, were detrimental to Africans. They construed the African territories they had occupied as their property, and kept other powers from trespassing. Like their European counterparts, they treated Africans as their property, and robbed Africans not only of their resources, but also robbed them of their labor. Congo, the very heart of Africa, was taken over by King Leopold of Belgium as his personal property, and that included the inhabitants of this territory. Thus, he could have the hands of the inhabitants of this territory mutilated if they resisted conscription into forced labor. The African territories occupied by the Portuguese were considered by the Portuguese as overseas provinces of Portugal until armed struggle by Africans led to their liberation. At the period the Portuguese considered them overseas provinces of Portugal, to be Portuguese possessions. Africans in these territorieswere not accorded the rights and the privileges accorded to the Portuguese citizens in Portugal. Africans were legally considered as being nothing more than resources for the enrichment of Portugal. As stated above they were Portuguese property. The Portuguese enacted and interpreted the laws in ways that secured this property. That is, they enacted and interpreted laws in ways that secured and promoted the dehumanization of Africans.

Despite the rivalry among them, European colonial powers were united in instituting a legal system in Africa and an interpretation of laws that legitimized the subjection of Africans to European oppression and exploitation. Africans were conscripted to assist in the administration of the oppression and exploitation of fellow Africans. They were not permitted to participate in either law making or in the interpretation of the law. Their participation, moreover, was confined to the servicing of the colonial regime on lower levels of colonial administration. In this role, they acted as chiefs, headmen, police assistants, or as assistants in keeping order in prisons. When domestic colonialism (the apartheid regime) was instituted in the Republic of South Africa in 1948, a similar situation prevailed. This regime enacted laws and interpreted laws in ways that dehumanized Africans and in ways that robbed Africans of their property. The enactment of laws and interpretation of laws legitimized the homelessness of Africans in their own motherland. It is ironic that people who had come to Africa apparently to civilize Africans were bent on brutalizing Africans. The interpretation of the laws that prevailed among European jurists and legal scholars failed to reveal this state of affairs if only because it was not intended to bring about this revelation.

The ideological character of the theory of the European legal interpretation that prevailed in Africa is paralleled by the ideological character of the theory of legal interpretation in the so-called New World. The word "parallel" in this case, perhaps, conceals more than it reveals. The historical fact is that the European regimes that were engaged in the dehumanization of Africans and robbing Africans of life, liberty and property were also involved in the European invasion and occupation of the Americas. Each invading European power transformed the territory it occupied into its own property and kept others from trespassing. The inhabitants of these territories became the property of the occupiers. To develop these territories, these European powers turned to Africa, a turn that was facilitated by the fact that they already constructed Africans as beasts of burden. Even before these powers formally colonized Africa, they had already commodified Africans, and were selling them as slaves. European slave traders (who had the support and the protection of their respective national regimes) could readily supply European settlers in the Americas with slave labor. By buying and conscripting Africans to slave labor, these settlers conspired with their European cousins in committing crimes against the common humanity of Africans. When these settlers organized themselves into nations, the resulting nations continued to commit this crime, and they sanctioned it legally. Laws were enacted and interpreted in ways that condemned Africans into inhumanity. As was the case in colonial Africa, Africans had no say in making the laws or in interpreting the laws. Like their counterparts in colonial Africa, their role was to service the dehumanization of Africans—that is, to facilitate their own self-dehumanization.

In the Americas, the roles that laws and the interpretation of the laws have played in the dehumanization of Africans is yet to fully unfold. Although it must be conceded that the debate on legal interpretation in the United States has benefited or can benefit from the contributions made by those involved in Critical Race Theory, skin fixation by those involved prevents them from raising the debate to a level where such fixation gives way to a debate on the more fundamental issues. The fundamental issues bear on what it is to be a human being, and in the case of Africans, it bears on what it is to be an African. To embrace the view that what is fundamental is to be bound in one's skin is precisely to embrace the racist creed that racists have attempted to impose on Africans. To embrace the fundamental issues is not to concede to the view that race does not matter anymore. It is rather to go beyond race for the sake of having a more fundamental grasp of what racism is. Racism is symptomatic. One must decipher this symptom to get to the truth of what is symbolized. In the case of the African, it must be recognized that being an African is not being an African in isolation from other Africans. One is an African in the context of other Africans. Being African is a communal mode of being. Of necessity, being African is being Pan-Africanist, and has to be interpreted accordingly. It is precisely in this regard that one must fault Critical Race Theory. This theory is practice in a concentration camp or in a reservation, in an apartheid homeland. It cuts off a segment of Africans and sets it off from the organic linkage it has with other segments of Africans. This cutting off is a criminal cutting off. It is undertaken by those who are bent on subverting the humanity of Africans. The organic linkage of the segment of Africans is not to be understood on the biological level. Being African is not to be sought in the so-called black genes. Being African and being black (whatever may be meant by being black) are not identical. Being African is being African. Genuine legal interpretive interests of an African or of an Africanist must be Pan-Africanist. An African theory of legal interpretation has to be emancipatory in a Pan-Africanist sense. It must contribute to the liberation of Africans from the overall bondage they are subjected to in concentration camps/reservations/apartheid homelands. Critical Race Theory in the US is practiced in these institutions of bondage. A genuine African legal interpretation seeks a locus outside these institutions. It contests not only oppressive Eurocentric legal interpretation, but also it must contest the legal interpretation that is advocated by those in the Critical Race Theory. The latter is to be contested because it is not radical enough and because, for the most part, it is nothing more than a disguised perpetuation of the Eurocentric tradition of liberal legal interpretation. It furthers the interests of the Civil Rights tradition of legal interpretation. It is an attempt to attain a more radical integration into a Eurocentric social regime—a regime that has distinguished itself in the elemental process of brutalization of Africans. It does not pose a credible threat to this process. By not being Pan-Africanist, it reinforces the balkanization of the African humanity, which, from the perspective of pan-Africanist legal interpretation, could be construed as a crime against the humanity of Africans. That it is for the most part integrationist is made evident by the inattention it has received in the Eurocentric legal interpretation and especially in being embraced by those in the Critical Legal Studies Movement and by those in the Feminist jurisprudence movement.[99] Those in the Critical Legal Studies Movement faulted traditional legal education, legal scholarship, and legal practice for concealing dishonesty in the liberal legal theory, and for concealing the role ideological and class interests played in the formation of legal consciousness. Partly, by going along with those in the Critical Legal Studies Movement, feminist legal scholars faulted the Movement for marginalizing women in legal discourse and in legal practice for failure to take into account the patriarchal dominance in legal education, in legal scholarship, and in legal practice. Generally, feminist legal scholarship is not a threat to the Euro-centered empire of law. It is largely liberalization or a democratization of this empire so that it can make room, primarily, for European women. It is a part of the European liberal legal theory. By seeking to accommodate itself to this tradition, it legitimizes it. In turn, partly in agreeing with feminist legal scholars and with those in the Critical Legal Studies Movement, the advocates of the Critical Race Theory faulted both camps for ignoring the role that race plays in legal education, in legal scholarship, and legal practice. Now the three camps are to be faulted for forming an unholy trinity that functions to conceal the global negative impact the American/Western legal education, legal education and legal practice has had and is having on Africans.

Another interpretive legal tradition that has some impact on Africans is the socialist/interpretive legal tradition. Although this tradition has usually been portrayed as if it were different from the Western legal tradition, for the most part, it remains intrinsically tied to it. It is an outgrowth of the internal contradiction within the Western/interpretive legal tradition. It is largely a result of the Marx/Engels critique of the Western capitalist/bourgeois legalism—the legalism embodied by both the civil and the common law traditions. According to Marx and Engels, this legalism concealed the nature of law in bourgeois/capitalist society. It depicted law as if it were a neutral force in society, and as if it were beyond class conflicts in society while, in reality, it was a tool used by the ruling class to oppress and exploit the working class. According to Marx and Engels, it was the historic task of the proletariat to institute a radical conception and interpretation of law whereby law would be transformed into a revolutionary weapon to rid society of class domination and exploitation, leading to a communist society in which man's inhumanity to man would be eliminated and in which true humanity would prevail. The historic inauguration of this revolutionary view of law was launched in the 1917 Revolution that saw the emergence of the Soviet Union. The Maoist revolution in China was fueled by this view of law. The writings of Marx, Engels, Lenin, and Mao became the official legal documents for anyone who wanted to study law, teach law, make law, administer law, or interpret law. These writings embodied the dialectical materialist theory of legal interpretation that was to guide the proletariat understanding in the construction of the classless society.

The appeal of the dialectical materialist legal theory of interpretation to Africans was understandably seductive. Africans were suffering from colonialist oppression and exploitation. The European capitalist bourgeois class had enriched itself and was enriching itself at the expense of Africans, and the American capitalist bourgeois class had enriched itself by using Africans as slaves. The use of law as a weapon to eliminate colonialism and the attendant oppression and exploitation attracted the attention of a few African leaders. Marx's claim that "The philosophers have only interpreted the world, in various ways; the point, however, is to change it"[100] was music to the ears of leftist African political leaders, not to speak of the masses of Africans who immensely suffered from colonialism. The masses of Africans wanted change. Here, it is important to bear in mind that Marx was a dialectician. One should not think of interpreting the world and changing the world as mutually exclusive. Interpreting the world could harbor changing the world and changing the world could harbor interpreting the world. Put differently, interpreting the world provides guidance to changing the world and changing the world could provide guidance for interpreting the world. Each corrects the other and enriches the other as they interact with each other in the world. Moreover, the world should not be seen as container of both, for the worldhood of the world is such that it is constituted by them. The world is the world as it is interpreted, and is what it is in its changing. The temporality and historicity of the world are essential aspects of the world. They are venues in which and through which the worldhood of the world is constituted.

The power of the dialectical materialist view of law and its attendant ideological interpretation of law was particularly attractive to African leaders such as Kwame Nkrumah of Ghana, Sekou Toure of Guinea, and to a certain extent, Nyerere of Tanzania, who were among those leaders who attempted to institute a socialist interpretation of law in Africa. The revolutionary movements in Angola, Mozambique, Guinea Bissau, and Zimbabwe also were significantly influenced by socialist interpretation of law. Although this interpretation of law was given an African face, it remained an alien force in African societies, and it never really took root in Africa. During the Cold War, African societies were under intense pressure to take a side with either of the two warring camps: either to side with the Soviet Union and her satellites or with the West—the so-called free world. There is an African saying that when elephants fight it is the grass that suffers. This is what precisely happened to Africans during the Cold War. Africans were merely pawns at the hands or the feet of the warring giants. Neither of these giants had the interests of Africans at heart, and the law, as understood and interpreted by either of them, was detrimental to genuine African well-being. Both treated Africa as if it were a *tabula rasa* on which they could inscribe legality. In the aftermath of the end of the Cold War, and the collapse of the Socialist-communist theory of legal interpretation, what appears to prevail in Africa is the conventional Western version of legal interpretation that is masked as a globalist interpretation. The Western version of legal interpretation has now assumed what appears to be a hegemonic status in the world.

Another factor to be taken into consideration in legal interpretation in Africa is the impact that Islamic legal tradition has had, and still has on Africans. Millions of Africans are influenced by Islamic legal tradition. To the extent that such a large number of Africans are Muslims and, hence, governed by Islamic law, Islamic legal interpretation is a factor to be taken into account in delineating African legal interpretation. However, an impression should not be given that Islamic legal interpretation is synonymous with African legal interpretation, or that African legal interpretation is synonymous with Islamic legal interpretation. What needs to be recognized is that in some African societies there is an intersection of the two. And paying attention to this intersection contributes to our knowledge of both African and Islamic legal interpretations. Africa has witnessed and continues to witness a conflict between the Christian and the Islamic legal interpretations as each seeks to gain absolute dominance. The conflict between the two legal interpretations has been going on for centuries not only in Africa but also in other areas of the world. Today, Nigeria is one of the countries in Africa where this drama is playing out.

In general, the conflict between Christianity and Islam had an impact on African jurisprudence, as it had on other areas of African thinking. During the classical period of the expansion of Islam, Muslims attempted to get rid of any Christian vestiges in Africa by forcing Christians and would-be Christians to convert to Islam. From Africa, the holy Islamic war was extended to the Iberian Peninsula. When Muslim power declined, the Christians, in turn, forced the Muslims and Islam out of this peninsula. The Muslims retreated and consolidated their gains in the northern part of Africa. Islam was effectively institutionalized therein, and became the religion of this territory. Islamic jurisprudence was the jurisprudence of the territory, and any other jurisprudence, including indigenous African jurisprudence, was either eliminated or suppressed. In this territory, to think like a lawyer was to think like an Islamic lawyer, since at the heart of Islamic jurisprudence is the Koran and Sunna that inform any true legal interpretation. The Koran, as the word of Allah, is not only the supreme source of law and jurisprudence for those under Islam. It is the supreme guide in legal interpretation. One may look at Hadithi, the words and deeds of the Prophet, or what Moslem jurists have said for guidance in interpreting the law, but ultimately it is the Word of God itself (the Koran) that is the source of ultimate authority.

The resurgence of Christianity, which was, in part, evidenced by the triumph over Muslims, made a historic impact in Africa too. During the period of European exploration in Africa, explorers were paving the way for Christianity. Where they successfully invaded and established colonies, they instituted Christianity, and fought against the attempts to establish Islam. Along with the imposition of Christianity came the imposition of the European ideas about law. Since it was the European view that Africans had neither religion nor law, the imposition was deemed by Europeans to be a gift or a blessing to Africans. The denial, however, was a cover-up for a systematic destruction of indigenous African religion and a systematic destruction of African ideas about law. Moreover, since in indigenous Africa, religion was intertwined with law, from the perspective of Africans, the so-called European gift was a Trojan horse, and the so-called blessing was a curse. In other words, from the African perspective, what the Europeans did was not only sacrilegious but also illegal. Unfortunately, Africans were not in a position to successfully resist the crime that was being perpetrated. Africans were not in a position to fight off this sacrilege or to prosecute and punish Europeans. In a sense, the triumph of Christianity in Africa was not only a triumph of the Christian conception of law; it was also a triumph of the Christian interpretation of law. The Christian conception of law was to reign and so was the Christian interpretation of the Christian Divine Law. Both the Christian conception of law and the Christian interpretation of law were to serve as instruments for securing and furthering the interests of the Christian world. Indeed, the Christian worldview was antithetical to the African worldview. African religions were not otherworldly. They were this-worldly. Moreover, the so-called Christian worldview was essentially the view of Europeans. The African conception and interpretation of law was anathema to Christian Europe. It was a pagan/heathen interpretation that had to be eradicated.

It should be evident now that one of the consequences of the Muslim and Christian invasions of Africa was a concerted effort to eradicate African ideas about law and African traditions of legal interpretation. This effort saw the rise of two legal interpretive systems: the system established by Muslims and the system established by Christian Europeans. The African was a victim of the rivalry between the two systems. His or her task then was and still now is to eradicate this victimization by asserting an autonomous African legal interpretation. This assertion requires that he or she think like an African lawyer, and that he or she undertake a legal interpretation that secures and promotes an African worldview. It also requires paying attention to what being African is, for an African lawyer is the mirror of an African and what is at stake in the African interpretation of African law is the interpretation of what it is to be African.

A major obstacle that lies on the way is the unearthing of the sediments that have been heaped on Africans in the course of the de-Africanization of the African that has been brought about by the Islamization (Arabization) and Christianization (Europeanization) of the African. The integrity of Africa has to be restored. The split of Africa into northern Africa, which erroneously has been depicted as Arab, and the southern Africa that has been depicted as African compromises the integrity of Africa. There is only one Africa, and dividing Africa into geographical areas should not obscure this fact. Whether they are Arabs or not, the inhabitants of North Africa are as African as Africans who inhabit any other part of Africa. The distinction between Arab Africa and Black Africa, as is the distinction between Arab Africans and Black Africans, is a racist distinction and should be abolished.

Whereas it may make sense to speak of Arab Africans, it is senseless and racist to speak of Black Africans. If there is a problem in distinguishing Arab Africans from other Africans, it is a pseudo-problem. The distinction can be made without resorting to racist words. Africans who are not Arabs do not suffer from a need for non-racist words of self-identification. If others suffer from such a need, it is purely imaginary, and what they need is psychoanalysis and psychotherapy. It must also be noted that the view that northern Africa should be a private domain of Islamic law and, hence, subject to Islamic legal interpretation, and the South should be the domain of European law is a view that is detrimental to an African understanding of Africa. Despite the diversity of Africa, Africa must be construed or constituted as a whole, because it is a whole. As their home, Africans should not cede any part of Africa to other people. Thinking like an African lawyer must be a thinking that preserves and that promotes the integrity of Africa. Here one must bear in mind that the borders of Africa are fluid and open, thereby, problematizing them. This also applies to what is understood as Africa. The fluidity and the openness of borders reflect the fluidity and the openness of what is bordered. What is African about Islamic jurisprudence is an integral aspect of African jurisprudence. Since there are African Muslim jurists, in determining what it is to think like an African lawyer, it is essential that what it means to think like an African lawyer in Islam be taken into account. It must not be forgotten that Africa played an important role in the development of Islamic jurisprudence. For example, Cairo, a major center for the study of Islam and Islamic jurisprudence, is where Muhammad b. Idris al-Shafi`i taught and wrote *Risala,* perhaps the first major systematic Islamic documentation of Islamic jurisprudence.

Initially Islam, found its way to Africa through conquest. Today, millions of Africans, especially in the northern, northwestern, and northeastern parts of the African continent, are Muslims. The Islamic holy war (Jihad) led to a forced conversion of millions of Africans to Islam, and with this conversion, Islamic law was imposed on Africans. Initially Arabs waged this war, and later, the war was conducted by Africans and directed against fellow Africans. Later on, Africans played a major role in imposing Islam and Islamic law on the Iberian Peninsula. The success of the conversion of Africans to Islam and of the reception of Islamic law has led to a situation where millions of Africans either think of themselves as Arabs or cannot distinguish their African identity from Arab identity. For example, this is the case in Sudan. Whereas it may be the case elsewhere, in Africa, an African is not defined by the color of his or her skin, nor is the Arab defined by the color of his or her skin. There are those who have the so-called black skin but they do not identify themselves as Africans. They think of themselves as Arabs. Even in the Arabian Peninsula and in the Middle East, there are so-called black skinned people, and they do not think of themselves as Africans. And to be sure, there are those who are both African and Arab at the same time. This problem of identity has a direct bearing on legal identity and on legal interpretation in Africa. There are Africans who fully identify with Islamic legalism and reject being identified with indigenous African legalism. In some places the distinction between Islamic legalism and indigenous African legalism has become blurred as Islamic legalism has become indigenized. The distinction may even be false when one bears in mind that, for Muslims, the Koran is the basic and the only basic legal text. Anything that falls outside this text is not law unless it can somehow be related to the text. The sayings of the Prophet (Muhammad), the stories told about him (hadith) by his companions, the writings of the Islamic jurists, and the utterances of the Islamic holy men have the force of law only if they do not contradict the Koran. Since indigenous African legalism lies outside the Koran it is not recognized as bona fide legalism. One must also take note that Islamic legalism is fundamentally religious and theological. The Koran is the Word of God as revealed to his Prophet. The Koran says there is but only One God, Allah, and Islam is the only way to this One God. Koran is the cornerstone of the only true religion and the only true theology. By inference, it is the only expression of the only true legalism. Islam is one of the most if not the most radical monotheism. To this extent it is more likely to advocate a monotheistic legal interpretation.

As is well known, Africa is polytheistic and harbors multiple religions. Even where one finds monotheism in African communities, one discovers that Africans are not bent on imposing their god on other Africans or on any other people. This is for a reason that is obvious to Africans. To Africans, religion is bound so much to a people's culture that converting one people to the religion of another people is to ask them to relinquish their own culture. There is a tolerance of multiple Gods and multiple religions. It is, perhaps, this tolerance that led the Muslim invaders to treat Africans the same way the Christians treated Africans: that is, as pagans or as heathens. Since, allegedly, the Koran is the latest and the last Word of God, and since this Word encompasses what can be truly deemed legal, it nullifies any claims by Africans to find or create true law outside of the Koran. True jurisprudential interpretation can only take place in the context of the Word. Since outside the context of this Word there is no law or true interpretation of law, an autonomous African law, or an autonomous African interpretation of law, is ruled out a priori.

We have linked the socialist legalism with the civil law legalism, and with the common law legalism. These legalisms are aspects of European legalism. It is time now to link these legalisms with Islamic legalism. The linkage should not be taken as a denial of the autonomy of each of them, or denial of the diversity that is embodied in each of them. If all of them have a common link or a family resemblance, it can be expected that they share a common view on legal interpretation. All of them have canonical written texts in which law is embedded. In common law legalism, there are written constitutions, written acts of parliament, written statutes enacted by legislative bodies, written administrative laws or written judicial decisions. It is the task of the judicial officers to interpret these legal documents in the process of adjudication. The training of lawyers consists in learning the art of interpreting these written documents. In the civil law legalism, judicial officers focus on interpreting legal codes, and the training of lawyers consists in the art of interpreting these codes. In socialist legalism, jurists interpret Marxist, socialist or communist legal texts and lawyers are trained in the art of interpreting these texts. In Islamic tradition Islamic texts are the texts to be interpreted and Islamic jurists are trained to interpret them.

It is obvious that it is only those who can read who have a direct access to written legal texts. Those who cannot read depend on those who can for the interpretation of what these texts say. Even if one can read, the legal texts are written in such an arcane and technical language that only those who are trained in law can read and understand them. It is also to be borne in mind that, although in many societies legislators make laws, the drafting of the laws requires the assistance of lawyers since legislators are not necessarily drawn from the legal profession. Even if non-lawyers can read and interpret them, societies tend to make lawyers the official interpreters of the laws. That is, it is the lawyers who have the final and authoritative say in determining what the legal texts say. The majority of Africans today either cannot read or their reading level is relatively low. This is especially the case in rural areas where the majority of Africans are concentrated. The writing culture is more developed in the urban areas. In modern Africa, colonial government was instrumental in creating this situation. Colonial governments were primarily responsible for creating modern African cities. These cities were established as the headquarters of the government. Educational institutions that were essential for servicing colonialism were established. These institutions provided basic education to Africans—an education that consisted of elementary reading and writing, and handwork knowledge. It was an education suitable for colonial subjects; for intelligent understanding and obeying of colonial orders. It was not an education for law making or for ruling. Colonial governments understood very well the subversive nature of education and they were not about to introduce to Africans the kind of education that would undermine the colonial regime and that would lead to a revolt against colonial oppression. In this effort the government had the full cooperation of European religious orders. Christian missionaries taught the natives how to read and write and great stress was put on how to read the Bible so that they can be better Christians. The interpretation of the Bible that the Christian educators emphasized was consistent with oppression and exploitation of Africans. The so-called brotherhood of men did not include the brotherhood between European men and African men, at least not here on earth. To European colonizers African men were not really men. They were boys who would never grow up. The secular schools that colonial governments established were also designed to infantilize Africans and prevent them from any aspiration to equality with Europeans for the obvious reason that this would be inconsistent with colonial designs. The education that the missionaries provided, as was the case with the education provided by the government, was fully sanctioned by law; that is, it would have been illegal to provide the kind of education that would undermine colonial design. It is not only the case that Africans were excluded from law making in the colonial period. They were also excluded from interpreting law and, similarly, they were excluded from upper levels of law enforcement.

In the case of the Africans who fell under the regime of Islam, the central text to be read, interpreted and understood was the Koran. The Education that was provided to Africans centered on the Koran. It started with the Koran and ended with the knowledge and the recitation of the Koran. It was especially important to read and understand and, if possible, memorize the Koran in Arabic, and when the interpretation of a Koranic word or phrase was at issue the tendency was to look for an Arabic meaning. There was very little in the way of higher education as understood in the West.

Whereas under colonialism there was an institutional effort to prevent Africans from obtaining anti-colonial education, in the United States, during the period of slavery, laws were passed making it a crime for an African to learn how to read and how to write, and also making it criminal for anyone to teach an African how to write or how to read. Reading and writing were construed as means of facilitating insurrection among Africans. Forbidding Africans from knowing how to read or how to write was a means of inhibiting the rise of such an insurrection. Oral Christian exhortation was intended to inculcate obedience in Africans. Obedience to slave masters was presented as if it were a religious duty, and hence as obedience to God. Although there was much suffering due to slavery, the afterlife would be a life of happiness. Although European colonial powers in Africa did not pass laws forbidding Africans from learning how to read or write, they appropriated education and made it an instrument of furthering colonial interests. Again, the education presented by missionaries stressed obedience. Obedience to colonial government was presented as a religious duty and as obedience to God. The reading of the Koran and of the related texts was intended to inculcate submission to Allah. And since Allah is the Supreme lawmaker, the Supreme Judge, and the Chief Executive of the laws binding oneself to the Koran became the ultimate form of submission. Any non-Koranic or anti-Koranic education was anathema in the Islamic community. An attempt was made to eradicate indigenous African education, or at least to subject it to Islamic education.

It is more appropriate to think of Western/European jurisprudence as well as Islamic jurisprudence as the jurisprudence of the book. Those who make up the Islamic community, those who make up the Judeo-Christian community and its secular expression are People of the Book. This is the way they come across. The book is the expression of Truth and it is the locus of Truth. Those who are outside the Book are outside the Truth and are not in possession of the Truth. The truth of our being as human beings is to be found in the Book. Thus, those who are in the Book are in possession of their being and in possession of the truth of their being. Those who are not in the Book are not, and obviously, if they are not, they cannot be in possession of the truth of their being. If they are, their being human is in question, and the truth they profess to have of their being is, in truth, untruth. Apparently Africans are among those human beings whose humanity is in question, for they are a people without a book. When Europeans turned their eyes to Africa, apparently, there were no books to be seen. Consequently, there were no people to be seen. Africa was a continent full of wild people—savages and heathens. Europeans introduced the book, and out of the book they introduced, they created human beings out of the savages. They made sure that these creations were marginally in the book, marginally in the human community. It is this marginality that made up the core of colonialism. The book in which Europeans had their being, and that they set out to introduce to Africans, and to which they set out to subject Africans, was the Bible—the Book of Books.

Those who introduced Islam to Africa had the same attitude towards Africa and towards Africans. Africa was a continent without a book. Africans were people without a Book, and consequently, a people who had no access to the truth of their being. The crusaders of Islam had to introduce the book, the Koran—the Book of books. Anyone outside of the Koran had his or her humanity put into question. Thus, to the members of the Islamic community, the humanity of Africans was questionable. To be fully human and hence access the truth of their being, Africans had to submit to Allah. In earlier times this meant submission through the sword. Those who resisted submission to Allah were put to death. Although, many may have forgotten, millions of Africans today belong to Islam because their ancestors were forced into Islam. As People of the Book, members of the Islamic community share this peoplehood with the members of the Judaic community, and with members of the Christian community. Regardless of the conflicts that exist among the members of this community of the Book, they are all united by the cult of the Book, by the fixation to the Book, their belief that they are the Chosen People, and that they have the monopoly of the Truth of what it is to be human. Despite the occasional quarrels they have with one another, they reinforce one another in the belief that they are Brothers and Sisters in and of the Book. The weight of the Koran, the Bible, and the Torah weighs heavily on Africans, reminding them that they are without a Book, and without a Book, they are outcasts in the human community, and are also outcasts in the realm of Truth.

The Book is the Law. As previously stated, in Islamic jurisprudence the Koran expresses the fundamental law. In the Islamic community those who want to know what the law is must study the Koran. A jurist or a lawyer must learn to interpret the Koran, since it is this interpretation that forms the foundation of all other legal interpretations. The Koran is not just the fundamental religious document in the Islamic community; it is also the fundamental legal document. In the community of Judaism, those who want to know what the law is must study the Torah, the Talmud. The legal interpretation of the Torah is the foundation of all other legal interpretations. The Torah is not only the fundamental document in the Judaic community; it is also the fundamental law. In the Christian community, those who want to know what the law is must study the Bible, especially the New Testament. The legal interpretation of the Bible is the foundation of all other legal interpretations. The Bible is both the fundamental religious document and the fundamental legal document among Christians. That one document can be both a legal document and a religious document has created a serious tension. One notices this tension in the State of Israel where there continues to be a debate on whether what is legal and what is religious are one and the same. The rise of various fundamentalist states in the Islamic world such as Iran and Sudan raises the same debate. In the West, the debate is far from over. In the United States, for example, what is called the Religious Right continues to have a powerful voice in the legal world and in legal interpretation. This is done by pushing the sort of legislation that takes into consideration the Judeo-Christian values.

The Judeo-Christian God is evoked in many official ceremonies, including the swearing in of the President of the United States. Judicial robes and the architecture of the courts continue to remind one of the ecclesiastical robes and architecture. The history of the Western legal tradition indicates that once the Romans became Christian converts, canon law merged with secular law, and the attempt mounted by the architects of liberalism to separate Church from State is still in progress.[101] The same difficulty that one sees in the attempt to separate church from state can be seen in the attempt to separate philosophy from theology. The assimilation of philosophy to theology was effected in the medieval period. As indicated earlier, during this period, philosophical jurisprudence was a part of theological jurisprudence. Today, contrary to what may appears to be the case, philosophy is yet to fully emancipate itself from theology and philosophical jurisprudence is yet to separate itself from theological jurisprudence. This is not to deny that in the Western world secularism appear to be the official faith in the legal world. It is a matter of recognizing that secularism is correlative to theologism and that secularism makes sense only in opposition to theologism. Contrary to what many believe, theology is humanism and as such it expresses the same humanism that secularism expresses. Secularist interpretation is the other side of religious interpretation. They are two sides of the same coin.

Even if one were to grant a separation between theological jurisprudence and secular jurisprudence, it remains a part of the liberal Western tradition that the locus of law is in a written document. This is the case whether what one has in view is the civil law tradition or the common law tradition. What is merely oral is not given as serious legal attention as what is written. There is an enormous implication of this state of affairs on African legal traditions. Although there is some evidence that writing was invented in Africa, and is much older than the writing tradition in Europe, the prevailing view is that the African continent is an oral continent. If Africans are depicted as not being people of the Book, it is because there is no Religious Book to be found among them. There is no Book that is analogous to the Bible, the Koran and or even the Hindu Vedas. There is no Book that expresses the word of God. There are no written commandments of God, and if God be construed as a lawmaker, there is no written documentation of his law. Hence, it is not a fundamental task of the lawyer to interpret the law if the interpretation of the law entails an interpretation of the written world. In indigenous Africa, there are no written constitutions that could make up the fundamental law. There were no codifications of the laws. This does not mean that there were no laws or that there were no interpretations of the laws. Perhaps one of the reasons, other than the fact that in many African societies writing did not exist, is that the knowledge of law could be passed by word of mouth or by practices of law. The communities in which Africans live were small enough to render the knowledge of the law unproblematic. There could have been and indeed there were legal disputes, but these disputes did not stem from the conflict in the interpretation of the laws since laws were not written. For the most part, the disputes arose in connection with conflicts in perception, in evidence or in the way a given dispute was to be adjudicated. The text of law was the world, life itself. What needed to be interpreted was the world, the life. There was no disagreement in textual interpretation. Older people, because they had more experience, were called upon to settle disputes. The objective of the settlement was to restore or promote harmony within the community. In case a witness was needed, he or she was expected not to give partisan evidence, but to state the truth of the matter in question in such a way as to enable the adjudicator to reach a just decision.

The creation of large social entities in modern periods has brought different groups of people who have different customary laws and the task of lawmakers and legal interpreters has become complicated. Writing has become one of the media for stating what the law is and for making law accessible to as many people as possible. This has given rise to a class of people who can read and write, people with special training to draft laws and interpret laws. The right of making laws and interpreting laws has been delegated to this class of people, a class of people whose location in society is problematic. It is problematic in that it has increasingly become a self-serving class. As Robert Gordon has noted,

> Lawyers both individually and in the guilds they organize to regulate themselves and further their collective purposes, have their own agendas, ideologies and interests. Their dominant interests lie in establishing and protecting reliable sources of fees, social status and privileges; and in controlling markets for their services.[102]

Writing and knowing how to read and interpret legal documents have become an ambiguous adventure. On the one hand, it is an effective way of codifying and disseminating laws. On the other hand it is a means by some individuals to empower and enrich themselves at the expense of fellow citizens.

In Chapter Two, it was indicated that African jurisprudence is situated at the intersection of other traditions of jurisprudence. Thus, in part, African legal interpretation is situated at this intersection. The implication of being so situated is that it cannot be entirely foreign to legal interpretations in other traditions of jurisprudence. A student of African legal interpretation does her or his job in conjunction with colleagues in other traditions of jurisprudence. He or she is subject to the scrutiny of his or her colleagues in other traditions just as they are subject to his or her scrutiny. The place of intersection, that is, the place where this reciprocity takes place, is not a place where an African legal interpreter loses her or his identity as an African. It is not a burial ground for African identity. On the contrary, it is a ground for the constitution and for the safeguarding of Africanness. As is the case with every other particular mode of human being, an African is an African in the context of every other human being. In this regard, it should be clear that legal interpretation is more than interpretation of law. It is more in the sense that it is an interpretation of what it is to be a human being. It is a determination and a constitution of what it is to be a human being. We are now in a position to appreciate with greater depth what is involved in legal interpretation. The interpreter has in view not only what she or he is, but also what each one of us is. Prioritizing the concern with whether a legal interpretation is subjective or objective, whether it is true or untrue to the legal text transforms what is secondary into what is primary. What is primary is the view of being human that the legal interpreter has in view. To truly bring into view what is essential in the legal text is to bring into view the picture of being human that is constituted in the legal text.

To see legal interpretation as pointing to what it is to be human is to question a claim by any legal interpreter who assumes the monopoly of legal interpretation. It is precisely for this reason that we have to be on guard against the usurpation of legal interpretation by lawyers and judges: in short, by the officers of the court. It is also for this reason that we must pay closer attention to the so-called experts in legal interpretation. Those we assume to have mastered competency in legal interpretation must be individuals who have mastered competency in understanding what is at stake in being human. Here lies the pitfall of pretentiousness. It is not self-evident what is involved in gaining this competency. Simply because one has gone to law school, or simply because one is a judge, a lawyer or a professor of law, it does not necessarily mean that one is competent in elemental matters that bear on what it is to be human. African law schools have organized along the pattern of Euro-Western law schools where these matters are marginalized.

Another crucial feature in African legal interpretation ought to be the appropriation of the decolonization of Africans. An important aspect of this feature is the decolonization of the legal interpretation in Africa. During the colonial era the primary objective of legal interpretation was to serve colonial order. It was to subject the African to a colonial order, to transform the African into a colonial subject. Integral to this role of legal interpretation was to transform Europeans into sovereigns in relation to Africans. It was to empower and to consolidate European power over Africans. Today, the objective of African legal interpretation is to eradicate this situation. It must be a source of empowerment for Africans. It must aim at the restoration of African agency—the agency in which Africans determine who and what they are. Moreover, the determination is not simple a reversal of what European colonizers did. It must not be a determination that is predicated on depriving other human beings of their role in determining who or what they are. It must not be parasitic or simply a reaction to European colonialism. It should open up a space in which humanity in extension and in intention can come into relief. Moreover, it is not to be simply a blind recovery of pre-colonial African existence. It should be a recovery of whatever it is that secures and promotes the humanity of the African, and a rejection of whatever stands on the way to such recovery. For example, there is a need to rethink the role that African feminist jurisprudence can play in guiding such recovery. The rule of African males over African females is one of the rules that prevailed and that still prevails in many African societies, and it must be eradicated. Such prevalence is incompatible with human dignity. African legal interpretation must be carried out in such a way as to facilitate the eradication of this rule. It is to serve the cause of human dignity, and not the cause of depriving human beings of their dignity. Law ought to be interpreted in a way that eliminates masculinist legal interpretation. Moreover, since the cause of human dignity is the cause of all human beings, African legal interpretation is to be carried out in such a way as not to enclose the African in an African cocoon and cut him or her off from other human beings. The dignity of human beings is indivisible. Hence, properly carried out, African legal interpretation should be such as to open an indivisible space where all human beings and not just Africans can affirm and practice the kinship they have with one another. If it is to serve human rights as it must, it must be from the standpoint of this indivisible human space. It is this standpoint—a standpoint in which the African is not a foreigner to any other human being, and in which no non-African is a foreigner to the African—that is to guide the perception and interpretations of promulgated Human Rights documents. It is that on which the legitimacy of the trial of those who violate these Rights is to be grounded. One of the obstacles in the realization of universal human rights in Africa and in the constitution of the attendant legal interpretation is the nation-state—a modern European creature. Under the assumption that every nation-state is sovereign, intervention of nation-states in each other's jurisdiction to implement the enforcement of human rights faces severe obstacles.

One of the objectives in what has been said above is to distinguish legal interpretation from other types of interpretation. Whether this objective has or has not been met, there is a presupposed assumption that must be considered if one is to have a more comprehensive understanding of a legal interpretation. One of the objectives of making distinctions is to attain clarity. Greater clarity is expected to lead to greater or better understanding. This expectation is sensible. The clarification that comes about through making distinctions improves our understanding. But where distinctions ought not to be made, making them does not fail to improve our understanding. It may also be a stumbling block to our understanding. For example, the liberal (Western) understanding of human society construes human society as consisting of nothing more than an aggregate of autonomous individuals. Whatever individuals have in common with one another is artificially constructed. To claim that what one human being has in common with other human beings is artificially constructed is to make a claim that obscures what it is to be human. Being human is an indivisible mode of being. That is to say, each human being, qua human being, has an intrinsic bond with every other human being and it is this bond that makes each human being a human being. Analogously, it may be worthwhile to point out that, although one may attain greater clarity and better understanding of what legal interpretation is by setting it apart from other types of interpretation, this setting apart may be a hindrance to a comprehension of legal interpretation. To the extent that legal interpretation is disclosive of what it is to be a human being, it is bound to and is inseparable from other interpretations in so far as they too are disclosive of what it is to be human. The implication here is that legal interpretation is fully what it is by implicating and by being implicated by other interpretations. Thus, it does not outrage our understanding to note a political or an economic dimension in legal interpretation. This is especially the case if we have a fuller understanding of politics or a fuller understanding of economics. By fuller, it is to be understood a conception of politics or a conception of economics that is the site of the disclosure of what it is to be a human being. In regard to African legal interpretation, it should therefore be clear that at stake is the political and economic direction to being African. This does not amount to reducing African legal interpretation to the political or to the economic interpretation of being African. Such reduction, especially in the latter case, can lead to a simplistic notion that one finds in orthodox Marxism where capitalist economics is depicted as the sole engine of human history. It is a matter of recognizing the full import of what is at stake in African legal interpretation.

The pursuit of African legal interpretation is multi-dimensional. It cannot be solely a re-action to the colonial era or to the neo-colonial era. It has an important intra-African role to play. It ought to highlight the obstacles that lie on the way in the effort to realize and constitute the dignity of being African in the African. With such highlighting, a path opens up leading the way to the success of this effort. On the instrumental level, African legal interpretation should be a resource for the reconstruction and the construction of Africa for Africans. In the colonial era, and unfortunately in the post-colonial era, legal interpretation was a resource for the reconstruction and the construction of Africa for non-Africans. Even where it is not used as a resource for the acquisition and maximization of non-African interests, for the most part, it is used for the acquisition and maximization of individual, class, gender, and ethnic interests. It has been privatized and used for self-gain rather than for African public well-being. The privatization of African legal interpretation has been sanctioned by modern professionalism. Whereas it ought to be a public resource, it is largely owned and controlled by private interests. The pressure to privatize, especially emanating from the West and embraced by the rising African bourgeoisie, is eclipsing the legal interpretation that can rescue Africans from the deterioration of their dignity as human beings. Whatever else can be blamed for such ills as the corruption and political difficulties we are having in Africa, the way that law has come to be understood and the manner that legal practice is carried out play an important role in institutionalizing these ills.

African legal interpretation is one of the pre-eminent African resources—a resource for the constitution and re-constitution of what it is to be African. It should be perceived and understood as such not only by those who are formally designated as the custodians of legal interpretation in Africa (lawyers, judges, and those formally charged with the administration of law), but also by each and every African. When what is at stake is being African, no African is dispensable. Indeed to the extent that an African is mindful of his or her Africanness, legal interpretation is a practice to which every African has to pay attention. Every African should and ought to have a say not only in determining what it is to be an African but also in the practice of self-reconstruction. In the latter case it is to be borne in mind that no African is unaffected by colonialist and neo-colonialist viruses. Here, it would be naïve and disingenuous to claim that what stands on the way to the establishment of the reign of human rights in Africa is exclusively of foreign origin. For the most part, intra-African legal interpretation and, in general, legal practice in Africa have contributed and are contributing to the dehumanization of Africans. The struggle for a liberating legal interpretation in African continues. What has been and what is patently clear is that legal education in Africa is not a part of this struggle, and with an exception here and there of isolated practitioners of law, the legal profession appears to be unconcerned. Legal interpretation in Africa today is a resource or a commodity in the market economy. For the most part, it benefits the few who are rich, or the few who are politically powerful. For the many, it is a curse, and a source of deep seated pessimism.

Just as it has been claimed in the previous chapter that a legal mind which is detached from what it cannot be detached from is an obfuscation of legal mind, so is a legal interpretation that is detached from what it cannot be detached from. African legal interpretation is animated by African culture and is a part of African history. It is beneficial in the interpretation of the interpretation of African legal interpretation to stay away from the missionaries of interpretation from foreign cultures, from foreign histories, or from their African converts. In regard to African legal interpretation, African African interpreters can better be guided by Chinua Achebe's observation that "proverbs are the palm-oil with which words are eaten".[103] This is true not only among the Ibo of Nigeria. It is a part of general African culture. There is what is proverbial about what is said about African interpretation of legal interpretation. Normally, what is said and what is heard cannot be chewed or digested without palm oil. Palm oil sweetens what is said or heard so that it can be digested and properly nourish the audience.

In indigenous Africa, proverbs were central to the art of communication and expression. Communication of important matters intended to have a long-lasting effect was subject to specific modes of communication and expression. Proverbs performed this task. This is especially important in communicating with younger people. Younger people lack maturity and experience, and are impatient. The use of proverbs by the elders was intended to help the young in the process of maturation. The assumption was that elders had lived long enough to have a deeper and broader cultural and historical experience to provide wiser guidance in the making of important decisions, among which were legal decisions. Accordingly, for the most part, legal interpretations were undertaken by the elders. Since, at times, instant gratification can be hazardous, advice from the elders was intended to protect young people from making unwise decisions. It is the council of the elders that was in charge of making legal decisions and other decisions that were essential for the preservation of the community. Within the family, parents were expected to provide advice to children on how to live well as members of the community, and blessed was the family that had grandparents. Grandparents rather than parents were the ones who played a major role in the transmission of ancestral wisdom. They were the custodians of cultural gems and were closer to the ancestors. Ancestors were the bedrock of cultural and historical knowledge within which law was to be understood.

Today, the embrace of foreign aid in legal interpretation dislocates young Africans from their parents, from their grandparents, and from their ancestors. With this dislocation they get adopted by non-African parents, grandparents, and by non-African ancestors. They get attached to non-African cultures, and, at times, to anti-African cultures and histories and use these new acquisitions consciously or unconsciously to undertake legal interpretation. By doing so, they replace the elders as the custodians of legal interpretation with non-African custodians. How to communicate the knowledge of legal interpretation has also undergone radical changes. The use of proverbs in communication and expression is gradually dying out. Proverbs now appear anachronistic and are deemed to be obstacles to communication and expression. What appears to prevail is what is instantly grasped. Time for reflection is taken to be a waste of time. What is not immediately understood is almost instinctively set aside, not to be picked up later but to be permanently forgotten.

Lack of insight into African cultural and historical knowledge renders young people easy prey to foreign cultural and historical underpinnings of the apparently neutral legal interpretation. Legal interpretation that is detached from what it cannot be detached from is presented to them as if it is detached from what it cannot be detached from. This obfuscation is called legal education. Our law schools foster this kind of education. They have an open door to the young, doors that have become closed to African elders. The young are without the mentoring of African elders. The professors, whether expatriates or domestic, have very little knowledge of African culture and historical heritage and dismiss this knowledge either consciously or unconsciously as a hindrance to legal education. The use of African culture and African history as integral to carrying out legal interpretations appears to have no place in the legal academy. What matters is European culture and history. In legal interpretation what matters is the legal culture and legal history of Europeans, which is a part of the general European culture and history.

Legal education in Africa has become a process of alienating African youth from African culture and from African history. This process is carried out in legal interpretation. The elders are deemed illiterate and primitive in matters of legal interpretation, and this perpetuates the European colonial project in a new guise. Colonial legal education is a preparation of a cemetery for the continuation of the burial of African culture. Those of us who shave our heads as a sign of mourning do so every time we think of what is happening to our youth in law schools. Other Africans can do what mourning time calls for in their communities. If our governments allow it and if the heads of the law schools allow it there should be a poster at the entrance of the law school campuses saying "Attending law school here can be hazardous to your life". Unfortunately, most of our government leaders and deans of our law schools are listening to a different drummer, most likely the drummer of death.

Chapter 5
Otieno Case and African Jurisprudence

> We do not claim, of course, that the Bantu are capable of formulating a philosophical treatise, complete with an adequate vocabulary. It is our job to proceed to such systematic development. It is we who will be able to tell them, in precise terms, what their inmost concept of being is. They will recognize themselves in our words and will acquiesce, saying, "You understand us: you know us completely: you 'know' in the way we 'know'.[104]

The above words were uttered by a Belgian missionary who served in Africa in the colonial phase of African history. What he means by "we" is not restricted to the Belgians. It covers all European peoples. He was speaking on their behalf. For the time being, let us set aside whether European peoples had consented to have him speak on their behalf. What appears to be an indisputable fact is that Europeans who read these words, to my knowledge, did not dispute what they say. Silence speaks volumes. Moreover, what the Belgian missionary says about the Bantu is not restricted to the Bantu. The Bantu he speaks about encompass all Africans. To my knowledge, he did not ask the Bantu whether he could speak to his fellow countrymen on their behalf, and neither did he ask Africans whether, in general, he could speak on their behalf. This did not bother fellow Europeans. To my knowledge, the fact is that this was not contested by fellow Europeans. This, however, should not come as a surprise to Africans. During the colonial period, Europeans had taken on themselves the liberty and responsibility of speaking to fellow Europeans about Africans without the consultation of Africans. In the post-colonial period, it is debatable whether Europeans have ceased to do so. To be sure, what Tempels said about Africans is not fashionable today. Very few of his kind have the courage to speak the way he did. Apparently, speaking this way has become anachronistic. Although it does not make sense to flog a dead horse, language has a chameleonlike quality to it. What disappears can assume a different form and continue to thrive. By conceiving Africa as underdeveloped, Tempel's kind are tempted to come to Africa as missionaries of development, since the assumption is that Africans are not in position to do so by themselves. The development of African legal philosophy, as is the case with the development of African jurisprudence, in Africa falls under the regime of the Western missionary project. Jurisprudence in Africa is one of the theaters where Europeans and Anglo-Americans have unilaterally assumed the right to speak about Africans without their consent—a consent that cannot be given without sacrificing self-determination.

Whereas European modernity has distinguished itself in pushing for self-determination, Europeans distinguished themselves in the colonial period by ensuring that the African will to self-determination was systematically suppressed or liquidated. Europeans restricted the privilege of self-determination to themselves and inhibited it in others. Evidently, colonizing others hinders their self-determination. Anti-colonial struggle on the part of Africans had as its goal the stopping of this European hubris and injustice by defending the African will to self-determination. Africans wanted to speak for themselves to themselves and to non-Africans. They wanted to bring to an end European dictatorship in the course of self-determination. One of the theaters of this dictatorship was in the domain of law. Colonial laws and judicial decisions were in the service of the colonial order. The stream of these laws and decisions did not dry up when African countries attained formal political independence.

In the light of what the Belgian missionary says, the vocabulary of the language of law in colonial Africa and in post-colonial Africa calls for special scrutiny, and so is the language of African legal philosophy. One of the issues is whether, in regard to Africa, legal discourse has been purged of paternalistic legalism. Today, authentic African legal discourse cannot come into relief without decolonization of this discourse. Formal political independence in Africa was not accompanied by formal independence of African legal discourse. The legal vocabulary introduced during the colonial period continues to dominate African legal discourse. Substantive independence in these and other spheres of African social existence is still in the making. A part of this process must entail a rethinking of the language that is to guide this process. What is to be taken as African legal philosophy or African jurisprudence has to be subjected to a dialectical assessment. Otherwise, a perpetuation of what is detrimental to African well-being will be reinforced. How African legal philosophy is to be understood matters substantially and so is the way that legal adjudication is to be construed. Either is essential for African renaissance and for the promotion of African well-being. Judicial decisions in Africa have a prominent role in this renaissance and in the promotion of African well-being. These decisions are to be made in the light of these objects and are to be interpreted and evaluated accordingly. To be made and interpreted this way is to recognize their grounding in the course of justice. The practice of justice is at the center of African well-being. It is this practice that must animate law-making, legal interpretation, and adjudication.

A legal case in Africa can be understood or interpreted in a way that makes it paradigmatic of the jurisprudential situation in Africa. This approach situates African legal interpretation, thinking like an African lawyer, and African jurisprudence. What was said at the introductory chapter is likewise herein situated. This is not exclusively the case because at issue is African jurisprudence. Every legal decision is not only a mirror of the jurisprudence within which it is situated but also a mirror of what is understood as jurisprudence in general. It implicates all those who become involved in it in a discussion of jurisprudence in its particularity and its generality.

Normally, in a legal case, what catches our attention is the dispute that brings litigants to court. Also, our attention may be readily drawn to litigants, lawyers, and judges depending on their prominence or the prominence of the case in which they are involved. What, for the most part, lies beyond our immediate attention is the law—not the law in the sense of the law that is applicable to the dispute at hand, but to the nature of law generally. It can be assumed reasonably that neither judges nor lawyers in the normal course of their work pay serious attention to law in this general sense, even if it has a direct bearing on what they do. The fact that it has direct bearing on what they do is not self-evident. It is the task of the legal philosopher to render what is not self-evident in law or about law self-evident. This making self-evident is an ongoing process. That is, what a legal decision stands for is subject to an endless inquiry. It is this open-ended articulation of the foundation of the legal decision that constitutes the heart of jurisprudence. Let us turn to a Kenyan case, Virginia Edith Wambui Otieno v. Joash Ochieng' Ougo and Omolo Siranga (hereafter referred to as the Otieno case) for an illustration of African jurisprudence.

Silvanus Melea Otieno, a prominent lawyer in Kenya, died on December 20, 1986. His body remained unburied for 154 days. The delay was occasioned by the events that took place between his death and his burial. After Mr. Otieno's death, his wife, Virginia Edith Wambui, started making funeral preparations. When the word of her husband's death got around, Mr. Joash Ochieng Ougo, Mr. Otieno's brother, and Mr. Omolo Siranga, a representative of the clan to which Mr. Otieno belonged, came to the Otieno residence to offer condolences and to render assistance with funeral arrangements. At a point in the conversation, Mrs. Otieno indicated that she wanted her husband's body to be buried at their Ngong farm, located near Nairobi, the capital of Kenya. On it, she and her husband had already built a house, where they resided for several years. She claimed that her husband had expressed the desire to be buried there. Mr. Ougo and Mr. Siranga wanted the body to be buried at Nyamila village in Nyalgunga, a Sub-location in Siaya District in the Western part of Kenya. It is at this village where Mr. Otieno was born, and where they alleged was his real home. When it proved impossible to reach an agreement, Mrs. Otieno decided to go ahead and make arrangements for her husband's burial at the place of her choice without any further consultation with Mr. Ougo and Mr. Siranga. She announced that the burial would take place on January 3 at the family's farm in Ngong. Mr. Ougo and Mr. Otieno announced that the burial would take place the same day at the same time hundreds of miles away at Nyamila village. To ensure that Mr. Ougo and Mr. Siranga would not remove the body from the mortuary, Mrs. Otieno and her lawyer, John Khaminwa, obtained a court injunction restraining the two gentlemen from removing the body. Mr. Ougo and Mr. Siranga appealed the ruling and the Court issued an injunction blocking the removal and burial at either place pending the final determination as to who had the legal custody of the body, and who had the legal right to bury it. Mrs. Otieno went to the High Court and specifically prayed that the court grant her the custody of her husband's body, and the right to bury it at the place of her choice. The Court, presided by Judge Shields, an Englishman, ruled that Mr. Otieno and Mr. Siranga had no standing, and ruled in favor of Mrs. Otieno. Thereafter, Mr. Ougo and Mr. Siranga with Mr. Richard Kwach as their lawyer appealed to the Court of Appeal and argued that Judge Shields had failed to consider relevant law in his decision. The Court of Appeal ruled in their favor and indicated that the matter was to be referred back to the High Court for another trial taking into account the relevant law. This time, the Court ruled in favor of Ougo and Siranga. Mrs. Otieno appealed to the Court of Appeal and lost. Mr. Ougo and Mr. Siranga were awarded the custody of the body, and were allowed to bury it at Nyalgunga. Mrs. Otieno was informed that she could participate in the funeral arrangements, but she declined to do so. Finally, on May 23, Mr. Otieno's body was laid to rest at Nyamila village.

At the time the Court rendered its final decision, Kenya did not have a national law of burial. But, simply because the country did not have such a law, it does not mean that once a burial dispute is brought into the court, it should be dismissed for lack of appropriate national law. To kick the disputants out of the court may tempt them to resort to an illegal means of settling their dispute, an action that could lead to social disturbance which would undermine law's objective to secure social order. Since they brought the dispute into the Court because they were unable to bring it amicably to a resolution, it would have been senseless to toss the matter out of the Court and expect a reasonable resolution. A society that is governed by "the rule of law" cannot tolerate such a resolution. To do so is to invite anarchy. The court has to find a way for peaceful resolution of the dispute. In the case at hand, the highest court in Kenya's judicial system, having no statute to guide it, and having no relevant precedent, or by ignoring the quest for a relevant precedent, turned to the applicable African customary law. Whether this turning is consistent with the rule of law depends on how the rule of law is understood and how African customary law is construed.

Secondly, Kenya is a land of many customs corresponding to many ethnic, religious and cultural communities that make up the country's population. The country is made up of many indigenous groups that Euro-western anthropologists call tribes. Each group has its own customary law. African customary laws are recognized by the national Constitution. If these laws are not in violation of the Constitution, and are not repugnant to justice and morality, or inconsistent with any written law, they may be used to resolve legal conflicts that are not otherwise covered by a standing law. To preserve order in the country the President and the Parliament have recognized the importance of retaining a plurality of customs, and of ensuring that the custom of a given group is not imposed on other groups. In addition to the indigenous groups, there is a diverse European community, and a diverse Asian community. Since what is customary in one community may be unacceptable or inappropriate in other communities, to keep inter-community peace, tolerance of diverse customs is encouraged. In matters of burial, for example, the Hindus are permitted to exercise Hindu burial rituals, the Jews are permitted to exercise Jewish burial rituals, the Sikhs are permitted to exercise their burial rituals, the Muslims are permitted to exercise their burial rituals, and the European communities are equally permitted to exercise their burial rituals.

Mr. Otieno was a member of the Luo community—a community that is largely settled in the western part of Kenya around Lake Nyanza, at times erroneously called Lake Victoria. (An African lake named after a British imperial monarch is a disgrace to Africans. It is a constant reminder of British oppression of Africans. An African lake deserves an African name.) Mr. Otieno was born in this part of the country, and received his early education there. When he finished high school he went to study law in India. Upon graduation, he returned to Kenya, and thereafter, started practicing law. With an exception of a few months, he lived in Nairobi, the capital of Kenya, where he had a lucrative law practice. In the late fifties he met Virginia Edith Wambui in Nairobi and the two became friends. Wambui comes from the Kikuyu community—a community that is largely settled in the central part of Kenya. Like her husband, she received her education in Christian school. Ultimately, their relationship led to marriage in the early sixties. Both were married in a Christian church, in an urban setting.

Traditionally, intermarriage between the Luos and the Kikuyus has been rare, and by not marrying within the Kikuyu community, Wambui, though not the first one, broke a long established tradition. While preserving their different ethnic identities, the Luos and the Kikuyus collaborated in the struggle for Kenyan independence, and for several decades they were major supporters of the Kenya African National Union (KANU), the major political party in Kenya. There are some customs that are unique to each community, and some of these customs have created some prejudices. For example, the ritual of circumcision that Kikuyu boys had to undergo which the Luo boys did not was a source of tension between the two communities. For the Kikuyu, circumcision was a rite of passage to manhood. Since the Luo men were uncircumcised, the Kikuyus disparaged them and thought of them as boys. But given the fact that each community has for the most part lived and continues to live in isolation from the other community, the tensions never reached a point of serious conflict. Contrary to the impression that Patricia Stamp gives, that the inter-community marriage of Wambui and Otieno was a political act intended to breach the gap between the two communities and that it aimed at establishing a trans-ethnic national Kenyan identity[105], the Otieno marriage was nothing more than a private affair. The personal was not political. That is, it was not a conscious attempt by either Otieno or Wambui to create a trans-ethnic Kenyan national identity. Like many other marriages, their marriage was not a political marriage. At most, it was a marriage between two petty bourgeois individuals in Kenya.

To get a better grasp of what is at stake in this case, let us begin by noting that a legal case does not exist in a vacuum. It is a part of a legal system. Moreover, a legal system is a part of a socio-cultural system, and because a socio-cultural system is a particular expression of what it is to be human, ultimately a legal case exhibits a particular expression of what it is to be a human being. Jurisprudence, therefore, is inevitably sociological. Every legal theory is a social theory. A human being, after all, is a social being, and in law, it should be evident a human being expresses and retains this mode of being. Thus, Judge Frank Shields' decision in the Otieno case was a reflection of an English legal system, which in turn, was a reflection not only of an English socio-cultural system, but also a reflection of a modern European understanding of what it is to be a human being. Thus, although the litigants are Africans, Judge Shields' decision expresses an English sense of social justice. He appears to have mistaken an English sense of social justice for a universal sense of justice. This was not an accidental mistake. The Englishman has a way of creating the world in his own image, and this applies to his sense of justice—a sense that he has sought to impose throughout the world. At least, in classical English colonialism, it appeared to be a part of English wisdom that the whole world was either English or ought to be English. It is in the light of such wisdom that Judge Shields' decision is to be understood.

Regardless of the merits of Shields' decision, what is remarkable about it is his ignorance of the African socio-cultural life. His reasoning does not take into account the cultural ground of social justice in Africa. Alternatively, if he takes it into account, he appears to be of the opinion that African culture is legally irrelevant to the issue that the case raises. The African sense of being human is set aside as irrelevant. This is precisely the approach the British colonialism adopted in its dealings with Africans. If British colonial authorities did not destroy African culture they sought to retain it primarily as an instrument for the advancement of colonial social policy. Although the Otieno case was brought to the court more than thirty years after Kenyan independence, Judge Shields reasoned in ways that are consistent with colonialist reasoning. Mrs. Otieno's opponents wanted to introduce African culture as an important element in the adjudication of the case. The issue that was subject to adjudication had African cultural underpinnings that had to be taken into account if the settlement of the dispute was to be just. Justice, they appeared to argue, has a cultural grounding and has to be culturally constructed. In this particular case, African culture has to be taken into account. The marriage between Mr. Otieno and Miss Wambui was a Kenyan African marriage, a marriage that was deeply rooted in African culture despite the fact that the two had a Christian marriage ceremony. It was not an English marriage or a European marriage. The bride and the bridegroom were Africans.

Traditionally, in Kenya, and for the most part, in many African societies, when a woman marries, in significant ways, she ceases to be primarily a member of the community in which she was a member before getting married. Although she continues to have social ties with her original community, she effectively becomes a member of her husband's community. She ceases to be bound by the customs of her parents' community, and is bound by those of her husband's community. Moreover, if there is an offspring in the marriage, it is bound by the customs of her husband's community, and not those of her community. In many African societies a man marries and a woman is married. The question that one often hears in the West where a man is asked whether he is or is not married, in indigenous African culture, is highly insulting to men. To ask a man this question is to mistake a man for a woman. It is to treat a man as if he were a woman. It is a terrible insult to call a man a woman, and it is likely to trigger a fight. One can imagine how much worse it would be if it were directed to a man by a woman. It is only a woman who is married. Girls are raised to be married and boys are raised to marry.

Unlike the change of status by the wife, the husband continues to be bound by the customs of his community. A man retains his identity throughout even at death and after death. It is in this context that Mr. Otieno's brother argued that Mr. Otieno was born a Luo, lived and died a Luo, and hence, deserved a Luo burial—an argument that the highest Court in the land accepted. Mr. Otieno could not have an identity outside his Luo community. His individuality made sense only in the context of the Luo community. He could not have individual rights that contravened the right of the Luo community unless the contravention was ordained by the national government. The national government has a constitutional mandate to make laws that would contravene the laws of the communities if the former are deemed to protect or enhance national well-being.

Once Wambui got married to Otieno, her identity as an individual was submerged in the identity of the community of her husband. Strictly speaking, she did not lose her individuality. There was a shift in the context of her individuality. The locus of her individuality changed. She became a Luo wife, a Luo woman. She ceased to be a Kikuyu woman and, henceforth, could not be thought of as a Kikuyu wife. Her Kikuyu identity was largely extinguished by marrying a Luo. Somewhat, her marriage estranged her from the Kikuyu community. As a Luo, she fell under the regime of the Luo customary law. In the most significant sense, the death of her husband was not the death of her husband. It was the death of a Luo husband, the death of a Luo man. Or, more appropriately, it was the death of her husband and, at the same time, the death of a Luo husband. A Luo wife had lost a Luo husband. A Luo man had died, and a Luo woman had been left without a husband. The loss was both personal and communal, the communal loss being more elemental. It is precisely this mode of reasoning that Wambui found perverse. She resisted a construction of marriage that would undermine the priority of a nuclear family. She resisted being submerged in the community of her husband to the point at which she would be deprived of the sole "possession" of her husband's "remains".

In the Court, Wambui pressed for an exclusive claim of the custody of her husband's body, and for an exclusive right to bury it at the place of her choice. She argued that after her husband died she was the next of kin and the sole legal representative. She stated that she was married to him in a Christian wedding, and that Christianity rather than Luo customary law had created the bond between them. It was this bond that ought to have been decisive in the disposition of the dispute on the custody of the body, and in the dispute on who had the right to bury it. She further argued that both she and her husband were educated in modern Western ways, and that they were no longer bound to traditional customary Luo customs. The Luo customs regarding marriage and death had no binding force on them since, from the time of their marriage, they rarely observed Luo customs, and rarely visited the Luoland. They had no intention of reverting to the traditional Luo customs—customs that they regarded as anti-Christian and primitive. She asserted that she was married to Mr. Otieno and not the Luo community, and having lived with him as a wife, and he as a husband to her, she had the sole right to dispose of her husband's body as she saw fit. Lastly, she argued that if she could not be permitted to bury her husband's body in the place of her choice, this would amount to discriminating against her on the basis of her gender and sex. Her contention was that a woman was being deprived of the right to bury the remains of a man who was her husband at the place of her choice, whereas men were accorded rights to bury their wives at the place of their choice. She was being denied the equal protection of the laws. Equality under the law was what justice called for. In this regard, she took a "feminist" perspective, and appealed to the Court not to embrace patriarchy and not to rule in a manner that would reinforce patriarchal jurisprudence. Ultimately, as has been already indicated, the Court was not persuaded by her arguments.

Whether one agrees or disagrees with the decision, it is important to bear in mind that feminism does not exist in a cultural or in a historical vacuum. One must also be sensitive to the missionary factor, to feminist missionarism. A feminist missionary assumes that she or he is in possession of absolute truth regarding feminism and, hence, the right to preach to the savages—among those who are ignorant about the evils of patriarchy and those who condone the exploitation and oppression of women. In the post-colonial world, such a missionary perpetuates the preaching psychology inherited from the colonial history.

Contrary to what Judge Shields stated, Mrs. Otieno's opponents argued that Mr. Otieno did not cease being a Luo by becoming a Christian, by entering into a Christian marital contract, by attending Western schools, or by being urbanized. Once a Luo, always a Luo. Once an African, always an African. Likewise, marrying a non-Luo woman did not make him a non-Luo. It would be against his interest and the interest of the Luo community to treat him otherwise. According to Luo customs, when a Luo man dies, it was alleged, he must be given a Luo burial. It is a part of these customs for a Luo to be buried at his home. Not having established a home elsewhere, Mr. Otieno's home remained in Nyalgunga, the place of his birth. The house that he and his wife had in Nairobi was a house and not a home. A house is not a home and a home is not a house. The house they had in Nairobi was a temporary place away from home. Christianity, Western education, Western urbanization, and Western modernization had no power to transform a house into a Luo home or into an African home.

As stated by Wambui's opponents, among the Luos there are specific rituals and ceremonies that are involved in establishing a home. One's father or uncle must point out a certain parcel of land where one is to set up one's home. This pointing out is not simply a physical designation of a geographical space. The pointing is a ritual conveyance of a geographical place, and the geographical place so pointed out becomes a cultural space upon which a human being is to culturally root himself, that is, to establish a home. It is only on such a place where a human being can be buried. Since, according to Wambui's adversaries, Mr. Otieno had not established a home anywhere, he could only be buried at home in Nyalgunga where his father had a home. To bury him elsewhere was to cast him out among the wild animals. If he were buried in the wild, the guardian spirits of the Luo community would haunt the Luo community and bring untold suffering to the members of the community, to their animals, and to their crops. Mrs. Otieno, with the support of her children, claimed that this is precisely the Luo superstition that she and her husband had rejected by being Christians and by being modern. Neither she, her children, nor her lawyer demonstrated why Christianity was not equally superstitious. In fighting superstition in Africa, Europeans have an entrenched habit of not recognizing that what they perceive as African superstition is replaced by a European superstition. Nowhere is it demonstrated to the African that Christianity itself is not a form of superstition. The replacement of one superstition with another superstition does not get rid of superstition. It is difficult to imagine a greater superstition than a belief in Heaven, in Hell, or in the Holy Communion. If being civilized calls for a rejection of superstition, one must wonder how civilized Europeans are.

It is indeed the case that some members of the Luo community have died away from Luoland without a home, and were buried wherever they died. It also appears to be the case that in the conception of what a home is or in what it takes to establish a home, there is no unanimity among the Luos. Given this state of affairs, it can be argued that there was more to the dispute than a mere determination of who should have the custody of the body, or who should determine the place of burial. There are those who say that it was indeed an attempt to determine who is to inherit the family's property that was at issue. Mr. Otieno had amassed a lot of wealth and there may be those among the Luos who did not want the property to be left in the hands of non-Luos. But even if this were to be conceded, the case's importance in highlighting the conflict between African jurisprudence and Euro-western jurisprudence ought to be taken into account. After all, property is property in a cultural context. It is a cultural construction. It is not to be assumed that the Euro-Western understanding of property is the same as the Luo or, more generally, the same as the African understanding of property, or indeed, superior to the African understanding. Understanding of property is culture-specific. The law of property in Dutch Roman law is the law of the Dutch Roman culture, just as the law of property in Western European law is a law of Western-European culture. Africa is not an exception. Property law in Africa is the law of African culture. In the Otieno case there is a cultural conflict and to resolve this conflict in favor of European culture is to perpetuate European cultural imperialism. One should not confuse European or Anglo-American brands of feminism with an African brand of feminism. If there is universal feminism, African feminists do not need non-African spokespersons. It would make greater sense to speak of pluriversality of feminism rather than universality of feminism, but speaking this way may face severe obstacles that are raised by the friends of globalism. In a world where the imperial West pilots globalism, globalism tends to be an imposition of what is provincial.

It is asserted by Mrs. Otieno's opponents that according to Luo customs, a woman has no say regarding the burial of her husband. Burial matters are left to the male elders of the community. They represent the spirit of the people and they are the ones that are responsible for ensuring that the relationship between the people and the spirits is not disturbed, and are also responsible for ensuring a proper transition from the living to the departed ancestors. Wives, or women generally, are not supposed to get near the dead body. They must stay away lest the community be afflicted with evil spirits. Since a man is not the exclusive "property" of his wife, but more so, a "property"of the community, the community has the last say as to his final resting place. Furthermore, since according to Luo custom, a woman has no home of her own because her home is the home of her husband, she cannot bury or have her husband's body buried at a place other than her husband's home. Her home is determined for her and, in the case at hand, it was the community's determination that her home be at Nyalgunga where her husband, having failed to establish a home for himself, had a proper home, the home of his father. This construction of a woman or of a wife is what Wambui contested and is what infuriated her "feminist" friends.

The main issue here is not whether this construction should or should not prevail. There is no social formation that is eternal. The issue is one of the direction of the change in the social construction of marriage. The Court of Appeal refused to allow the direction of the change to be handled by those whose interests did not lie in the promotion of genuine African cultural interests. It abstained from indulging in judicial activism. It recognized the primary role that African communities must play in charting the course of their social and cultural history. Its decision was not intended to silence the debate among Africans on what this course should be.

The Luo community to which Mrs. Otieno belonged since her marriage, according to her adversaries, did not interfere with her rights as a Luo wife, as a Kenyan, as an African, or as a woman. The man she married was an integral member of his community. The children she had with him were equally the children of the husband's community. If a woman does not abide by the customary laws regarding the burial of her husband, it can be assumed that she has divorced him, and having divorced him, she can no longer lay a claim to his body. Mrs. Otieno had two choices: she could either be a Luo wife and participate in the burial of her husband's body according to Luo customs, or she could consider the death of her husband as a divorce, and she could thereby cease to be a Luo wife. Apparently, according to her adversaries, she chose the latter and became an outcast in the Luo community. It is indeed the case that the Luo community was not and is not static. As a human community, it has perimeters that are constantly changing. The Court, however, did not want to play a role in directing the change. It was up to the community or the national legislature to initiate change.

As indicated earlier, after listening to the arguments from both sides the highest Court in the country ruled in favor of Mrs. Otieno's opponents. After noting that there was no national law covering the issue at hand the court said,

> At present there is no way in which an African citizen of Kenya can divest himself of the association with the tribe of his father if those customs are patrilineal. It is thus clear that Mr. Otieno having been bred a Luo remained of the Luo tribe and subject to the customary law of the Luo people.[106]

When the court concluded that it was the Luo customary law that controlled the case, the court had to determine whether the Luo customary law was repugnant to justice and morality, or inconsistent with any written law. The Court could not find any written law with which the Luo customary law was inconsistent. On the issue of repugnance to justice and morality the court noted that,

> We are persuaded that our perusal of the evidence and from a summary of the ebb and flow of the argument... that there is nothing in the Luo customary law which a reasonable man in Kenya would find repugnant to justice and morality.[107]

It can be argued that what the court meant by reasonable man was a reasonable Kenyan male, which could invite a rejoinder from a feminist that this is precisely what was unjust and immoral about the decision. The decision favored a patriarchal justice and patriarchal morality, and this compromised the right of a Kenyan female. But it is not clear how such a right could have been compromised, for it could be argued that the right that Wambui fought for was not the right of a Kenyan female, or the right of an African female; it was the right of a pseudo-European female. This is the kind of a female that Wambui fought for since she had sought to flee from being Kenyan to being "urbanite/cosmopolitan/modern". She may have believed that she was a "new" Kenyan female, but as construed by her, such a female appears to be indistinguishable from the neo-colonial female that neo-colonialism sought to construct. The judiciary would not assist her in her quest for the recognition of her new identity. Clearly, this case enriches the conversation on feminism by reinforcing the possibility that feminism is subject to multiple interpretation or to multiple constructions. Orthodox Christianity finds this thought abhorrent. There is only one true form of marriage, and this is the Christian form. Western feminism is deeply rooted in Western culture, a culture that is deeply Christian. One should be suspicious of the utterances of Western feminists, for what is parochial in them may surreptitiously come across as universal.

Although the Court pointed out that there was no way an African citizen of Kenya could divest himself of his tribal affiliation, the affiliation was flexible enough to allow for deviation. For, example, if Mr. Otieno wanted to be buried in Nairobi he could have done so by having his father or uncle perform the necessary ritual to enable him to establish a home in Nairobi. Once a home is established, he could have been buried there. As he did not avail himself of this opportunity, he died without a home, and he who dies without a home according to Luo customary law is to be buried at his father's home. Moreover, he could have written a will that would indicate what was to be done with his body after his death. The Court found nothing unjust or immoral in Luo customary law, and allowed its application in the disposal of Otieno's body. Whether the decision was or was not consistent with justice and morality poses a difficult question, for it is not clear that the Court (as construed in the Euro-western context) is the proper forum for addressing this difficulty. Following a modern Euro-western trend, today, the legal training that is offered to lawyers and judges in Kenya dispenses with courses on justice and morality. There is little attention paid to African theories of justice or to African moral theories. Moreover, courses on Kenyan sociology and Kenyan cultural anthropology are not a part of the law curriculum. The vacuum is easily filled by non-African sociology and by non-African cultural anthropology.

In rendering its decision the Court did not single out Mrs. Otieno to bear the brunt of its decision. If Wambui was singled out, it was to dramatize the crisis of the institution of marriage in Kenya. As said above, Wambui was not advancing the cause of Kenyan women or the cause of African women. She was advancing her own cause. Perhaps this is one of the reasons that Kenyan African women gave her little support. Clearly, there is no doubt that patriarchal jurisprudence was at work. The decision had a bearing on most of the African communities in Kenya since they are patrilineal and patriarchal. The Court's message was clear: for the most part, at present, the ontological bond—the bond that ties men and women together—will continue to be given social and cultural contours by men until social changes are brought about by the essential organs of the community. That is, it is through African men that African women will continue to receive their being. By essential organs, the Court primarily meant the councils of the elders. It is these elders that the court refers to as the custodians of the African customary law. These male custodians form the patriarchy that conceives and administers gender relations. To be sure, the national legislature could enact a law overriding what in customary law was repugnant to the constitution, or what is inconsistent with national interest. The legislature could abolish patriarchal conception and administration of gender relations, but in the absence of such abolition, the status quo would prevail. The legislature in Kenya, as is the case in practically all African countries is largely a male institution. This is also the case in the majority of legislatures in the world. The Court could have legislated on this matter, but doing so would open a pandora's box in gender relations in the country. Most likely, it is not the devotion to the separation of powers that led to the Court's restraint. The Court was patriarchal and, apparently, this was the legal issue facing the Court.

If we bear in mind that law is not only a feature of culture but also a means by which a culture preserves and develops itself, it should be clear that the elders, as custodians of African customary law, are also custodians of African Culture. Faced with the question as to whether it should render a decision that would subvert traditional African culture, the Court answered in the negative. Its decision was essentially conservative. The Court refused to play an activist role; its decision provided a legal justification of the status quo: the subjection of women to men. The court found nothing repugnant about patriarchal justice or about patriarchal morality in this status quo, and went as far as to claim that no reasonable man in Kenya would find the Luo customary law repugnant. In other words, the Court was not simply rubber-stamping the wisdom of elders. It concluded that this wisdom was a product of reason. In addition, it should be noted that the court had in view the development of a jurisprudence that would ultimately have a Kenyan, African "identity". Apparently, the Court viewed its decision as a reasonable step towards establishing such jurisprudence.

It is tempting to investigate whether this was, indeed, a reasonable decision and, in so doing, meet the Court's decision head-on, but I will not succumb to this temptation if only because it may obscure what I believe to be a fundamental aspect of this case. Besides, whether the decision taken by the Court was reasonable or not cannot be fully determined unless the reasonableness of the wisdom of the elders is investigated. This is precisely the type of investigation that the Court did not undertake, and, perhaps, for a good legal reason. Such an investigation may have constituted a transgression of its mandate as understood in the modern Western organization of government, which ironically is the form of government that Kenya seeks to establish. It is not within the province of the judiciary to evaluate the wisdom of the legislature. Its province is to interpret the laws that the legislature has enacted. An investigation of the reasonableness of the wisdom of the elders must be carried out extra-judicially, and must be done with all the care that one can muster lest the investigation lead to a disrespect of the elders. A respect for the elders may be essential to reasonableness.

In the Otieno case, it appears that conformity with the wish of the elders constitutes an element of reasonableness. Elders provide the "glue" that holds society together. Whether the holding is or is not reasonable is, indeed, an issue that elders must face; otherwise, they may fail in their duty to hold society together. The court, perhaps wisely, was not about to open Pandora's Box, and be accused of undermining social order. It is not accidental that such respect appears to be recognized in practically all cultures. Once the Court accepted this case, however, Pandora's box became open. The traditional spousal relationship was irreversibly placed in the public arena for broader discussion. A part of the discussion should include the idea of reason itself. Like all of our other ideas, it is an idea that is shaped culturally and historically, and one must also include the role that racism has played in the construction of this idea. This is being suggested in the light of the fact that during the colonial phase of African history, Europeans assumed that Africans were irrational, and it appears they never questioned the rationality or the reasonableness of this assumption. Taking the Greek idea that man is a rational animal, they believed and acted as if it was they and only they who were rational, which tells us the view that they had of Africans and other non-European peoples. There is reason to be paranoid whenever the word reasonableness is uttered by them.

In the Otieno case, there appear to be two opposing views of a marital relation. The first, shared by Mrs. Otieno, is one in which the act of marriage establishes an exclusive relation between the spouses. In the context of law, such an exclusive relation establishes a contractual relationship in which each spouse acquires exclusive legal rights over the other. Since it is two individuals who enter into a marital contractual relationship, it is only they who can seek an enforcement of their respective legal rights unless, of course, compelling state interests or rights override those of the spouses. It is in the context of this interspousal contract that Mrs. Otieno sought exclusive rights regarding the custody and the burial of her husband's body. In one of her press conferences, Wambui stated, "Every woman in Kenya should look at this case keenly. There is no need of getting married if this is the way women will be treated when their husbands die".[108] This statement is to be understood in an adversarial context. Most likely, what she had in mind was to have every woman look at this case from her personal perspective as a wife or as a possible wife. She appeared to assume that all women share her view. She was not calling for an open-minded re-appraisal of the marital relationship. She was assuming that there was a consensus among women on what it means to be a wife. What she meant by "her" husband is not what her adversaries meant by "her" husband. Her adversaries were claiming that "her" husband was also "their" husband. He was a Luo husband, not just her husband. She sought to personalize "her" husband while her adversaries sought to socialize him. Her advocate, Mr. Khaminwa, stated that according to the Kenya Law of Succession, the next of kin was the legal representative of the deceased. He and Wambui assumed that she, as the deceased's wife, was the next of kin and, hence, the legal representative. Apparently, in her eyes, once she got married to Otieno, she replaced anyone else as the next of kin and thereby replaced anyone else as his legal representative. Her understanding of the next of kin was not only different from but also in opposition to what her adversaries understood as the next of kin, thereby disagreeing on who the legal representative ought to be. She was speaking and thinking from the standpoint of the nuclear family. Ougo and Siranga claimed that they represented the next of kin and, hence, were the legal representatives of his brother. Moreover, she appeared to believe that her need to get married was the need or ought to have been or to be the need of every other woman. If her statement can be construed as feminist, it is one of possible versions of feminism.[110] Her view appears to be a Western bourgeois feminism view. She was crusading for a monopoly of marital relationship by individuals who enter into marriage, and for the nuclear family that is generated from such a monopoly. This is precisely the view that her adversaries were contesting even though contestation was not explicitly driven by anti-bourgeois sentiment. The Court ruled against her without appealing to anti-bourgeois sentiment.

The second view on marital relation is the one that was advocated by Mrs. Otieno's adversaries. Contrary to what Mrs. Otieno advocated, they took the position that in a marital relation a woman is incorporated into the community of the man who marries her, and what the marriage establishes is a corporate relationship. The married woman becomes a member of the community in which her husband is already a member. Once membership is established the community acquires both legal and non-legal rights over the new member of the community. It is this legal right that came into being once Mrs. Otieno became a member of the Luo community that her adversaries in the case sought to have legally enforced. Her adversaries were acting as the agents of the community whereas she was acting as her own agent. Ostensibly, her adversaries sought no personal gain in the matter at hand. Obviously, the matter at hand was concretely personal for her. To her, marriage was a personal affair, whereas her adversaries thought that marriage was a community affair. If her adversaries are construed as anti-feminist, their anti-feminism may be construed as anti-Western bourgeois feminism. Theirs is explicitly a position that endorses patriarchal conception and administration of gender relations.

If one is to take sides regarding this conflict, to do so intelligently, an investigation of what marriage is, is in order. Such an investigation must deal with the marital relation, for marriage is essentially relational. Contrary to the claim made in liberalism in the West, relationality is not a matter of isolated subjectivities. It is shaped by the prevailing material conditions. The investigation of marital relationship does not take place in a cultural, historical, political, or in an economic vacuum. The adjudicator is not an abstraction divorced from cultural, historical, political, economic circumstances. The prevailing ideology of gender must be taken into consideration. When a dispute on marital relation is brought into Court these factors must be taken into consideration if one is to fully understand the jurisprudential presuppositions. The court is not an island in the sea of culture. It has its roots and nourishment in the culture in which it exists.

Secondly, marital relation is essentially historical. That is, the way it is now is not the way it has been from time immemorial, and it does not appear that the way it is now is the way it is going to be forever. Moreover, this relation is manifested differently in different cultures, and in different historical periods. It is therefore important to take its historical and cultural context into consideration if it is to be adequately understood. In this regard, it would be an error to essentialize an African marital relation. To be sure, this does not mean that the historical/cultural context of this relation is to be ignored. Moreover, as far as we know, it is only human beings who enter into this relationship. If this is the case, it is reasonable to assume that this relation defines what it is to be human. To be sure, this relation is not intended to be essential to what it is to be human for, clearly, human beings remain human even if they do not enter into a marital relationship. To the extent that it is a relation that appears to be entered into exclusively by human beings, the jurisprudential aspect of it bears witness to what being human is. Mrs. Otieno was asking the Court to construe her humanness in a particular way, and her adversaries were asking the court to construe her humanness in a way that was inconsistent with the way she understood her humanness.

Although it is not necessary that every human being realize his or her humanness by entering into a marital relation, once this relation is entered into, it should be entered into in a manner that does not subvert the humanity of those who enter into it. By humanness, it is meant the worth or the dignity that is inherent in every human being, and in the relation that he or she has with other human beings. Thus, a marital relation preserves humanness to the extent that it is the source and the means of preserving or enhancing human worth or human dignity. It is this standard that must be used to evaluate the Otieno case. The measure of such worth is not to be placed exclusively in an isolated individual. Such an individual is not human. He or she represents abstract humanity. The concrete, human individual is such only in the corporate context.

If we bear in mind that the Court based its decision on African customary law and, hence, on African culture, what it seemed to say is that there was no reasonable basis to think that marital relation as it exists in African culture does not bear or embody human dignity. Obviously, Mrs. Otieno thought otherwise, and undoubtedly, there are those who sided with her. But not only did she think otherwise; she thought that modernity, more precisely, Western European modernity, was the vehicle for human dignity. Initially, when Mrs. Otieno went to Court to ask for the sole custody of the remains of her deceased husband, she was granted her request by the English judge. In his decision he said,

> He (Otieno) was a metropolitan and a cosmopolitan, and though he undoubtedly honored the tradition of his ancestors, it is hard to envisage such a person as subject to African customary law and in particular to the customs of a rural community.[110]

The words "metropolitan" and "cosmopolitan" are code words referring to someone who had left the so-called tribal life for a so-called civilized life. Metropolitanization and cosmopolitanization testified to de-tribalization of Otieno. In their colonial or neo-colonial contexts, these processes aim at Europeanization of Otieno. Otieno was an evolue. He had evolved from the primitive world to the world of civilization, and as evidence for this, he is said to have loved to quote Shakespeare often. Apparently, no African was worth quoting. His evolving had reached such a level that even the judge observed that "it is hard to envisage such a person as subject to African customary law and in particular to the customs of a rural community". The English judge was applying English common law to an African under the assumption that Otieno had left behind his Africanness and should be treated the same as an Englishman ought to be treated. In his eyes, Otieno had become an African Anglo-Saxon, and ought to have been treated as such. Mrs. Otieno and her advocate were trying to convince the judge of what he already believed. Let us not forget that Mrs. Otieno claimed that she and her husband had already left behind the archaic and primitive Luo customs, and that she was a Christian, a product of modern European education and an urbanite. Her children repeated this claim in court in support of their mother's contention. Her advocate even brought the human rights argument to support her case, that is, human rights as understood in the West. In the West, the individual rather than the community is the depository of human rights. It should not come as a surprise that her idea of the marital relation that Mrs. Otieno sought to promote is essentially Western or, more specifically, an idea that is a product of modern Western culture. The drama in Court was essentially a conflict between African and Western cultures. Let us delve further into this conflict to get a clearer picture of what was going on in the Court.

The German philosopher Immanuel Kant has formulated one of the dominant views about the marital relationship in Western culture. In a lecture on ethics, he describes how human beings can engage in sexual intercourse in a manner that preserves human dignity. Such an activity may easily lead to a situation where an individual can treat another individual as an object, thereby compromising her or his humanity. It is Kant's view that the only way that sexuality can be pursued without compromising one or the other's worth is through matrimony. He asserts,

> Matrimony is an agreement between two persons by which they grant each other equal reciprocal rights, each of them undertaking to surrender the whole of their person to the other with a complete right of disposal over it. We can now apprehend by reason how a commercium sexual is possible without degrading humanity and breaking the moral laws... If then, one yields one's person, body

> and soul, for good and ill and in every respect, so that the other has complete rights over it, and if the other does not similarly yield himself in return, and does not extend in return the same rights and privileges, the arrangements are one sided. But if I yield myself completely to another and obtain the person of the other in return, I win myself back; I have given myself up as the property of another, but in turn I take the other as my property, and so win myself back again in winning the person whose property I have become. In this way the two persons become a unity of will. Whatever good or ill, joy or sorrow befall either of them, the other will share it.[111]

It should be clear that for Kant, in sexual matters, adultery is immoral and violates human dignity. Once the individual fully exhausts himself or herself in a matrimonial relationship with another individual, the individual fully exhausts himself or herself in this relationship, and there is nothing that remains that he or she can sexually share with another human being. Marital sex defines what being married entails. It joins two individuals in a manner that categorically excludes any third party and all third parties. Thus, whether sex is or is not involved, a matrimonial relationship is an exclusive relationship. It is a monogamous relationship. We should also bear in mind that Kant is a Western modern man who reflects the modern Western Christian culture—a culture which, in its modern version, considers the individual and the individual relationship as definitive of what it is to be a human being. It is this culture that Mrs. Otieno has taken on as her very own, and she asks the Court to settle her complaint in the light of it. Patricia Stamp calls our attention to an event that reinforces this observation. She says,

> Once the High Court decision went against her, Wambui startled and titillated the huge audience following the case by declaring she had been "born again" in her Presbyterian church. Consoled by them, she told them that it was God who gave her Otieno, and only He could take away what He had provided. Tomorrow, I will go court but this time I am going with Jesus. Her message for the clan: "Go and tell Joash Ochieng to get saved".[112]

In her zealousness to dramatize Wambui's victimization by clan, judicial and political patriarchies, Stamp fails to have a critical look at this declaration. She also overlooks another patriarchy, that is, Christian patriarchy. Wambui says that she will go to court with Jesus, the Son of God, Jesus the male God, the God who gave her Otieno. God did not consult with Mary, the so-called mother of Jesus, to see whether she would be willing to bear His Son. Clearly, this was an invasion of a woman's body. There was a violation of Mary's right regarding her body. As Christians celebrate the birth of Jesus, they forget that there was a crime committed. It is not an excuse to claim that God created her and He could do whatever he wanted to do with her body. Such an excuse could readily lead to the view that since a woman was taken from the rib of a man (Adam), man could do whatever he wants to do with a woman. He could rape her and get her pregnant.

When Wambui said she was born again, she was not born again as a Kikuyu woman, as a Kenyan woman, as an African woman, as a woman. She was born again as a true Christian, as a saved Christian. Apparently, up to this time, she was not a true Christian since she was not saved. Even when she claimed that she had a Christian wedding, the wedding was not truly Christian. A true Christian wedding was a wedding of the saved. One might even say that before being born again she was living in sin, for being married outside salvation meant she was not living the way a true Christian ought to have been living. One cannot but recall the words of St. Paul who said that just as Christ is the head of the church the husband is the head of the family. Christian feminism is a round square. It is both a misunderstanding of Christianity and of feminism. Stamp underestimates the devastation that Christianity has had on Kenyans and Africans in general. When she looked at the Christian Church in Kenya, she saw it as a force of democratization, as a force that challenged what she depicted as Moi's political-patriarchal repression. Had she paid closer attention, she would have discovered that Christianity has been responsible for subordinating women to men by socializing them into obedience to their husbands. The Presbyterian Church in which Wambui was raised and in which she was "born again" is one of the most fundamentalist and the most reactionary Christian Churches in Kenya. It is patently absurd for Stamp to think of the Christian church as engaging in Kenya's own "liberation theology"1 What Kenyans and other Africans need is not a Christian liberation theology. They need to liberate themselves from Christian theology. African women cannot be liberated by or under Christian theology. A genuine feminist African theology must be inspired by African gods and by African goddesses.

Kenya has had no meaningful liberation theology, and none appears to be on the horizon. During the colonial days, the Christian Church was in the service of colonialism. It was engaged in a religious and spiritual conquest of Africans for Christianity and for colonialism. Jesus, the man-god that Wambui claimed to take to court with her, was never and will never be a liberator of Africans from colonial or neo-colonial jurisprudence, not even if he is blackened, as was the case in the United States in the Sixties. In his name, havoc has been wreaked in Kenya, in Africa and in many parts of the world. During the war of independence in Kenya, it sided with the colonial forces and urged Kenyans to stay away from the Mau Mau, and from other anti-colonial forces. Financially and ideologically, the "white" church officials continue to shape the nature and the direction of the Christian church in Kenya and in Africa generally. After all, African churches were franchises and still are franchises of the parent churches in Europe or in the United States.

If an authentic African liberation theology were to come into being in Kenya or in Africa, it would seek the emancipation of Africans from Christianity. It would run Jesus out of Africa and hand him back to Europeans who, were they to undergo their own liberation theology, would hand him back to the residents of the Middle East. The God of the Old Testament, a tyrannical and patriarchal God, would be banished from Africa, and his so-called son would have to meet the same fate. This God has solidified the subjection of African women to male authority more than any African theology could ever have done. Wambui did herself a disservice as a woman and more particularly as a Kenyan African woman by embracing this god. In her being born again, her African identity was erased. To ask an African court to legitimize this act is to seek the complicity of the court in undermining the Africanness of an African.

During the colonial period, Christianity in Kenya, and in most of Africa, was an ideology of colonization, and in post-colonial Africa, it is an ideology of neo-colonialism. As a force in the European colonization of Africa, the version of Christianity that Europeans introduced to Africa has been an ideological force in the process of nuclearization of the African family. This process consisted of an effort to reduce African societies and cultures into an aggregate of autonomous nuclear families. The nuclear family that Europeans wanted to construct would consist of mother, father and offspring or husband, wife, and offspring (if there were any). The process of the nuclearization of African societies and cultures was a means of systematically destroying indigenous African societies and cultures. It sought to replace them with societies and cultures that would preserve and promote colonial interests. One of the most effective ways of accomplishing this task was to destroy the institution of the extended family in indigenous African societies and cultures. In this process there was a conspiracy of Christianity and capitalism. The institutions of fatherhood, motherhood, husbandhood, wifehood, and offspringhood, as was the case with the relationships that linked these "hoods", and which were essential for the being and intelligibility of these institutions, derived their being and intelligibility from the institution of extended family. Colonial judicial processes and decisions were grounded in these institutions and were construed in ways that were supportive of these institutions. It is these institutions that came under assault and which were subverted during the colonial period. Colonialist jurisprudence presided over this subversion and assault. As the engine for the construction of the colonial society, it favored the nuclear family over the extended family.

Since in post-colonial Africa, de-colonization of jurisprudence in Africa did not substantially take place, neo-colonial jurisprudence prevailed. Nuclearization of the African family continued as a neo-colonial process. Generally, it was construed as an important element in modernization. The judicial remedy that Wambui sought for the alleged harm she would suffer if she were not awarded the custody of her husband's body and the right to bury it in the place of her choice was neo-colonialist. She had embraced a neo-colonialist conception of family and sought a judicial legitimation of such an embrace. If she thought that she was advancing the cause of Kenyan women or the cause of African women, it was an advancement that was in the service of neo-colonialism, and as such, it was not in the African interest of Kenyan or African women in general. European Christianity has subverted the identity of the African woman. It has instituted a re-birth of the African woman into a woman who is not only un-African but also anti-African. Under the influence of European Christianity, she no longer has a taste for her own African identity. It has attempted to construct her in the image of the European woman or into the image of woman constructed by Europeans from the Christian Bible. By constructing her as such, it has subverted her identity as an African wife, as an African mother. That is, it has distorted her relationship with her husband, and her children. This distortion has been contagious. By distorting and subverting her African identity, Wambui became a neo-colonial agent. She wanted the Kenya judiciary to assist her in a process that furthers the colonialist project. Wisely, the Kenyan judiciary said no.

In rejecting the remedy she had prayed for, the Court did not necessarily strike a blow for the adversaries of neo-colonialism. An adversary of neo-colonialism does not simply seek to return Africans to a pre-colonial African culture. Such a return is not possible. Even if it were possible, it would not necessarily be a return to a golden age of justice in Africa. There is no culture that is static. Change is inherent in every human culture. Moreover, the impossibility of return does not entail a blind embrace of the colonialist culture, or the embrace of a neo-colonialist culture. It is a matter of looking for what is salvageable in indigenous African society and culture, and fusing it with new elements. Since no society or culture can exist in isolation from other societies or cultures, the construction of post-colonial African society and culture requires critical conversation with other cultures. Neo-colonialism seeks to reduce Africans to junior partners in such a conversation. It is precisely such junior membership that Africans must combat. The combat must be extended to the jurisprudential level. Jurisprudence can be a potent ideology for keeping a people under subjection or for liberating a people from subjection.

As previously indicated, Wambui's adversaries had taken the position that marriage—the kind of marriage to which she had subjected herself, was a communal affair. They argued that human dignity lay in the community. That is, the dignity of the individual and of the relation that the individual may enter with others lies in the community. Specifically, in marriage, an individual woman surrenders herself, not to a man who is to be her spouse, but to the community of the man she is to marry. If there is a contractual relationship with her it is with the community. The individual enters into such a contractual relationship as an agent of the community. Obviously, the Court decided that the African conception of marital relationship did not only preserve the dignity of human beings, but was also consistent with the effort to develop a jurisprudence that was unique to the Kenyan situation. The Court's recognition that its decision was a part of the developmental process provides a horizon for further reflection on the nature of the marital relation. Or differently stated, the status of the marital relationship as a bearer of human dignity continues to be problematic. Kenya cannot uncritically embark on the task of institutionalizing a foreign understanding of what a marital relationship is, or what it ought to be. As a bearer of human dignity the sense of this relationship must be determined by every culture in its historical context. No culture can live on a borrowed humanity. It must not be forgotten that Kenya has been and, to a certain extent, is still a victim of Western cultural imperialism, and her sense of human worth should prevent her from falling prey to this imperialism. At the same time, she should not use her culture to enforce the subjection of women or to further a dehumanizing patriarchy, or to shield herself from critical engagement with the thinking that is going on in other cultures.

The conception of marital relation in the West cannot be used as a paradigm for the location of human dignity. It is up to Kenyan women and men in conjunction with women and men everywhere to work out the parameters of culture where the dignity of all will become a reality. They have to find a way of ensuring that spouses do not become each other's hostage, and that neither of them should be a hostage to the community. To do so, it is imperative that spouses recognize that they cannot establish a relation where the dignity of each is realized without the existence of a culture that would give birth to and nourish such a relationship. Given that culture is an affair of the community, the community will inevitably have a decisive role in establishing the parameters of the spousal relationship. After all, one cannot be a human being in a community vacuum.

Apparently this is a lesson that Western individualists have yet to learn. Kenyans themselves, as is the case with many other Africans, must work out away where communities do not reduce individuals to mere automatons. Individual women and men should take it as their task to generate the kind of community that will sustain a spousal relation that embodies human dignity.

Remaining unanswered is this question: What right can a human being have in another human being? Whatever the answer to this question may be, clearly, it cannot be that this right is a property right. A property right in another human being is inconsistent with what it is to be a human being, for a human being is not a property that can be owned. That is, a human being is not a piece of property. The right that a human being can have on another human being is a human right. It is not, however, evident what a human right is. Wambui sought to individualize this right, which is what, generally, Westerners have come to define as a human right. Whether viewed from a moral or a legal standpoint, this right is a product of modern Western construction of human right. Wambui was asking the court to vindicate such a right against any claimant who sought a trans-individual vindication of the marital right. In Africa, a human right has its location not only in an individual but also in a human community and in human community. Every spousal relation should aim at defining what it is to be a human being or, more specifically, every spousal relation is already a statement of what it is to be a human being. It would be ideal for individuals to reflect on this statement before entering into a spousal relationship but, unfortunately, for many of us, it is only after we have entered into it that the question as to its meaning begins to impose itself on us. On the other hand, it is not evident that those who raise this question before entering into a spousal relationship have a decisive advantage over those who do not. When it comes to things human it is not clear what having an advantage or not having an advantage means.

The African saying that "When two elephants fight, it is the grass that suffers the pain" is relevant here. In the Otieno case, the grass was the African culture. If Wambui lost, what she lost is not self-evident. Likewise, what her opponents won is not self-evident. Moreover, thinking of the outcome of this case in terms of who won or who lost does not exhaust the sense of this case. For the most part, it appears that Wambui lost the custody of her deceased husband's body and the right to bury it at a place of her choice. Her opponents appear to have won what she lost. A part of her implicit loss—a loss she did not truly appreciate because she was not aware of it, is the loss of her consciousness as a Kenyan woman, as an African woman, and as a woman. She may have thought that she embodied a true identity of a Kenyan woman by marrying someone from a different Kenyan ethnic group as if to demonstrate that she had transcended a mere ethnic identity, and was thus a true Kenyan nationalist. She appears to have been of the opinion that to be a true Kenyan nationalist, one had to emancipate oneself from one's ethnic group, and legally from one's customary law. Similarly, her adversaries may have thought that the Luo custom and the rights derived from it were vindicated by the decision. This thinking, however, may have done injustice to the Luo custom by shielding it from critical scrutiny which may have affirmed this custom as a living custom. The celebration of the victory may turn out to be a celebration of the death of the Luo custom. When a custom fails to embrace historicity, it becomes fossilized, thereby robbing it of its humanness. But it must be noted that the historical trajectory that Wambui embraced was not the historical trajectory that was either good for her, for African womanhood, or for Africans in general. The spousal claim she embraced promoted a Christo-Eurocentric ideology of spousal relationship.

The Otieno case provides a forum for examining not only African jurisprudence but also a forum for inter-cultural and cross-cultural conversation on jurisprudence. Inevitably, the notions of morality, politics, gender, race, and the very notion of reason will enter into this conversation. How they enter should likewise be a matter of critical conversation. Shielding these notions from critical scrutiny may give rise to a false notion of jurisprudence. It is such a scrutiny that can bring into relief false notions of what constitutes the rule of law. It should not be forgotten that the rule of law is the law's rule, and as the law's rule can be tyrannical, the rule of law may be a cover-up for political tyranny or other types of tyranny. It is especially important to bear in mind that the rule of law, contrary to what is generally claimed in the West, is the rule of man, not man in general, but the rule of particular men—men in their historical, social, political, and cultural contexts. What the case has done is to open space for multiple conversations, conversations that evaluate the past in the context of the present, and that evaluate the present in the context of the future. These conversations would truly get traction if they are not limited to lawyers, judges or to legal scholars (narrowly construed). They get traction if ordinary citizens are involved. Although one should not make the mistake of believing that pre-colonial Africa harbored the golden age of marital relationship, to confine conversations on this relationship to a small elite that is trained in law or that researches law is to disempower the majority of Africans. It is especially important to involve those who dwell in rural Africa since they are custodians of a major segment of African Culture. Today, most of them are excluded from domestic conversations of law and are effectively cut off from meaningful conversations on law with non-Africans. The class aspect of jurisprudence is particularly pernicious. A small "educated" elite group has reserved for itself the conversations on African jurisprudential matters. It ignores and is contemptuous of the majority of Africans. It is this group that has arrogated to itself the right to enter into conversation with non-Africans on behalf of fellow Africans on matters that pertain to jurisprudence. The so-called democratization in Africa is yet to get a foothold in these conversations. For the most part, marital relationship has been introduced to Africa as a commodity to be purchased and consumed by Africans. Thinking about law has become a major facilitating means for the purchase and consumption, and has itself become a commodity made out of Africa for intra-African marketing and consumption.

Even on the level of scholarship, given the multi-contextuality of the Otieno decision, it should be obvious that the case is not exclusively a concern of those in legal scholarship or legal practice. It implicates all social sciences as well as the humanities—not in isolation from each other, but in conjunction with each other. Failure to recognize this state of affairs may lead one to fall into the professed autonomy of legal science, a failure that is bound to obfuscate this science. An understanding of the issues raised by the case, as is the case with the understanding of the decision that was rendered, calls for an interdisciplinary approach. This calls for a critical rethinking and for a critical restructuring of the faculties of law in Africa. Moreover, since these faculties of law are a part of general education in Africa, the critical dimension should be extended to general education. The breakdown of African education into disciplines or into faculties is without African cultural roots, and is a commodity produced in the non-African world for marketing and consumption in Africa. It may not be obvious but this dependent economy radically and concretely affects spousal lives in Africa. This dependent economy has led to the constitution of a particular brand of African that is marked and consumed by Africans—an African without legs who is compelled to ride on the shoulders of others, an African on a wheelchair who has to be pushed around by others.

The Otieno case offers a forum for intra-women conversations, and a forum for intra-men conversations. It also offers us a forum for conversations between these two sets of conversations. There is a need to secure these multiple fora and a need to nurture and promote the multiple conversations that take place in them. In law and through law, African women have their own story to tell about themselves to themselves, and a story to tell about African men. In turn, African men have their own story to tell about themselves to themselves, and have a story to tell about African women. In these gendered stories, there is also an intersection of stories, and no doubt, African women have their own story about this intersection to tell, and men have their side of the story to tell about it. These stories too have an intersection that may invite a continued bi-gender and inter-gender storytelling. To complicate this seemingly endless dialectical storytelling there is a constitutive dimension. The story to tell is not always a story of what is already there, for story telling is, in part, story creating. A further and inevitable complication is that this story telling and story creating necessarily implicates storytelling and story creating of non-African women and of non-African men. No one is an outsider in this process. Every story teller and every story creator who is conscious of storytelling and of story creating is conscious of his or her indispensability in this process. And even if one is not, one is still a part of it, for no human being can be human in isolation from other human beings. This is a part of the telling and creating of a story of jurisprudence. Although this story will inevitably have a contingent grounding, ultimately, it must have a contingent grounding that opens up to other contingent groundings. It must reflect the human condition. In reference to being human, Jean Paul Sartre has pointed out that,

> Strictly speaking, we should never say of him that he is at all. He is what he is not and he is not what he is; he is the nihilation of the contingent In-itself in so far as the self of this nihilation is its flight ahead toward the In-itself as self-caused.[113]

The "not" here is what is decisive. It arises out of the nothingness that founds the sense of our being. It is the "not" that is evoked by Nietzsche in *Beyond Good and Evil*, when he tells us,

> More and more it seems to me that the philosopher being of necessity a man of tomorrow and the day after tomorrow, has always found himself, and had to find himself, in contradiction to his today: his enemy was ever the ideal of today.[114]

This philosopher must not be yesterday's philosopher or just today's philosopher. It must be a philosopher who is subject to temporal and historical reality. To be of tomorrow and of the day after tomorrow is not to be at all. This ontological status is not exclusively the status of a philosopher. It is the status of all of us. The philosopher is all of us. We are without any sense of substantiality, without essence. This "without" is not negative. It is a positive mode of being. It names what we are. It seems to me that it is this sense of being what we are that summons us if we are truly in the neighborhood of an elemental understanding of what is at issue in being or not being married. Today, marriage is largely a societal gender disciplining of the indisciplinable. Indisciplinability characterizes our condition as human beings. The gendering of human beings (which has implications for the gendering of marriage) is under severe strain, and it may be to our interest to deepen and broaden this strain. This is not solely because of the pressure to recognize gay/lesbian or transgender or bi-gender marriages. It is primarily because the gender inscription of being human is relentlessly under challenge. There is a rejection of the view that a human being is eternally gendered. What I have been trying to do is to draw your attention to a thinking that draws and sustains us in the kind of beings that we are. For me, this is where the conversation on being married or not being married leads. When properly understood, philosophical thinking summons us to converse with each other. The goal of this conversation is to find out how we can live well. This is precisely the kind of thinking that was inaugurated by Socrates in Greece. One cannot truly understand Socratic thinking without being compelled to think about oneself not in isolation from other human beings, but in conjunction with them. Moreover, Socratic thinking is the kind of thinking that one cannot flee from. Socrates, it appears, was fully aware of this, for he tells us that he was sent to Athens as a gadfly to ensure that fellow Athenians were not immunized from self-examination. He did this by examining himself. It can be said, and, I believe, validly so, that the Apology was about Socrates' self-examination. Differently stated, Socrates had put himself on trial, and dares us to put ourselves on trial. Whether one is examining oneself or examining others, primarily, philosophical self-examination aims at living well. Today, we need to be reminded of this because of the variety of distractions that marginalize concern with living well. We are constantly seduced by sophists—clever men and women who delight in rhetorical victory over their adversaries. Socrates was aware of this seduction and tried to avoid it, and that is why at the beginning of his trial he tells the jury that he is not to be taken as a clever speaker who uses any linguistic artifice to win an argument. Finally, the invocation of Socratic thinking is not an invitation for us to kneel at the altar of Greek thinking. This would be an insult not only to Greek thinking but also to philosophical thinking, to human thinking. Socratic thinking is more than Socratic thinking. It is African, and more than African. It is your thinking and my thinking; it is our thinking. Socrates is one of us. In an elemental sense, his thinking is no better than the thinking of any one of us as long as we fully and truthfully respond to the call of human thinking.

Let us not forget that a philosophical journey begins at home and ends at home. A human being does not live and cannot live on a borrowed humanity, unless one has decided that one does not want to be what one is, unless one has decided to flee from oneself: a ridiculous flight since one flies with oneself wherever one flies. As Fanon observed,

> Because it is a systematic negation of the other person and a furious determination to deny the other person all attributes of humanity, colonialism forces the people it dominates to ask themselves the question constantly "In reality, who am I?"[115]

This is not the kind of question that is likely to be raised in the context of legal education in Africa or in any other place. The absence calls for critical assessment of what normally passes for legal education—an education that for the most part suppresses the question as to what law is. Professors of law are busy with this or that branch of law and their students are busy taking in what is taught to them by their professors. What each branch is the branch of, namely law, appears to be taken for granted and, to the extent it is taken for granted, so is any of its branches. The question regarding the reality of what one is is the kind of question that is normally left to philosophy, an area that is not taken seriously either by law professors or by law students. Even in philosophy, and particularly in the area of legal philosophy, the question is not taken seriously. For example, in Western legal philosophy, contrary to what I claim in the introductory chapter, legal philosophy tends to be a study of law rather than the study of philosophy. As I said, an honest philosophical study of law is at the same time an honest study of philosophy. Philosophy discloses itself in every subject it undertakes to study. Accordingly, a study of African legal philosophy directs us to the study of African philosophy, and in the context of this philosophy the question "In reality, who am I?" is of central significance. It is a question that opens up the being of the African as questionable. It is the question that European modernity has compelled Africans to ask of themselves. The Otieno case provides us with an ideal environment to ask this question. After the ordeal that Wambui went through, it was appropriate to ask herself, "In reality, who am I?' And when appropriately asked, it opens up the following interrelated series of questions: "As a Kenyan woman, who am I?", "As an African woman, who am I", "As an African, who am I?", and ultimately, "As a human being, who am I?" Her case was pregnant with these questions, and, ultimately,none of us is outside them. They are a part of our innermost sense of being. The failure on her part to nurture this pregnancy is our failure too if we fail to take up the project of prenatal care and to assist in the birth of the answers. Moreover, once birth takes place, we have an obligation to nourish these answers. This is a project of justice. It is what the Otieno case calls for.

Failure to recognize the call of Justice in the Otieno case, which would amount to self-evasion on the part of Africans, has a counter-part on the part of Europeans. This case is their case too. Europeans may be under the regime of self-evasion, but they too are haunted by the same question. They too are under an inevitable imperative to ask themselves, "In reality, who are we?" If the colonial experience forces the African to ask himself or herself, "In reality, who am I ?", the experience ought to awaken in the European the same question. He or she has to ask himself or herself, "In reality, who am I?" If the question does not arise, most likely it is because by colonizing the African the European made himself or herself comatose. In this situation, authentic African jurisprudence can have a therapeutic effect on the consciousness of a European. It would have a revolutionary effect on European jurisprudential consciousness. It can have a civilizing effect on European self-consciousness. To expect Africans to play this role is analogous to a Copernican revolution. It seems incredible. The same incredulity knocks at the door of the African since decolonization of jurisprudence, for the African, is itself a revolutionary act. If it does not appear that way, one possible reason is that it is not yet clear to the African what decolonization of African jurisprudence calls for. In the hurry to finish legal education so that they can begin practicing law, this question is not awakened in law students. Any student who enters law school with an interest in the question sees this interest gradually suppressed and eradicated in the course of being trained to think like a lawyer. To bring about this condition is the normal task of the law professors. It can be expected that in their zeal as missionaries of legal education in Africa these professors consider themselves to be doing their job successfully if they can succeed in making African law students forget the question as to who they are. The bulk of African professors are likewise helping to accomplish the same end. Law schools or the faculties of law in Africa are places of African self-oblivion. They are places where Africans are sacrificed or where they sacrifice themselves. The question that is called to our attention by Fanon cannot but have a volcanic effect in these places if it is truly heard. It is where the Otieno case eventually leads us, where African legal interpretation leads us, where thinking like an African lawyer leads us, where African jurisprudence leads us, and it is to what we are introduced by African legal philosophy.

It is important to note that the question "In reality, who am I?" is a question that makes sense in multiple contexts and so does the answer to it. It can be taken in a Cartesian sense, in which the "I" refers to an isolated individual. This is the central sense that prevails in European modernity, and accordingly the answer is to be provided by the individual in his or her singularity. The human community in this context is an aggregate of individuals with no internal linkage, no sense of communal identity. It characterizes the sociology generated by Hobbes, Locke and by other architects of modern Western European sociology. It is also a sociology that Westerners have attempted to impose on the rest of the human beings in modern history and continues doing even today. From an Africa perspective, the sense of the question "In reality, who am I?", the "I" does not refer to an isolated individual, to a singular individual. It refers to an "I" that is communal in an organic sense. It is a question that Africans ask themselves collectively and communally in the face of the European onslaught. It is also the way Africans perceive Europeans in this onslaught. Europeans do not come across to Africans as isolated singular individuals. Europeans also do not perceive Africans the way they perceive themselves in their own society. They perceive Africans as a primitive undifferentiated whole—a whole to be dismantled by the Europeans in the course of civilizing Africans, although this is done in such a way that no "equality" with Europeans is intended. The African individual is intended to be an inferior individual. A philosophy that is individual-centered, a philosophy that is anti-communal centered, may express a Western European sense of philosophy, but clearly it is not African. It is not that there is no sense of individuality in African society, but an individuality that takes shape outside the communal context signifies ignorance or madness. One, after all, is a human being among other human beings. The difference gives rise to two different legal philosophies.

Asking the question "In reality, who am I?" is deeply and broadly traumatic in the African. This existential trauma is yet to be fully diagnosed. The African is beset by persistent concerns that paying attention to it is likely to strike one as an affordable luxury or as frivolous. Without in-depth diagnoses the remedy, if there is one, will be elusive. That being an African can be taken by an African as a luxury or as frivolous is indicative of the extent to which being African has become foreign to the African. Being married can be a site where this self-estrangement can take place. It can also be a site where the struggle against this estrangement can take place. The legality of the Otieno case plays out at this site.

Chapter 6
Concluding an African Legal Philosophy

Pretentious. Unequivocally pretentious. A work on African legal philosophy is inconclusive, and has to be so. It is ongoing and, as long as there are workers, it will go on. Even if there are no workers it will be left unfinished. But then, there will be no one to witness it. It will be without a witness and, perhaps, it has been without a witness all along. It began without a witness and will end, if it ever ends, without a witness. Workers are merely caretakers of what surpasses them. Accordingly, one should not overestimate what a legal philosopher can accomplish. He or she is merely a caretaker of what he or she does.

In conventional wisdom, a conclusion is expected to be a summary of what precedes it or to state a resolution of the issue raised by the work. This conclusion differs in that intentionally it frustrates this expectation. The hope is that the frustration will preserve and sustain us in a state of openness to the thinking that this work calls for. Accordingly, nothing definitive has been said about African legal philosophy, and nothing can be said about it that is definitive. In this regard, this conclusion does not conclude.

At the core of African legal philosophy is the question that Fanon raises; that is, for the African, the question is "In reality, who am I?" It is in the environment of this question that we apparently situate concluding remarks. This question is not a typical question one encounters in mainstream texts on legal philosophy. The agenda in them is different. What has been said so far in this work should not be taken as a tributary to this mainstream. If it is a tributary, it is leading to a different mainstream or it is laying down the foundation of a different mainstream. It is the kind of question that befits a conclusion on a work on African legal philosophy if this work is taken seriously. It is not an easy question to answer if only because it is a question that demands a philosophical answer. Because it is in the nature of a philosophical question to be difficult, the answer will equally be difficult. In response to this question it is not enough to say "I am an African" for it is precisely the being of the African that is in question. The difficulty lies neither in the conceptual nor empirical domains if only because, primarily, the domain of philosophy is neither conceptual nor empirical. Philosophy sets the contours of these domains and, as such, it cannot be subject to them. For the African the difficulty is essentially the difficulty in being African. Because this difficulty abides, this conclusion is not a conclusion. Nothing concludes and, perhaps, this is because nothing begins. Beginning and ending follow each other seamlessly, inevitably, and endlessly.

There is what can be learned from the apparent movement of the sun. In the morning the sun rises only to set in the evening. In the evening it sets only to rise in the morning. The movement seamlessly repeats itself without end. It is also a part of our experience that there is no morning that is identical with any other morning, and there is no evening that is identical with any other evening. There is no day that is identical with any other day, and there is no night that is identical with any other night. Recurrence may appear to be recurrence of the same, but it is not. Even the sun as it appears and disappears endlessly is not the same sun. Its movement is not self-identical. Each day has its sun, and each sun has its own day. This is the rhythm of nature, the rhythm of life. African legal philosophy is not exempt from this rhythm. If there is elusiveness in grasping African legal philosophy, this is because what African signifies, what law signifies, or what philosophy signifies is elusive. This elusiveness is what experienced and what has to be experienced by each one of us, whether we are or are not Africans. An African proverb says one cannot defecate with another's anus. The proverb is a part of African ethics of autonomy. African people are autonomous just as are Chinese or any other people. This ethics, however, is not the kind of ethics that one finds in Kant or in most of the modern European ethicists of autonomy. It does not cater to individuals existing as monads. Autonomy is a "we" nomos. It is a "we" nomos, not "we" as solely an aggregate of individuals, but "we" in a communal organic sense. In this "we"nomos lies what is essential about African legal philosophy. If one does not forget what Europeans intended to do with Africans—that is, alienate them from the community of human beings—the "we" nomos that is expressed in African legal philosophy is not exclusively African. It encompasses all human beings, even those who have attempted to exclude Africans from the community of human beings. It is the source of human rights and also the source of human rights law. One should not be misled by what may appear to be a tirade against Europeans. Europeans too are a part of the human community unless they want to exclude themselves from such a community as they attempted to do by enslaving, colonizing, and neocolonizing Africans and other non-Europeans. There is nothing irreversible in what they have done, and in what they may be doing. It should not be forgotten that what they have done can be done and may be done by Africans and by any other non-European people. It is a possibility in all human communities. As evidenced in the Rwanda genocide, Darfur genocide, the Idi Amini murderous foray, Sierra Leone and Liberian massacres, the continuing atrocities in the Republic of Congo and Somalia, Africans are not immunized from crimes against humanity. One misunderstands what has been said in the name of African legal philosophy if one sees it from a Manichaestic point of view, where Europeans inherently represent the force of evil and where Africans inherently represent the force of the good. Thinking this way would make Africans guilty of what they are charging Europeans with. They become co-conspirators against humanity.

There is much to be learnt from Fanon's book *The Wretched of the Earth*, a quintessential text on colonial violence. Fanon warns against a possible move by the colonized to emulate the colonizer's way of thinking. He insightfully says,

> If we want to turn Africa into a new Europe, and America into a new Europe, then let us leave the destiny of our countries to Europeans. They will know how to do it better than the most gifted among us.[116]

What he says is vitally important for those of us who are servants of African legal philosophy. If African legal philosophers seek to turn African legal philosophy into a European or Anglo-American philosophy, European and Anglo-American legal philosophers can do a far better job than any one of them will ever be able to do. So, we might as well let them carry out their legal missionarism. Should this be the case, we might as well settle for being junior partners in the carrying out of this project, that is, we might as well resign ourselves to being nothing more than junior partners in the propagation and evangelization of the European and Anglo-American legal philosophy. There is no question that the senior partners will readily be willing to assist us in this effort as long as we demonstrate that we have the knowledge and the skill to do this work. Aid in helping us acquire the knowledge and skill will readily be forthcoming. They are more than willing to help us in building capacities to do so, that is, eventually to be like them. We should not be under the delusion that they will ever allow us to be full partners. Even if they would it should not be in their terms.

Should we decide that we do not want to be parasitic to European and Anglo-American legal philosophy or in reducing African philosophy to being nothing more than writing footnotes to Western European legal philosophy, and of Western European philosophy in general, our work is cut out: we have to engage in "we"nomous legal philosophizing, in Ubuntu philosophizing. As can be inferred from what has been said previously, this philosophizing cannot in principle exclude genuine European and Anglo-American legal philosophers. What should be expected of them is that they affirm and cultivate "we"nomos, that is, they affirm and cultivate Ubuntuism. It is precisely Ubuntuism that we have in mind when we speak of "we"nomos. This is precisely the notion that Ramose

Mogobe seeks to convey in his description of Ubuntuism.[117] It is the same idea that Nyerere sought to convey in his notion of Ujamaa.[118] If Europeans and Anglo-Americans are to effectively participate in this Ubuntu project, they have to know us by the way we know them, and they have to know themselves the way we know them. This prescription is difficult to bear. In reference to fellow Europeans in connection with the process of the de-colonization of Africans, Sartre says,

> Let us look at ourselves, if we can bear to, and see what is becoming of us. First we must face that unexpected revelation, the striptease of our humanism. There you can see it, quite naked, and it's not a pretty sight. It was nothing but an ideology of lies, a perfect justification for pillage, its honeyed words, its affection of sensibility were only alibis for our aggressions. A fine sight they are too, the believers in non-violence, saying that they are neither executioners, nor victims. Very well then; if you are not victims when the government which you've voted for, when the army in which your younger brothers are serving without hesitation or remorse have undertaken race murder, you are without a shadow of doubt, executioners.[119]

European and Anglo-American philosophers will find it difficult to resist evangelization for their culture—a culture that is deeply steeped in Christianity. This culture has primed them for engaging in missionary work in legal philosophy and in philosophy in general. It is worth noting the words of Carl Schmitt. He says,

> All significant concepts of modern theory of the state are secularized theological concepts not only because of their historical development—in which they were transferred from theology to the theory of the state, whereby, for example, the omnipotent god became the omnipotent lawgiver—but also because of their systematic structure, the recognition of which is necessary for a sociological consideration of these concepts. The exception in jurisprudence is analogous to the miracle in theology. Only by being aware of this analogy can we appropriate the manner in which the philosophical ideas of the state developed in the last centuries.[120]

Schmitt has Christian theology in mind. It is to be borne in mind that Christianity is one of the major building blocks of this history and culture. It is indeed the case that under the apparent drive for secularism, a term that is for the most part synonymous with modernism, or at least the other side of secularism, Christianity has been swept under the rug but continues to nourish what rests on it. This rug is to be lifted if one is to understand what rests on it. Europeans may have succeeded in expelling Islam from Europe, but they miserably failed to expel Christianity from Europe. Christianity decisively conquered and subjected Europe. It has become so indigenized that resistance is nowhere to be seen on the horizon. European secularism merely reinforces Christian subjugation. To expel

Christianity from Europe would amount to a creation of a new Europe. Europeans would have to expel themselves from being European, and this because Christianity has become so much a part of what they are that they could not expel it without expelling themselves from Europe. Islam, however, was not as damaging to Europeans as Christianity has been and, clearly, this religion and its attendant theology has been worse than the so-called Black Death, the plague that decimated Europeans in the fourteenth century. Nietzsche thought that it would take a "mad man" to alert them to what had been done to them by Christianity, but according to him the "mad man" had come too early. The chance of reaching the pre-Christian Europe is too remote for Europeans and their descendants. Without reaching such a Europe, neither Africans nor any other non-European people can hope for a dialogue with them. A missionary psychology has been so deeply rooted in them that it has for the most part taken the place of the pre-Christian European psychology. No dialogue is possible with a people who are animated by such a psychology. It is a pseudo-imitation of such a psychology that Europeans have attempted to generate in the African, so that like them, they can forget who and what they are.

The mainstream of European and Anglo-American legal philosophy distinguishes itself in silence regarding African legal philosophy and in African philosophy in general. For the most part, African philosophy in general is taken up by European and Anglo-American social scientists and especially by social and cultural anthropologists. These are individuals with no philosophical training, and what they do is for the most part what Hountondji refers to as ethnophilosophy, which he correctly regards as a pseudo philosophy. They pose as the spokespersons of African philosophy. Nothing less than a philosophical revolutionary turn-around can create genuine interest in African philosophy in European and Anglo-American philosophers. Without such an act, a genuine African legal philosophy will not register in their consciousness.

The position of the African philosophers who take up African legal philosophy is equally difficult. They have to wean themselves from the tutelage of European and Anglo-American legal philosophy, and from European and Anglo-American philosophy in general. They have to decolonize philosophical space in Africa, in part by decolonizing African legal philosophy and by decolonizing African philosophy in general. The historic undertaking here should not be underestimated. Let us recall the words of Martin Heidegger, one of the major and influential European philosophers. In his statement on the nature of philosophy he asserts "The statement that philosophy is in its nature Greek says nothing more than that the West and Europe, and only these, are in the innermost course of their history originally 'philosophical'"[121] and adds "The word *philosophia* appears, as it were, on the birth certificate of our own history; we may even say on the birth certificate of the contemporary epoch of world history which is called the atomic age".[122] Evidently, not every European or Western philosopher explicitly embraces this view and, indeed, there may be some who reject it, but it appears to be taken for granted so much that it does not require to be stated explicitly every time. What is unmistakable here is the Europeanization of Hellenic philosophy and philosophy in general, and equally unmistakable is the Christian spirit that animates it. Apparently, if Africans and other non-Europeans are to be philosophical they are to be so by grafting themselves to European philosophy; that is, by being parasitic to European philosophy. They are without an indigenous philosophical birth certificate. African legal philosophy and philosophy in general must lay claim to an indigenous African philosophical birth certificate. They have to say no to what passes as Christianized philosophy. They have to say no to Europeanized/Christianized Greeks. They have to say yes to Africanized philosophy. In so saying they have to say no to an African legal philosophy that is detached from African culture. They have to concern themselves with the renaissance and reconstruction of their own culture. They have to concern themselves with what it is to be an African today. African legal philosophy has everything to do with being African. Similarly non-Africans who have genuine interest in African legal philosophy cannot but have genuine interest in the question of being African. What prevails today in African legal education is systematic suppression of the question of what it is to be an African. Legal education schools or faculties of law have become or are increasingly becoming places for the generation and reaffirmation of amnesia regarding the question of being African. Like their Western counterparts, they are trade schools—places where they train to practice their craft.

I recognize that it is difficult for us as African legal philosophers to raise ourselves from being the junior managers of the Western jurisprudential empire. This empire is still a power to reckon with. Like every empire, it engages in militarized thinking. It is undeniable that the genuine philosophical work we are engaged in is taking place at the margins of this empire. If Afropessimism tempts us, it is worth recalling that apparent political independence from colonial regime was not handed to us on a platter. We had to fight for it, and we are still fighting for it. Jurisprudential independence is harder to fight for. It is a part of the continuing decolonization of the African life. It is the entire African person that has to be decolonized. Decolonization of the African mind will not get far without the decolonization of the heart. Ultimately, it is the decolonization of the whole person that is at stake. Moreover, this must be a decolonization of the existential and ontological environment in which the African lives. For the time being, most of us who concern ourselves with African legal philosophy and African philosophy in general are primarily busy footnoting Western European philosophy- Western European Christian theology. Mostly, we oil Western European imperial philosophy. We are yet to hear and dance to the drum of African philosophy. We are yet to hear the drum and the dance of African legal philosophy. Our African Gods weep for us, but we erroneously believe they are laughing. What has come to be thought of as modernization in Africa obscures this state of affairs.

The modern European mind has created a world and has also created itself as an axis around which the world it has created revolves. It has used law to secure itself and give itself legitimacy. Africans and other non-Europeans have paid dearly for the hubris and self-delusion in which it has shrouded itself. The theater of this operation of the European mind has not been confined within the boundaries of Europe, or within the colonies of European descendants. Its boundaries are like the boundaries of venereal disease. It knows no territorial boundaries. It is polymorphously perverse. What it cannot digest it destroys. This has been the course of European modernity. Africa has fallen under its regime and continues to languish under it. Its tyranny has concretely been experienced by Africans in the form of slavery, colonialism, neo-colonialism, and apartheid. These heinous institutions were creatures of European legalism and were given legitimacy by the European legal mind. It was a criminal offence to challenge slavery, colonialism, neo-colonialism, and to challenge apartheid. The desire to be free of oppression was evidence for criminal intent. In the prevailing environment in which the sense of Western European legal philosophy prevails, speaking of African legal philosophy is analogous to speaking to oneself. It appears that one has to be mad to do so. In Africa, a man who speaks to himself is viewed as a mad man—a man who is out of touch with the the Western European sense of reality—a sense that may be an extreme opposite of reality. But it should not be forgotten that, as Africans, we have suffered greatly for what passes as Western European sense of reality. This reality itself could be the flowering of madness. We do an injustice to embrace the madness of others as if it were sanity. As Aime Cesaire, an Afro-Martiniquan, has pointed out,

> ...for centuries Europe has stuffed us with lies and bloated us with pestilence,
> for it is not true that the work of man is finished
> That we have nothing to do in the world
> That we are parasites in the world
> That we have only to accept the way of the world
> But the work of man has only begun
> And it remains for man to conquer all prohibitions immobilized in the corners of his fervor and no race has a monopoly of beauty, intelligence, strength
> And there is room for all at the rendezvous of conquest and we know that the sun turns around our earth, lighting only the portion that our single will has fixed and that every state falls from sky to earth our limitless command.[123]

If what works itself in this work dwells at length with the thinking that prevails in the Christian West, this should not come across as a surprise. If Asian thinking had played or is playing a major role in African history and life, it would be proper to take it up in a reflection of African legal philosophy. Africans and Christianized Westerners have engaged and are engaged in an ongoing wrestling match. Western Christian missionaries have opened, or rather, have created a void in the African and have sought to fill it out with its brand of theology and religion—Christianity—with a particular brand of anthropology. Islam has done and is doing the same to the African. Both have been and continue to be formidable forces, for ultimately they have the same theological and religious root, the same sense of what it is be a human being. The success in generating the void in the African has been so successful that what they seek to fill it with has become the oxygen without which, apparently, the African would not be able to live. A part of what they want to fill it with includes more than theology and religion. It also includes jurisprudence and philosophy, elements that are secreted by Christian and Muslim theologies and religions. These secretions are intended to fill the void that Christians and Muslims have created in the African. It is a part of civilizing the African, a way of getting savagery and heathenism out of the African. Christian and Islamic legalisms fertilize this project.

The void that Christians and Muslims have created and continue to create in the African is the void that they have created in themselves, and perhaps creating it in the African is a way to fill the void in themselves. Beneath the cacophony of legal-philosophical discourse in both the Christian and the Muslim worlds is the gnawing nihilism. It is what European modernity has sought to flee from. It is an attempt to beautify what cannot be beautified. It is a project that leads to a dead end. Nietzsche has alerted fellow Europeans to this extreme danger but, apparently, they have not paid attention to what he says. The Muslims are yet to have their Nietzsche. Africans are prevented from sensing this danger to themselves. They tend to believe that the void created in them can be filled by Christianity or Islam, by the jurisprudence and philosophy that emanates from these faiths. Worldly salvation is sought by them in the pursuit of political power, wealth and the pursuit of formal education that is introduced by Westerners. They also appear to be on a crusade to benefit from science and technology. Consumerism of Western products that include philosophy has become an aphrodisiac. They see the West as the Savior incarnate. How they expect to defecate with someone else's anus is a proverb that has lost its historic sense. It is a miracle. In this context, a genuine African legal philosophy is diagnostic of this situation. It is also a diagnosis in quest for an indigenous African therapy. African legal philosophy is a medical philosophy. Where an African is to attend a law-philosophico-medical school remains an unanswered question. Wherever there is a site for such a school, the site must be the site where the question of being African is fundamental. The school must be the school of African self, a school where every African will experience the inevitability of the question regarding his or her being. It is also where the answer as to what he or she is is constituted and made available. The answer will not be constituted or available at a European site, at a Judaic site, at a Christian site, at an Islamic site, at a Taoist site, at a Buddhist site, at a Hindu site, at a Greek, or a Roman site. It is to come from an African site. The question of being African is bound to the question of this site. Ultimately, the question of African legal philosophy—a question that is integral to the question about African philosophy—is a question about the site where the African has his or her being. This is the question that Fanon poses. It is and, if it is not, it has to be the innermost question of every African. The answer to it directs the African's engagement with non-Africans. There are no shortcuts. It is the unenviable task of being African. Non-Africans also have an analogous task. They too must have their being in order before they can hope to engage Africans in a non-frivolous way.

One's culture is the eye with which one sees the world. Without it, one is blind. Colonialism sought to render Africans blind by dislocating them from their culture or by destroying it. It sought to replace it with an imitation of the imitation of European culture, giving Africans imitation of the imitation of the European eye. Decolonization of the colonial culture and the decolonization of the colonial eye become imperative. These processes are to take place on the cultural level. Law in any culture is rooted in and is the fabric of the culture in which it exists. The practice of law, legal reasoning, and legal philosophy are aspects of the fabric of one's culture. Law is both a way of seeing a cultural world and a way of creating a cultural world.

The longstanding imposition of European culture on Africans has undoubtedly induced cultural amnesia in the African. In this regard, it is worth recalling Powell's words. As he says, "If you think that you can think about a thing inextricably attached to something else without thinking of the thing it is attached to, then, you have a legal mind". The thinking that is at work in the production of the legal mind is not only similar to the thinking that is at work in the production of a philosophical mind. More accurately, it is a product of a philosophical mind that is detached from what it cannot be detached from. The European philosophical mind that is projected from what it cannot be detached from, namely European culture, has produced a legal philosophy that is detached from what it cannot be detached from, namely European culture. This is the legal education diet that has been fed to students of law in the West for centuries and it is what even today nourishes them. Since Western professors of law and professors of legal philosophy granted African students permission to study law and to study philosophy of law this is the education legal diet that they have been fed with. What has prevailed is a false belief in the universality of legal education. Having been rendered blind to European cultural underpinnings of the study of law, they have not only participated in promoting a false idea of law; they have also participated in the promotion of European culture, and in the dislocating of themselves from their own culture. Instead of recognizing that European legal philosophy is a part of the fabric of European culture, they have come to share the European belief that European legal philosophy is synonymous with universal legal philosophy and that the qualification of legal philosophy with the word European contributes nothing to the substance of legal philosophy. It is simply a geographical designation. This is the mentality they carry over to African legal philosophy. They see the qualification of this philosophy with the word African as designating nothing more than a geographical location. Viewing both African legal philosophy and European legal philosophy this way puts dialectical thinking about legal philosophy out of commission, and in the name of legal philosophy,

Western cultural imperialism is legitimated and promoted. African professors of law and legal practitioners become agents in the service of this imperialism. How teaching and studying law in Africa could be hazardous to Africans is a concern that does not appear to catch the attention of African educators or African political leaders. To this extent, their Africanness is questionable.

Given the fact that there is no culture that exists in isolation from other cultures today, the sovereignty of cultures has become problematic, and so is the sovereignty of legal philosophies. The avoidable temptation is to think in terms of global culture and, consequently, in terms of global legal philosophy. Given what has transpired in the past and what for the most part transpires today, globalism could be another disguised feature of Western European imperialism. The notions of the rule of law, democracy, world order, world peace, human rights, civilization, fighting terrorism and savagery, sugarcoat this imperialism. This is not a new song. Africans were robbed of their land and resources, were colonized, enslaved, exploited and oppressed under the European banner of freeing them from barbarism and savagery and providing them with a means of salvation from heathenism. The same banner that flew over the Berlin-Conference (1884-1885)—a conference in which European nations sat at the table to orchestrate and legalize their plunder of Africa and from which Africans were excluded—flies over Africa today despite the presence of African national flags. As Anthony Anghie has pointed out,

> The deep and enduring inequalities that afflict the planet might be attributed, simply to inequalities in power: the strong dictate and the weak must comply. But power rarely presents itself simply as brute force, as shock and awe. Rather, it presents its violence in terms of an overarching narrative, and there are few more compelling stories that power can relate itself when expanding than the great imperial narrative in which "we" are civilized, peace-loving, democratic, humanitarian, virtuous, benevolent, and "they" are uncivilized, violent, irrational, backward, dangerous, oppressed, and must therefore be sanctioned, rescued and transformed by a violence that is simultaneously defensive, overwhelming, humanitarian and benevolent. The furtherance of justice, the promotion of humanitarianism: these are the great goals that imperialism has traditionally set itself.[124]

In part, the imperial West has succeeded in Africa by the help it has received from some Africans. As is the case with all peoples, Africans are not immunized from the pursuit of selfish ends even if the pursuit entails inflicting suffering on fellow Africans. African history will amply demonstrate how the pursuit of selfish ends by some Africans has reinforced and promoted Western European self-interests. Whereas this may be evident in political, economic, and religious spheres, it is not readily perceived as self-evident in legal philosophy or in philosophy in general. Again as Anghie has pointed out,

> By 1914, after numerous colonial wars virtually all the territories of Asia, Africa and the pacific were controlled by the major European states and this resulted in the assimilation of all these non-European peoples into a system of law which was fundamentally European in that it derived from European thought and experience.[125]

Legal philosophy, as is the case with philosophy in general, stems from a people's thought and experience. African legal philosophy is not an exception. It is a product of African thought and experience. To the extent that this thought and experience has been distorted by European imperial colonialism, the identification and elimination of this distortion must be a part of genuine African legal philosophy. It is indeed incontrovertible that, today, no people can engage in legal philosophical thinking apart from the legal philosophical thinking of other people. The pressure to globalize legal philosophical thinking appears irresistible. The danger here is that Africans are subject to the vulnerability of a parochial legal philosophical thinking that is paraded as if it were universal. The recognition of this danger may come across as a luxury due to the more pressing subsistent needs that call for immediate satisfaction. In meeting these needs, for the most part, Africans look to the West for assistance, the same West that has been the source of their subjugation. To the extent that legal aid is required to meet these needs, it should not come as a surprise that rendering such aid is accompanied by Western legal aid. With this aid, the Western empire of law and Western hegemony of legal philosophy prevails. For the most part, what is construed as a legal mind today is a product of modern European culture. This product has been and is marketed throughout the world. Those who have resisted or who resist it are depicted as the enemy of law or as obstacles to the rule of law. Western law schools are factories for producing it. Today, the industry of legal discourse in philosophy and in the world in general is largely monopolized by the West. One of the products of this industry is the thinking that Powell calls to our attention. Again, it is worth repeating his view that "If you think that you can think about a thing inextricably attached to something else without thinking of the thing it is attached to, then you have a legal mind". This is a poisonous gift from the West. Its poisonous nature is sugarcoated and is not normally recognized as such. The historic task of the African legal philosopher is not only to call attention to this historic obfuscation, but to struggle against it. It is a struggle that not only benefits Africans but also benefits everyone who has interest in securing and promoting human dignity. There is what is universal in African legal philosophy. Whether African or not, all human beings have a stake in securing and promoting what is essential about this branch of philosophy. It is the work of humanity, a work in which human beings define what brings them together as human beings. A legal philosophical journey begins at home and ends at home. This home is the home of what is human about us. It is a home that is what it is by being cared for. This caring is inescapably an ethical caring.

In the history of human beings, the colonization of Africans by Europeans features the most extreme form of racism. Albert Memmi, an African from Tunisia, has noted that,

> Racism appears then, not as an incidental detail, but as a consubstantial part of colonialism. It is the highest expression of the colonial system and one of the most significant features of the colonialist. Not only does it establish a fundamental discrimination between colonizer and colonized, a *sine qua non* of colonial life, but it also lays the foundation for the immutability of this life.[126]

Today, if one wants to understand African legal philosophy, one cannot dance around racism. A major task of African legal philosophy is to ensure that such a dance does not take place. But exposing racism is not and should not be an end in itself. African legal philosophy must pave the way for an alternative world—a world without racism. Having noted that racism is a symbol and the sum of all oppression, he further observes, "Oppression is like an octopus: it is hard to tell which of its arms have the tightest strangle-hold".[127] Let us add that each arm is likewise an octopus, and it is hard to tell which of its arms has the tightest strangle-hold, and each of these arms is itself an octopus, etc. Moreover, each arm is the arm of the octopus, and has to be understood as such. It is a part of the octopus, and contributes to what an octopus is. Let us imagine law as an octopus. In colonial Africa, it penetrated every aspect of the African's life. Similarly, the colonizer's life was penetrated by racist oppression. The European sense of law was not immunized from this oppression. European/Western legal philosophy, like African legal philosophy, cannot be let alone to dance around this oppression. African legal philosophy has its task not only in rendering this explicit but also in bringing about the demise of the oppressive octopus. In the course of doing so, it opens a horizon for the possibility of the emergence of an alternative octopus—the octopus of liberty. Liberty too has arms—all of which belong to this octopus. Each of the arms has or ought to have a tightened stranglehold—a stranglehold that guards liberty and that protects what threatens it, and that advances it. Because racism has spread to all features of human existence, the task of the African legal philosopher must equally be pervasive. It has to engage and collaborate with all other branches of African philosophy. It has to issue a challenge to non-African legal philosophies and to non-African philosophy in general. Human well-being is indivisible. It is this perspective that is to guide legal education and legal practice. Legal practice must be a practice of human rights, and legal education should prepare students to engage in such practice. In post-colony, the practice must continue. Hopefully, one can now appreciate what was claimed at the beginning of this conclusion. The work of law, which is the work of being human, is not over yet. Every student of law, and every practitioner of law, whether African or non-African, has this as his or her task. It is a joint task in which every human being has a stake. It is an Ubuntu project. Neither the study of law nor the practice of law is a solo project. It is the project of us all. It is a project of being human and, in it, none of us is a stranger.

Notes

1. Frantz Fanon, *The Wretched of the Earth*, translated by Constance Farrington, (New York: Grove Press, 1963), 13
2. Calvin Schrag, *The Self After Postmodernity*, (New Haven: Yale University Press, 1997), 1-2
3. See generally Paulin Hountondji , *African Philosophy Myth and Reality*, translated by Henri Evans, (Bloomington: Indiana University Press, 1983). It is his view that the tradition of African philosophy is about fifty years old. He bases this view on his belief that African philosophy consists of written philosophy, and he does not see any evidence of strictly philosophical writings prior to this period. He offers no argument as to why writing is the only evidence for the existence of philosophy.
4. Hugh Trevor-Roper, *The Rise of Christian Europe*, (New York: W.W. Norton, 1989), 9
5. Alfred North Whitehead, *Process and Reality* eds. D.R. Griffin and D.W. Sherburne, (New York: The Free Press, 1979), 39
6. See Georg Friedrich Hegel, *Phenomenology of Spirit*, translated by A.V. Miller, (New York: Oxford University Press, 1977)
7. Leopoldo Zea, "The Actual Function of Philosophy in Latin America", in *Latin American Philosophy,* ed. Jorge J.E.Gracia, (Buffalo, New York: Prometheus Books, 1986), 220
8. Sir William Blackstone, *The Commentaries of the Laws of England*, (Oxford: Clarendon Press, 1992), 41
9. Martin Heidegger, *An Introduction to Metaphysics*, trans. Ralph Manheim, (New Haven: Yale University Press, 1939), 11

10. See, Edward H. Berman, "Tuskegee in Africa". Journal of Negro Education Vol.41. No.2, 1972, 99-112
11. See generally Mahmood Mamdani, *Citizen and Subject*, Princeton: Princeton University Press, 1996
12. Aime Cesaire, *Discourse on Colonialism*, trans. Joan Pinkham, (New York: Monthly Review Press, 1972), 31
13. Vine Deloria, Jr., *Custer Died For Your Sins*, (New York: The Macmillan Company, 1969), 2
14. Georg Wilhelm Friedrich Hegel, *The Philosophy of History*, trans. J Sibree (New York: Dover Publications, 1959), 93
15. Paulin Hountondji, *African Philosophy Myth & Reality*), 50
16. Ibid., 52
17. Baron de Montesquieu, *The Spirit of the Laws*, trans. Thomas Nugent, (New York: Hafner Publishing Company, 1975), 238-9
18. Joseph Raz, *The Authority of Law*, (Oxford, UK: Clarendon Press, 1979), 211
19. For a discussion of legal positivism see H.L. Hart "Positivism and the Separation of Law from Morals", 71 Harvard Law Review, No. 4, 1958
20. That Hegel is not a lone ranger in his thinking can readily be seen if one pays attention to other Western thinkers such as Hume and Kant. Kant claims that The Negroes of Africa by nature have no feeling that rises above the trifling. Mr. Hume challenges anyone to cite a single example in which a Negro has shown talents, and assets that among the hundreds of thousands of blacks who are transported elsewhere from their countries, although many of them have even been set free, still not a single one was ever found who presented anything great in art or science or any other praise-worthy quality, even though among the whites some continually rise aloft from the lowest rabble, and through superior gifts earn respect in the world. So fundamental is the difference between these two races of man, and it appears to be as great in regard to mental capacities as in color (*Observations of the Beautiful and the Sublime).* Hume, who Kant claims, awakened him from slumber, appears to have awakened Kant not only from slumber in matters of epistemology but also in matters of humanity. In a famous footnote, Hume says A. I am apt to suspect the Negroes and in general all the other species of men (for there are four or five different kinds) to be naturally inferior to the whites. There never was a civilized nation of any other complexion than white, nor even any individual eminent either in action or speculation. No ingenious manufacturers amongst them, nor arts, nor sciences. On the other hand the most rude and barbarous of the whites, such as the ancient GERMANS, the present TARTARS, have still something eminent about them, in their valour, form of government, or some other particular. Such a uniform and constant difference could not happen in so many countries and ages, if nature had not made an original distinction betwixt these breeds of men. Not to mention our colonies, there are NEGRO slaves dispersed all over Europe, of which none ever discovered symptoms of ingenuity; though low people, without

education, will start up amongst us, and distinguish themselves in every profession. In JAMAICA indeed they talk of one negro as man of part of learning; but tis likely he is admired for very slender accomplishments, like a parrot who speaks a few words plainly.
It has been the unfortunate to live in the northern part of Africa where Africans have come under the negative influence of Europeans. Ibn Khaldun of Tunisia has claimed that the only people who accept slavery are the Negroes owing to their low degree of humanity and to their proximity to animal stage. He also observes that Negroes are generally light headed, reckless and prompt to mirth, fond of every kind of dancing and everywhere renowned for their stupidity. P.46
21. Kwame Nkrumah, *Africa Must Unite*, (New York: International Publishers, 1963), xvii
22. Frantz Fanon, *The Wretched of the Earth*, 211-212.
23. John Locke, *The Second Treatise of Government,* (New York: MacMillan Publishing Company, 1985), 71
24. John Locke, *Second Treatise of Government*, (Indianapolis: Hackett Publishing Company, 1980), 69
25. Montesquieu, 151-2
26. See John Dugard, "The Jurisprudential Foundations of the Apartheid Legal Order", The Philosophical Forum Vol. XVIII, No 2-3, (Winter-Spring, 1986-87). Dugard correctly observes that during the apartheid regime, under the control of the Nationalist Party the South African Parliament was made the supreme branch of government and the judiciary was subordinated to it. The judiciary unquestioningly enforced the laws that the Parliament enacted.
27. See, Dugard, The Jurisprudential Foundations of the Apartheid Legal Order
28. A.V. Dicey, *The Law of Constitution* hereafter referred to as LC, (New York: St. Martins Press, 1965), 3-4.
29. Ibid., 4
30. See Hyun I. Kim, *Fundamental Legal Concepts of China and the West: A Comparative Study*, (Port Washington, New York: Kennikat Press, 1981). In part II he shows how the concept of nature in Western natural law is analogous to the concepts of The way of Heaven and Tao in Chinese "law". What he appears to miss is that the concept of nature in Western jurisprudence is highly Christianized, and as understood as such, one must have a highly distorted concept of The Way of Heaven or the concept of Tao to create an analogy in the two views of law. Although I claim no expertise on Traditional Chinese thought or Taoism, it seems to me that Kim has a very loose understanding of both.
31. *The Daodejing of Laozi*, translated by Phillip I. Ivanhoe (Indianapolis: Hackett Publishing Company, 2002), 4
32. See Linda Mulcahy. "The Architects of Justice: The Politics of Courtroom Design". Linda Mulcahy, Birkbeck University of London Social and Legal Studies Vol .16 (3) 383-403 , 2007
33. See generally John Austin, *The Province of Jurisprudence Determined*, (Indianapolis: Hackett Publishing Company, 1984)

34. See generally Frantz Fanon, *The Wretched of the Earth.*
35. Ramose Mogobe,"An African Perspective on Justice", Polylog: Forum for Intercultural Philosophy, Vol. 3, (2001)
36. Quoted in *Law as Culture* by Larry Rosen , (Princeton: Princeton University Press, 2006), xi.
37. Walter Kaufmann, *The Portable Nietzsche* , (New York: Viking Penguin, Inc., 1892), 43
38. Ibid., 42
39. See H.L.A. Hart critique of John Austin's Command theory of law in "Positivism and the Separation of Law and Morals." What Hart was criticizing is precisely what prevailed in European African colonies. Law in the colonies came through the barrel of a gun, police baton, and the whip. Law was the face of violence. The colony as the site of colonizers' violence has been exceptionally noted by Frantz Fanon in *the Wretched of the Earth*,
40. Hegel, See the previous note 12
41. Friedrich Nietzsche, *Beyond Good and Evil,* translated by Walter Kaufmann,, (New York: Random House, Inc., 1966), 71
42. Paulin Hountondji, *African Philosophy Myth & Reality*, 44
43. Kwame Nkrumah, *Africa Must Unite*, (New York: International Publishers, 1963), 1
44. See Cheik Hamidou Kane, *Ambiguous Adventure*, translated by Katherine Woods, (New York: Collier Books, 1969). Kane describes the predicament of African education during the colonial days, whereby the education that Europeans offered to Africans uprooted them from their cultural environment and turned them against it.
45. Lansane Keita, *African Philosophy and Development*, (Dakar: Codesria Publication, 2011), 161
46. See generally Caroline Elkins, *Imperial Reckoning: The Untold Story of Britain's Gulag in Kenya*, (New York: Henry Holt and Company, 2005).
47. See generally, Frantz Fanon, *The Wretched of the Earth*
48. Paulin Hountondji, *African Philosophy Myth & Reality*,53
49. Malcolm X, *Malcolm X On Afro-American History*, (New York: Pathfinder, 1990), 86
50. See generally Frantz Fanon, *Black Skin White Masks*, translated by Charles Lam Markmann, (New York: Grove Press, Inc., 1967)
51. Russell Banks, *Dreaming Up America*, (New York: Seven Stories Press, 2008), 27
52. W.E.B. Du Bois, *The Souls of Black Folk*, (Mineola, New York: Dover Publications, 1994), 9
53. See generally Kimberle Crenshaw, Neil Gotanda, Gary Peller, Kendal Thomas, *Critical Race Theory*, (New York: The New Press, 1995). Most of the articles in this anthology assume that being African American is synonymous with being Black American. This assumption obscures African American jurisprudence from Black American jurisprudence.

54. Frantz Fanon, *Black Skin White Masks*, 60
55. Frantz Fanon, *Black Skin White Masks*, 18
56. Ngugi wa Thiong'o, "Europhonism, Universities, and the Magic Fountain: The Future of African Literatures and Scholarship", Research in African Literatures, 31.1, (2001), 1-11
57. Edward P. Stringham, *Anarchy and the Law* (New Brunswick: Transactions Publishers, 2007), 178
58. David Luban, (New York: Cambridge University Press, 2007), 99
59. See generally Thomas Hobbes, *Leviathan* (Oxford: Clarendon Press, 1983)
60. John S. Mbiti, *African Religions and Philosophies*, (Garden City, New York: Double Day & Company, 1970), 141
61. Eugene Cotran, "African Law", International Encyclopedia of Comparative Law, Vol. II, chap. 2, 159
62. See Kant's assertion that "Thoughts without contents are empty, intuitions without concepts are blind". Immanuel Kant, *Critique of Pure Reason*, translated by Marx Muller, (Garden City, New York: Doubleday & Company, Inc., 1961), 55
63. See Lucien Levy Bruhl, *Primitive Mentality*, (London: Allen & Unwin, 1923)
64. See, Gibert Ryle, *The Concept of Mind*, (Chicago: University of Chicago Press, 1984)
65. Achille Mbembe, *On the Postcolony*, (Berkeley: University of California Press, 2001), 2
66. Ibid., 2
67. Na Aim tends to go along with this view although he hurriedly qualifies this. See *African Constitutionalism and the Role of Islam*, (Philadelphia: University of Pennsylvania Press, 2006)
68. By ethnophilosophy Hountondji is referring to a bogus philosophy which does not merit being called philosophy. It is a falsified notion of philosophy created by Europeans that claims that Africans think collectively and that individual thinking has no place.
69. This calls to mind the claim by European missionaries in Africa that African customs or cultures are impediments to Christian evangelization. For example, one cannot be a polygamist and be a Christian. The saying that one cannot put new wine into old wine skins is a typical refrain among Christian missionaries.
70. William Heffernan, "Not Socrates but Protagoras: The Sophist Basis of Legal Education", Buffalo Law Review vol 29, Summer 1980, pp. 399-400
71. H.L.A. Hart, "Positivism and the Separation of Law and Morals", Harvard Law Review, Vol. 71 February 1958, No. 4, 593.
72. Ibid., 592
73. Ibid., 594
74. John Dugard, "Some Realism about The Judicial Process and Positivism—A Reply", *African Law and Legal Theory*, 441

75. Maurice Merleau-Ponty, *Humanism and Terror*, trans. John O'Neil, (Boston, Beacon Press, 1969), 176
76. Dugard, p. 445
77. Aime Cesaire, *Discourse on Colonialism,* translated by Joan Pinkham, (New York: Monthly Review Press, 1972), 15
78. Morton J. Horwitz, "Why Is Anglo-American Jurisprudence Unhistorical", Oxford Journal of Legal Studies, Vol. 17, Winter 1997, p.551.
79. Ibid., 582
80. See Susan Estrich, *Getting Away with Murder*, (Cambridge: Harvard University Press), p.1. The "everyone" does not mean every one. It means every one who is recognized by law, and everyone who is recognized by law refers to everyone who is politically recognized.
81. Robert W. Gordon, "The Role of Lawyers in Producing the Rule of Law: Some Critical Reflections," Theoretical Inquiries in Law Vol. 1 January 2010 Article 15
82. Quoted in "Henry Lord Brougham and Zeal", by Monroe H. Freedman. Hofstra Law Review, Vol. 34, No. 4, 2006, 1322
83. David Luban, Legal *Ethics and Human Dignity*, (Cambridge: Cambridge University Press, 2007), 9
84. Monroe Freedman, "Judge Frankel's Search for Truth", University of Pennsylvania Law Review, Vol. 123, 1060, 1065, (1975)
85. Getting Away with Murder, 95
86. Friedrich Nietzsche, *Beyond Good and Evil,* translated by R.J. Hollingdale, (New York: Penguin Books, 1984), 67
87. Friedrich Nietzsche, *Beyond Good and Evil,* translated by Walter Kaufmann, (New York: Vintage, 1989), 69
88. Martin Heidegger, *Discourse of Thinking*, trans. John M. Anderson and E. Hans Freund, (New York: Harper & Row, Publishers, 1966), 45-46
89. *African Philosophy: Essential Writings,* ed. Tsenay Serequeberhan, (New York: Paragon House, 1991), 231
90. Ibid., 230
91. Lon L Fuller, *The Law in quest for Itself,* (Boston: Beacon Press, 1966), 2
92. Larry Alexander, "All in or Nothing at All" in *Law and Interpretation,* ed. Andrei Marmo, (Oxford: Clarendon Press, 1995), 358
93. Quoted in *Homo Sacer*, Giorgio Agamben, trans. Daniel Heller-Roazen, (Stanford, CA: Stanford University Press, 1998), ix
94. Hyung I Kim, *Fundamental Legal Concepts of China and the West*, (Fort Washington, NY: Kennikat Press, 1981), 5
95. Joseph Raz, See the online publication to Oxford Scholarship online. May 2009. DOI:10.1093acprof.oso/978019956288.oo1.0001
96. See Hart's famous article on the separation of law from morals. H. L Hart, "Positivism and the Separation of Law and Morals", Harvard Law Review, Vol. 71 February 1958, No. 4, 593

97. See Declaration of the Rights of Man and Citizen in *The Coming of the French Revolution*, by George Lebfebre, trans. R. R. Palmer (Princeton: Princeton University Press, 1971), 221
98. John Locke, *The Second Treatise of Government*, (Indianapolis: Bobbs-Merril Company, Inc., 1952) , 71
99. See Mark Kelman, *A Guide to Critical Legal Studies*, (Cambridge, MA: Harvard University Press), 1978
Mahmood Mamdani,. *Citizen and Subject*, (Princeton: Princeton University Press, 1996)
100. See Thesis XI in The Marx-Engels Reader, edited by Robert C. Tucker, (New York: W.W. Norton & Company, 1978)
101. John Austin made an attempt to separate divine law from positive law, and hence laid down the foundation of modern legal positivism. The attempt to expel God from the legal arena has largely failed because it is not fully appreciated the role that God plays in Western European culture. One recalls Nietzsche's immature proclamation of the death of God. God is still well and strong. He has multiple ways of manifesting himself.
102. Robert W. Gordon, "The Role of Lawyers in Producing the Rule of Law: Some Critical Reflections" Theoretical Inquiries in Law Volume II, Number 1 January 2010, Article 15
103. Chinua Achebe, *Things Fall Apart*, (New York: Anchor Books, 1994), 7
104. PlacideTemples,*Bantu Philosophy,* translated by Margaret Read, (Paris: Presence Africaine, 1959), 36
105. See Patricia Stamp, "Burying Otieno: The Politics of Gender and Ethnicity in Kenya", Signs: Journal of Women in Culture and Society 1991, vol.16, no.4, p. 817. Stamp writes, "Formed during the time of closest alliance between the Kikuyu and the Luo, it stood for many Kenyans' aspirations to a national rather than ethnic identity". The marriage between two individuals from two different ethnic groups does not necessarily imply that such a marriage is entered into with the political purpose of constructing or reinforcing national identity even if those who enter into it are nationally prominent.
106 .Eugene Cotran, *Casebook on Kenya Customary Law*, Nairobi University Press, 1987, p.336
107. Ibid. p.344
108. Quoted in Stamp, p. 808. See note above.
109. See Fatima Sadiqi article, "Changing Gender Dynamics in Africa" where she distinguishes Moroccan feminism from Western feminism. Codesria Bulletin Numbers 3&4, 2002, 35-36
110. Immanuel Kant, *Lectures on Ethics* translated by Louis Infield, (Indianapolis: Hackett Publishing Company, 1980), 167
111. Patricia Stamp, "Burying Otieno::The Politics of Gender and Ethnicity in Kenya", *Signs*, Vol. 16, No 4, (Summer, 1991), p, 817
112. Ibid., p. 808

113. Jean Paul Sartre, *Being and Nothingness*, (New York: Washington Square Press, 1984), 755
114. Nietzsche, *Beyond Good and Evil,* 137
115. Fanon, *The Wretched of the Earth*, 250
116. Ibid., 315
117. Polylog: Forum for Intercultural Philosophy 3 (2001). Online: http://them.polylog.org/3/frm-en.htm
118. See generally Julius Nyerere, *Ujamaa: Essays on Socialism*, (Oxford, UK: Oxford University Press, 1974)
119. Fanon, *The Wretched of the Earth*, 24-25
120. Carl Schmitt, *Political Theology*, translated by George Schwab, (Chicago: University of Chicago Press, 2005), 36
121. Martin Heidegger, *What Is Philosophy*, translated by Jean T. Wilde and William Kluback, .31
122. Ibid., 35
123. Aime Cesaire,, *The Return to My Native Land*, (Paris: Presence Africaine, 1968), 125
124. Anthony Anghie, *Imperialism, Sovereignty and the Making of International Law,* (Cambridge, UK: Cambridge University Press, 2004), 317
125. Ibid., 32-33
126. Albert Memmi, *The Colonizer and the Colonized*, (New York: Beacon Press, 1967), 74
127. Albert Memmi, *Dominated Man,* (Boston: Beacon Press, 1968), 19
William c. Heffernan, "Not Socrates But Protagoras: The Sophistic Basis of Legal Education", 29 Buffalo Law Review, p. 412, 1980

Bibliography

Achebe, Chinua. *Things Fall Apart*, New York: Anchor Books, 1994

Anderson, David. *Histories of the Hanged, The Dirty War and the End of the Empire*, New York: W.W. Norton and Company, 2005

Anghie, Antony. *Imperialism, Sovereignty and the Making of International Law*, Cambridge, UK: Cambridge University Press, 2004

Asante, Molefi Kete. *The Afrocentric Idea*, Philadelphia: Temple University Press, 1998

Bell, Derrick, *Faces at the Bottom of the Well: The Permanence of Racism*, New York: Basic Books, 1992

Cabral, Amilcar. *National Liberation and Culture*,Translated by Maureen Webster. Syracuse, NY: Syracuse University Press, 1970

———. *Return to the Source*. New York: Monthly Review Press, 1974

Cesaire, Aime. *Discourse on Colonialism*, New York: Monthly Review Press, 1972

———. *The Return to My Native County*, Paris: Presence Africaine, 1968

Crenshaw, Kimberle; Gotanda, Neil; Peller, Gary; and Thomas, Kendal. *Critical Race Theory*, New York: New Press, 1996

Du Bois, W.E.B , *Dusk of Dawn*, New York: Schocken, 1971

———. *The Souls of Black Folk*, Mineola, New York: Dover Publications, 1994

Dussel, Enrique, *Philosophy of Liberation*, New York: Orbis Books, 1985

———. *History and the Theology of Liberation. A Latin American Perspective*, New York: Orbis Books, 1976

Dworkin, Ronald. *Law's Empire*, Oxford, UK: Hart Publishing Company, 1998

———.*The Philosophy of Law*, Oxford, UK: Oxford University Press, 1977

Elkins, Caroline. *Imperial Reckoning: The Untold Story of Britain's Gulag in Kenya*, New York: Henry Holt and Company, 2005

Fanon, Frantz. *The Wretched of the Earth*, translation by Richard Philcox, New York: Grove Press, 2004

———. *A Dying Colonialism,* translated by Haakon Chevalier, *New* York: Grove Press, 1965

———. *White Skin Black Mask* translated by Richard Philcox, New York: Grove Press, 2007

———. *Toward the African Revolution*, translated by Haakon Chevalier, New York: Grove Press, 2007

Freire, Paulo. *The Pedagogy of the Oppressed*, New York: Continuum International Publishing Group, Inc., 1993

Hayek, F.A. *The Road to Serfdom*, Chicago, University of Chicago Press, 1994

Hegel, F. V. W. *Philosophy of History*, translation by J. Sibree, New York: Dover Publications, 1959

Heidegger, Martin. *What Is Philosophy?* Translated by Jean T. Wilde and William Kluback, Albany, NY: New College and University Press, Inc.1956

Hountondji, Paulin. *African Philosophy Myth & Reality*, Indianapolis: Indiana University Press, 1983

Janz, Bruce, *Philosophy in an African Place*, Lanham, MD: Lexington Press, 2009

Lao Tzu. *The Way of Life*, translated by Witter Bynner, New York: Perigee Books, 1972

Mamdani, Mahmood. *The Subject and the Citizen,* Princeton: Princeton University Press, 1996

M'Baye, Keba. "The African Conception of Law". In: 2 International Encyclopedia of Comparative Law. 138-158 (R. David ed., 1975)

Memmi, Albert. *Dominated Man,* Boston: Beacon Press, 1969

———. *The Colonizer and the Colonized,* Boston: Beacon Press, 1965

Ngugi wa Thiong'o. *Decolonizing the Mind: The Politics of Language in African Literature*. London: Heinemann Publisher, 1994

Nietzsche, Friedrich. *Beyond Good and Evil*, translated by Walter Kaufmann, New York: Random House, Inc., 1966

Nkrumah, Kwame. *Consciencism,* New York: Monthly Review Press, 1964

———. *Africa Must Unite.* New York: International Publishers, 1970

———. *Neo-Colonialism: The Last Stage of Imperialism*, New York: International Publishers, Inc., 1966

Nyerere, Julius. *Freedom and Unity: Uhuru na Umoja*. London: Oxford University Press, 1967

———. *Ujamaa; Essays on Socialism.* London: Oxford University Press, 1970

Odinga, Oginga, *Not Yet Uhuru*, London: Heinemann Educational Books, 1968

Ramose, B. Mogobe, and Boatamo Mosupye. *African Philosophy Through Ubuntu*, Harare: Mond Books Publishers, 1999

———. *The Land Is the Source of Law,* London: Cavendish Publishers, 2010

———. *The Development of Thought in Pan Africanism*, Dubuque, IA: Kendall Hunt Publishing Company, 2006

———. "An African Perspective on Justice and Race", vol.3, 2001, http://them.polylog/3/frm-en.htm>

Raz, Joseph, *Authority of Law*, Oxford: Oxford University Press, 1979

Schmitt, Carl, *The Concept of the Political,* translated by George Schwab, Chicago: University of Chicago Press, 1996

———. *Political Theology*, Chicago: University of Chicago Press, 2005

Serequeberhan, Tsenay, *African Philosophy: The Essential Reading,*. New York: Paragon House, 1991

———. *The Hermeneutics of African Philosophy*, New York: Routledge, 1994

Smith, Patricia. *Feminist Jurisprudence*, Oxford: Oxford University Press, 1993

Stein, Peter. *Roman Law in European History*, Cambridge, UK: Cambridge University Press, 1999

———. *Introduction to the Philosophy of History*, translated by Leo Rauch, Indianapolis: Hackett Publishing Company, 1988

Taiwo, Femi, *Legal Naturalism: A Marxist Theory of Law*, Ithaca, New York: Cornell University Press, 1966

———. *How Colonialism Preempted Modernity in Africa*, Bloomington, Indiana: Indiana University Press, 2010

Tempels, Placide. *Bantu Philosophy*, translated by Rev. Colin King, London: Presence Africaine, 1959

Trevor-Roper, Hugh, *The Rise of Christian Europe*, New York: W.W. Norton & Company, 1989

Unger, Roberto Mangabeira, *Law in Modern Society*, New York: The Free Press, 1976

———. *Critical Legal Studies Movement,* Cambridge: Harvard University Press, 1986

Walter, Rodney. *How Europe Underdeveloped Africa.* Washington,. D.C.: Howard University Press, 1974

Wiredu, Kwasi. *A Companion to African Philosophy*, Oxford, UK: Blackwell Publishers, 2004

———. *Philosophy and an African Culture.* New York: Cambridge University Press, 1980

Index

African culture, viii, 11, 18, 22, 23, 38, 68, 85, 94, 143, 144, 145, 169, 170, 178, 179, 182, 185, 188, 195, 196, 208
African customary law, 22, 46, 85, 176, 185, 189
African feminist jurisprudence, 166
African jurisprudence, 19, 20, 24, 27, 31, 35, 37, 38, 44, 45, 46, 47, 49, 51, 53, 55, 57, 59, 60, 61, 64, 63, 65, 67, 68, 69, 70, 88, 90, 96, 99, 104, 105, 111, 157, 159, 174, 175, 200
African lawyer, 69, 71, 73, 74, 78, 79, 80, 81, 84, 83, 84, 86, 87, 89, 90, 92, 93, 96, 97, 98, 99, 100, 101, 102, 103, 104, 105, 106, 109, 110, 127, 128, 130, 133, 134, 135, 141, 158, 159, 175, 200
African legal interpretation, 137, 138, 139, 140, 141, 142, 143, 144, 145, 147, 153, 156, 158, 165, 166, 168, 169, 175, 200
African legal philosophy, 1, 2, 3, 4, 5, 6, 7, 8, 9, 10, 12, 13, 15, 17, 18, 19, 20, 22, 23, 24, 26, 27, 28, 78, 96, 99, 104, 105, 108, 145, 174, 199, 200, 203, 204, 205, 207, 208, 209, 210, 211, 213, 214
African philosophy, vii, viii, ix, 3, 7, 9, 10, 11, 12, 13, 15, 18, 20, 24, 26, 63, 79, 88, 111, 141, 199, 207, 208, 210, 214, 217

Africanness, 7, 9, 23, 24, 34, 60, 69, 88, 92, 93, 98, 99, 101, 113, 134, 165, 168, 189, 192, 212
Afropessimism, 133, 208
Age of Darkness, 36
Allah, 27, 54, 139, 157, 159, 162, 163
Anghie, Antony, 212, 224
apartheid, 31, 42, 56, 73, 78, 116, 118, 123, 134, 136, 152, 154, 209, 219
Arab, 55, 56, 158, 159
Austin, John, 32, 37, 42, 57, 114, 115, 116, 119, 219, 220, 223

Banks, Russell, 95, 220
Bantu, 173, 223
Berlin Conference, 39
Bible, 52, 161, 162, 163, 164, 193
Blackstone, William, 16, 217
British, 9, 23, 36, 41, 43, 107, 123, 151, 178
Brougham, Lord Henry, 125
Bruhl, Levy, 107, 221

Calvin Schrag, 5, 217
Caribbean Islands, 91
Cartesian, 98, 105, 108, 128, 129, 200
Cartesianists, 98
Cesaire, Aime, 24, 118, 209, 218, 222, 224
China, 87, 110, 155, 222, 219
Christian missionaries, 21, 47, 52, 55, 77, 78, 130, 161, 209, 221
Christian theology, 3, 14, 17, 49, 51, 52, 77, 191, 206, 208
Christianity, 13, 14, 15, 17, 21, 25, 31, 48, 49, 51, 52, 53, 54, 57, 75, 76, 77, 78, 129, 130, 131, 157, 163, 180, 181, 184, 191, 192, 206, 209, 210
Colonial jurisprudence, 64
colonialism, 11, 15, 21, 24, 31, 37, 38, 41, 56, 64, 65, 73, 78, 82, 83, 84, 85, 86, 87, 102, 116, 122, 134, 135, 136, 142, 150, 152, 155, 161, 162, 166, 178, 184, 191, 192, 193, 198, 209, 213
communitarianism, 35
Conrad, Joseph, 36
Constantine, 48, 75
Cotran, Eugene, 107, 221, 223
Critical Legal Studies Movement, 154, 155
Critical Race Theory, 44, 95, 153, 154, 155, 220

Dark Continent, 36, 63, 65, 88
Deloria, Vine, 24, 218
Descartes, René, 18, 65, 77, 106, 107, 108, 109, 128, 129
Dicey, A.V., 42, 219
Dugard, John, 42, 116, 117, 118, 219, 222
Dutch Roman law, 182
Dworkin, Ronald, 32, 44

Estrich, Susan , 126, 222
Eurocentric legal interpretation, 154

Fanon, Frantz, 38, 64, 87, 93, 98, 99, 198, 200, 203, 205, 210, 217, 219, 221, 224
feminist African theology, 191
feminist missionarism, 179
Freedman, Monroe, 126, 222
Fuller, Lon L., 138, 222

genocide, 36, 205
globalization, 34, 58, 79, 81, 100
Gordon, Robert C., 122, 165, 222, 223
Greek philosophy, 13

Greeks, 14, 16, 50, 66, 67, 76, 89, 126, 208

Hasnas, John, 101
Hart, H.L.A., 32, 44, 114, 115, 116, 119, 120, 146, 218, 220, 221, 222
Hefferman, William, 113
Hegel, Georg, 15, 30, 31, 32, 35, 37, 47, 48, 217, 218, 220
Heidegger, Martin, 20, 21, 131, 207, 217, 222, 224
Hobbes, Thomas 37, 79, 80, 200, 221
Horwitz, Morton, 120
Hountondji, Paulin, 30, 48, 80, 81, 88, 89, 107, 111, 112, 207, 217, 218, 220, 221
Imperialism, 12, 77, 194, 212
Islam, 27, 54, 56, 57, 157, 159, 161, 162, 206, 209, 210, 221
Islamic jurisprudence, 12, 17, 53, 55, 56, 57, 157, 159, 161, 163

Judeo-Christian theology, 3
Judge Shields, 176, 178

Kant, Immanuel, 189, 190, 203, 218, 221, 223
Kenya, 43, 175, 176, 177, 179, 183, 184, 185, 186, 191, 192, 193, 220, 223
Khaminwa, John, 176, 186
Kikuyu, 177, 179, 191, 223
Kim, Hyung I., 50
Koran, 54, 157, 159, 160, 161, 162, 163, 164

Latin America, 26, 43, 93, 217
legal education, 21, 22, 23, 32, 33, 34, 39, 68, 69, 70, 80, 85, 93, 101, 104, 113, 120, 123, 127, 134, 135, 145, 154, 169, 170, 198, 208, 211
legal modernization, 46
legal philosophy, 1, 2, 3, 4, 5, 6, 7, 8, 9, 10, 12, 14, 15, 16, 17, 18, 19, 20, 21, 22, 23, 25, 26, 27, 28, 59, 78, 83, 96, 104, 105, 108, 174, 199, 203, 204, 205, 206, 207, 208, 209, 210, 211, 212, 213, 214
King Leopold, 152
Locke, John, 40, 41, 151, 199, 219, 223
Logical Positivists, 112
Luban, David, 102, 221, 222
Luo, 177, 179, 180, 181, 182, 183, 184, 185, 186, 187, 189, 195, 223

Malcolm X, 92
Mamdani, Mahmood, 22, 218, 223
Marx, Karl, 122, 155, 223
Mbembe, Achille, 109, 221
Mbiti, John, 106
Mill, John Stuart, 151
Missionarism, 78
modernity, 17, 23, 27, 36, 37, 40, 56, 64, 66, 73, 74, 77, 91, 107, 108, 129, 136, 143, 174, 188, 199, 200, 209, 210
Montesquieu, 31, 40, 108, 218, 219
Muslims, 54, 55, 57, 156, 157, 158, 159, 176, 210
mwananchi, 90

Na'im, 56
Nairobi, 175, 177, 181, 184
Negro, 29, 38, 92, 93, 99, 100, 218 219
neo-colonialism, 73, 78, 83, 86, 122, 135, 193, 209
Ngugi wa Thiong'o, 100, 221
Nietzsche, Friedrich, 72, 73, 74, 129, 130, 197, 207, 210, 220, 222, 223, 224

Nkrumah, Kwame, 38, 81, 82, 156, 219, 220
Nyerere, Julius, 156, 206, 224

Otieno, 175, 179, 181, 186, 190
Ougo, Joash Ochieng' 175, 187

Pan-African thinking, 96
People of the Book., 162
Portuguese, 41, 96, 152
Powell, Thomas R., 71, 72, 77, 78, 79, 211, 213

Raz, Joseph, 33, 218, 222
Romans, 14, 16, 52, 75, 76, 78, 164
rule of law, 18, 33, 34, 56, 64, 66, 70, 79, 80, 90, 95, 101, 102, 103, 112, 114, 121, 125, 136, 143, 147, 176, 195, 211, 213

Sartre, Jean-Paul, 2, 197, 206
Savigny, 143
Schmitt, Carl, 206, 224
self-knowledge, 2, 33, 83
separation of powers, 40, 41, 42, 124, 146, 150, 185
Sharia'h, 55
Siranga, Omolo, 175, 187
Socrates, 20, 113, 114, 121, 138, 198, 224
Socratic thinking, 33, 113, 198
St. Augustine, 49, 75
St. Paul, 191
St. Thomas Aquinas, 14, 18, 49, 50, 75
Stamp, Patricia, 178, 223

Tao, 50, 67, 219

Ubuntu, 68, 69, 135, 205
Ubuntuism, 68, 205
Ujamaa, 17, 224

Wamba dia-Wamba, 131
Wambui, Virginia Edith, 175, 177, 179, 180, 181, 182, 183, 184, 186, 190, 191, 192, 194, 195
Washington, Booker T., 21
webiogaphy, 27
West Indians, 91
Western, viii, 2, 3, 7, 11, 12, 13, 14, 15, 16, 18, 25, 27, 30, 31, 32, 33, 34, 35, 36, 37, 38, 40, 44, 45, 48, 49, 50, 51, 52, 53, 55, 56, 57, 63, 66, 67, 72, 74, 77, 78, 79, 81, 82, 90, 92, 103, 104, 106, 109, 110, 112, 113, 117, 118, 123, 124, 128, 129, 131, 132, 134, 135, 145, 151, 153, 156, 163, 164, 166, 167, 174, 175, 180, 182, 184, 185, 186, 188, 189, 190, 194, 199, 200, 205, 207, 208, 209, 210, 211, 212, 213, 218, 219, 223
Western jurisprudence, 12, 14, 27, 32, 34, 35, 45, 48, 50, 53, 58, 63, 68, 219
Western legal philosophy, 12, 14, 18, 27, 199, 214
Western philosophy, 12, 13, 49, 113

Leopoldo Zea, 15, 217